Laura Ingalls Wilder

FARM JOURNALIST

Laura Ingalls Wilder
FARM JOURNALIST

Writings from the Ozarks

Edited by Stephen W. Hines

UNIVERSITY OF MISSOURI PRESS
COLUMBIA AND LONDON

University of Missouri Press, Columbia, Missouri 65201
Printed and bound in the United States of America

5 4 3 2 1 11 10 09 08 07

Library of Congress Cataloging-in-Publication Data

Wilder, Laura Ingalls, 1867–1957.
Laura Ingalls Wilder, farm journalist : writings from the Ozarks / edited by Stephen W. Hines.
p. cm.
Summary: "Collects all of the essays by Laura Ingalls Wilder that originally appeared in the *Missouri Ruralist* between 1911 and 1924, offering Wilder's unique perspective on life and politics during the World War I era and her comments on the challenges of surviving and thriving in Missouri's rustic Ozark hill country" —Provided by publisher.
Includes bibliographical references and index.
ISBN 978-0-8262-1771-4 (alk. paper)
I. Hines, Stephen W. II. Missouri Ruralist. III. Title.
PS3545I342A6 2007
814′.52—dc22

2007028027

⊗™ This paper meets the requirements of the American National Standard for Permanence of Paper for Printed Library Materials, Z39.48, 1984.

Designer: Kristie Lee
Typesetter: The Composing Room of Michigan, Inc.
Printer and binder: The Maple-Vail Book Manufacturing Group
Typeface: Century Old Style

For all those who want to know more about Laura Ingalls Wilder

CONTENTS

1911–1915

1916

1917

1918

1919

1920

1921

1922

1923

1924

CODA, 1931

ACKNOWLEDGMENTS

Parts of this book originally appeared in *Little House in the Ozarks,* published in 1991. I want to acknowledge once again the enormous help I received from the staff at Ellis Library at the University of Missouri–Columbia, where I did my first research, and I also want to thank the staff of the Kansas State Historical Society Archives for their help as I rounded out my work.

The completion of this volume has been greatly facilitated by my wife, Gwen, and daughter, Megan, whose contributions were significant in ways too numerous to mention.

My sister-in-law Kaye Hines from Topeka, Kansas, helped out at the last moment when a few column copies and page numbers were needed which had been misplaced over the years.

Finally, I thank the University of Missouri Press, acquisitions editor Clair Willcox, and copyeditor Jane Lago—for their encouragement and guidance in completing this work. It has been the labor of many hands.

If it should happen that an alert reader knows of a work by Mrs. Wilder published in the *Ruralist* that I missed, please excuse the omission. It was not intentional. Perhaps the problem can be addressed if there are future editions.

All of us are hopeful that readers of this "new" Laura will love these writings as much as they have loved her original books about her pioneer experience as viewed by her from long ago and far away.

Laura Ingalls Wilder
FARM JOURNALIST

INTRODUCTION

In the late 1950s and early 1960s, the state of Kansas was finally closing its few remaining country schools. In the eastern part of the state, where I grew up on a dairy farm, the inefficiency of the old system gave rural schoolchildren only eight months of instruction while their town and city counterparts had the "advantage" of nine months of schooling. We country children thought we knew who had the best of it.

But, frankly, the school closings were long overdue. Town children had access to greater resources, better heated buildings, and teachers with their bachelor's degrees already earned. Some of our teachers, and they tended not to last long in the one-room-school setting, were often still working to earn their primary degrees.

Our school "library" at Victory School, Junction 200, was pathetic. We had approximately four shelves of books, which extended only partially along the west side of our small room. They fitted under the windows that we were inclined to stare out whenever the teacher wasn't looking.

Books were a salvation from ignorance and parochialism, but our choice of escapist literature was limited: stories about noble dogs and horses, a Bobbs-Merrill series on American heroes that read about the same from hero to hero, and Laura Ingalls Wilder's Little House series of books. With little hesitation I gravitated toward these "girls' books" on prairie life; they were a revelation to me, a widening of the narrow horizons of my youth.

In the Little House series, I found a family much like my own, with a strong father and mother and with children who mostly obeyed but who spent a great deal of time quarreling and competing with one another. They were a family who struggled against the elements of nature and misfortune, trying to make a more secure place for themselves in a challenging world. Yet they had an eternal constant in family love. From this love came the strength not only to meet life's challenges but also to be invigorated by them.

So it was that I came to hold Laura Ingalls Wilder in high regard. Out the west-facing windows of my own little school on the prairie, I could see the windswept buffalo grass and feel the vastness of the land on which the Ingalls family pioneered. I felt I knew this little family as I knew no other in literature. Their values of family loyalty and courage overcame all obstacles, and this message comforted and reassured me, as it has done the many fans of Laura's books to this day. Little did I know back then, however, that I was destined to encounter a far more multifaceted and profound Laura, whose writings as an Ozark journalist and farmwife were to give me a much greater respect for this complex woman.

My discovery of the adult Mrs. Wilder began with a serendipitous experience at a fine downtown Nashville, Tennessee, bookstore. Rare, Foreign & More no longer exists, but in 1989 it was a major part of my life. As an earnest idler over the lunch hour, I could get in a lot of free reading and still make it back to the newsletter publisher where I worked. Lunch itself was optional. Who cares about eating when there are books to be sampled?

One day in late summer, pursuing my obsession with works of biography, I chanced upon William T. Anderson's *A Little House Sampler,* then recently published by the University of Nebraska Press. In the preface, I found this passage: "Many of Laura's essays [found in the book] were published during her association with the *Missouri Ruralist,* years before she thought of writing the 'Little House' books." Although at the moment of reading that preface I couldn't be sure that there would be years' worth of her columns to be found, I thought it likely. It made sense that Laura Ingalls Wilder had had some sort of apprenticeship before she launched into the major task of writing a series of books about her family.

I decided almost on the spot that I wanted to learn more about this Laura of the Ozarks—known to her readers as Mrs. A. J. Wilder, as it turned out—and whether or not she would be like the person I had come to know as a Kansas schoolboy. Would the modern Laura of 1916 be the same person as the Laura of the 1880s who endured the long winter and taught school when she was sixteen?

I was lucky on two counts as I sought the answer to this question. First, I discovered that Ellis Library at the University of Missouri–Columbia had a complete set of bound volumes of the *Missouri Ruralist* for the years that Mrs. Wilder was reported to have written for the paper, 1911 through 1924. Second, when I actually began to go through those decaying volumes, I discovered that Mrs. Wilder had been given a byline. The fact that her articles were signed made it possible for me to rest assured that I was seeing almost all of what she had written, even though at that time papers commonly gave their writers no credit at all.

It is evident that Mrs. Wilder was regarded as a prized contributor almost from the start of her efforts with the paper. In 1918, John F. Case, the long-time editor, wrote an appreciation of her that provides insight into just how highly she was regarded, and his article does much to reveal what the real Laura of the Ozarks was like.

> Missouri farm folks need little introduction before getting acquainted with Mrs. A. J. Wilder of Rocky Ridge Farm. During the years that she has been connected with this paper—a greater number of years than any other person on the editorial staff—she has taken strong hold upon the esteem and affections of our great family. Mrs. Wilder has lived her life upon a farm. She knows farm folks and their problems as few women who write know them. And having sympathy with the folks whom she serves she writes well.
>
> "Mrs. Wilder is a woman of delightful personality," a neighbor tells me, "and she is a combination of energy and determination. She always is cheery, looking on the bright side. She is her husband's partner in every sense and is fully capable of managing the farm. No woman can make you feel more at home than can Mrs. Wilder, and yet, when the occasion demands, she can be dignity personified. Mrs. Wilder has held high rank in the Eastern Star.[1] Then when a Farm Loan Association was formed at Mansfield she was made secretary-treasurer. When her report was sent to the Land Bank officials they told her the papers were perfect and the best sent in." As a final tribute Mrs. Wilder's friends said this: "She gets eggs in the winter when none of her neighbors gets them." . . .
>
> "Our daughter, Rose Wilder Lane, was born on the farm," Mrs. Wilder informs us, "and it was there I learned to do all kinds of farm work with machinery. I have ridden the binder, driving six horses. And I could ride. I do not wish to appear conceited, but I broke my own ponies to ride. Of course they were not bad but they were bronchos [broncos]." Mrs. Wilder had the spirit that brought success to the pioneers. . . .
>
> . . . They came to Rocky Ridge Farm near Mansfield, Wright county, and there they have lived for 25 years. Only 40 acres was purchased and the land was all timber except a 4 acre worn-out field. "Illness and traveling expenses had taken our surplus cash and we lacked $150 of paying for the forty acres," Mrs. Wilder writes. "Mr. Wilder was unable to do a full day's work. The garden, my hens and the wood I helped saw and which we sold in town took us thru the first year. It was then I became an expert at the end of a cross-cut saw and I still can 'make a hand' in an emergency. Mr. Wilder says he would rather have me help than any man he ever sawed with. And, believe me, I learned how to take care of hens and to make them lay."
>
> One may wonder that so busy a person as Mrs. Wilder has proved to

1. Eastern Star is a masonic organization for women.

> be can find time to write. "I always have been a busy person," she says, "doing my own housework, helping the Man of the Place when help could not be obtained, but I love to work. And it is a pleasure to write for the *Missouri Ruralist.* And oh I do just love to play! The days never have been long enough to do the things I would like to do. Every year has held more of interest than the year before." . . .
>
> Reading Mrs. Wilder's contributions most folks doubtless have decided that she is a college graduate. But, "my education has been what a girl would get on the frontier," she informs us. "I never graduated from anything and only attended high school two terms." Folks who know Mrs. Wilder tho, know that she is a cultured, well-educated gentlewoman. Combined with inherent ability, unceasing study of books has provided the necessary education and greater things have been learned from the study of life itself.
>
> As has been asserted before, Mrs. Wilder writes well for farm folks because she knows them. The Wilders can be found ready to enter wholeheartedly into any movement for community betterment and the home folks are proud of the reputation that Mrs. Wilder has established. They know that she has won recognition as a writer and state leader because of ability alone.

For the astute reader of Mrs. Wilder's work, Mr. Case's encomium on the lady who "has won recognition as a writer and state leader because of ability alone" is both enlightening and puzzling. Having read the Little House books myself some six or seven times over a forty-year span, I am frankly at a loss to completely explain Laura Ingalls Wilder's transformation from someone who wanted to give up farming in *The First Four Years* to the person described by Mr. Case as a state leader in the farming community. He describes Mrs. Wilder as a farm booster, and no one will doubt his assessment when they read the ensuing columns.

Yet, in *The First Four Years,* she flatly tells Almanzo that she has never wanted to marry a farmer because "a farm is such a hard place for a woman. There are so many chores for her to do, and harvest help and threshers to cook for. Besides, a farmer never has any money."[2] How differently she seems to feel when she says to Mr. Case, "I learned to do all kinds of farm work with machinery. I have ridden the binder, driving six horses. And I could ride. I do not wish to appear conceited, but I broke my own ponies to ride." Laura's not conceited, just proud of her farm-related skills.

How can one explain this change of heart? I have no single, simple answer but can offer a series of insights as to how this change may have come

2. Laura Ingalls Wilder, *The First Four Years* (New York: Harper and Row, 1971), chapter 1.

about. For one thing, she may have simply respected Almanzo's competence and age: he was twenty-eight and she was eighteen when they married, and she may have been more deferential at the start of their marriage. For another, there was at least some truth in Almanzo's reply that only a farmer could be free and independent—at least as to the hours he worked. In this regard, the farmer answers to no one but himself. In *The First Four Years* he is reported to have said: "How long would a merchant last if farmers didn't trade with him? There is strife between them to please the farmer." He also jokes about the rich having their ice in the summer while the poor get theirs in the winter. "Everything is evened up in this world," he says.[3] For him, being free and independent compensated for the hard work of farming.

Such an argument would have hardly been compelling to Laura, who had already seen the struggles her own family endured in trying to till the soil of the unforgiving prairie. More to the point might be something she has Almanzo's father say at the end of *Farmer Boy.* In the last chapter of the book, which was written long after Laura and Almanzo had retired from agricultural work, Laura has Almanzo's father say, "A farmer depends on himself, and the land and the weather. If you're a farmer, you raise what you eat, you raise what you wear, and you keep warm with wood out of your own timber. You work hard, but you work as you please, and no man can tell you to go or come. You'll be free and independent, son, on a farm."[4] Yes, "free and independent," if you are willing to pay the price. In a January 5, 1920, column, Laura reports Almanzo saying, "I never realized how much work my father did. Why, one winter he sorted 500 bushels of potatoes after supper by lantern light. . . . he must have got blamed tired of sorting potatoes down cellar every night until he had handled more than 500 bushels of them."

As perplexing as Mrs. Wilder's change of heart was, I don't think she was being hypocritical about the perceived advantages of the farmer's life. From her perspective, she was "her husband's partner in every sense," as Mr. Case wrote. Her boast sounds genuine when she says that she could not only break horses but also "'make a hand' at a cross-cut saw in an emergency."

Yes, Laura was "free and independent." Yet in the passages Case quotes she refers to Almanzo as "Mr. Wilder," and throughout her 170-plus articles and columns for the *Ruralist* she refers to him only as "The Man of the Place." Is this appellation a term of endearment? Or is it an ironic commentary? I can't say.

When I interviewed people who had known Mr. and Mrs. Wilder for the book *"I Remember Laura,"* there was universal agreement that Laura "ran

3. Ibid.
4. Laura Ingalls Wilder, *Farmer Boy* (New York: Harper and Row, 1933), chapter 29.

the show" at the farm. She wore the pants in the family, yet there was no record of Almanzo's having resented her assertiveness, which he seems to have taken as a matter of course, more an aspect of her strong personality than anything else. Yet they loved each other and were married for sixty-four years. Their pet names for each other were "Manly" for Almanzo and "Bessie" for Laura.

Mrs. Wilder's relationship with her only daughter, Rose, is also complex and perplexing. As William Holtz makes clear in *The Ghost in the Little House,* Rose and her mother did not get along well, apparently from very early in their relationship. By her teenage years Rose was so independent that Laura thought it best to have her finish her high school education in Louisiana under the care of none other than Almanzo's sister, "lazy, lousy, Lizy Jane" of *Little Town on the Prairie.*[5] It was thought that the formidable Eliza Jane Wilder Thayer, who had homesteaded on her own claim while trying to teach recalcitrant students, including the young Laura Ingalls, would be better able to control the wild Rose.

The ostensible reason for Rose's going to Louisiana to finish her education was the inadequacy of the Mansfield school system. Perhaps that was the reason, but the folks I talked to in Mansfield who had known Rose and had heard of her conflicted relationship with her mother simply felt that Laura had lost control of her daughter and, for once in her life, didn't know what to do.

In fact, Laura and Rose were much alike, but they defined their freedom and independence in different ways. Laura was something of a feminist, but a conservative one. She wrote gleefully of women who were bold enough to leave the home and work in the factories during World War I. And she was proud that her daughter was a "bachelor girl" who traveled through Europe for the Red Cross and made her living by writing. Yet at the same time she expressed doubts about such a life. Might such a life make women independent of men and less likely to get married and rear children? New freedom seemed to present new dangers to womankind.

As far as women having the right to vote, Laura assumed this would happen, but she worried that women wouldn't be up to their responsibilities when the vote came, as it did in 1919. Thus, she urged women to become better informed and to take an active political role in their community. She wrote enthusiastically in "Who'll Do the Women's Work?" from April 5, 1919, that "never again will anyone have the courage to say that women could not

5. William Holtz, *The Ghost in the Little House: A Life of Rose Wilder Lane* (Columbia: University of Missouri Press, 1993); Laura Ingalls Wilder, *Little Town on the Prairie* (New York: Harper and Row, 1941), chapter 9.

run world affairs if necessary." But the phrase "if necessary" could be taken to mean that running world affairs is not a woman's primary task. Such statements seem to conflict with her enthusiasm over the new freedoms women were winning.

In her *Ruralist* columns, Laura urges mothers to teach strong moral values and not to forget that homemaking is a woman's sacred task, her primary task. Mothers are to raise their children to be honest, hardworking, and thrifty. She says nothing about what role fathers ought to play in child rearing, and perhaps she never thought about it. A man's place was in the fields.

In one of her more humorous columns from April 20, 1917, Laura puzzles over her increasingly hectic lifestyle. She observes: "We have so many machines and so many helps . . . to save time and yet I wonder what we do with the time we save. Nobody seems to have any!" Having more time because of labor-saving devices, Laura has enrolled in more clubs and joined more efforts for civic betterment. Ironically, she almost seems like the "modern" woman who wants to "have it all." A preoccupation with time management and how to enjoy an increasingly busy life runs through many of her columns. She wants back that time she "saved."

Rose's preoccupations lay in other directions. A more "radical" feminist than Laura, Rose had a long independence from the hassle of husband-keeping that left her free to work in California, to travel for the Red Cross, and to live in Albania. Her divorce from Gillette Lane, after nine years of marriage, did not seem to affect her much, though it must have shocked Laura, who put such value on home and family. In addition, Mrs. Wilder was deeply pious, and her daughter was a skeptic in matters of faith. Laura and Almanzo went to Methodist camp meetings and the like and kept up strict moral appearances, while Rose was more of a freethinker and shocked the little community by keeping company with male visitors past the accustomed hours of Mansfield standards.

Rose returned from Albania in 1928 to live with her parents and watch over their declining years, but she found Mansfield just as horribly parochial as when she was a teenager and had left to be a telegrapher in Kansas City. Rose worried about her mother's narrow world and penny-pinching ways. She encouraged "Momma Bess," as she called Laura, to write for the big markets and earn her way out of straitened farm life rather than save her way out of it. Her mother's habits of thrift drove Rose to distraction.

Laura would have been concerned that Rose had lost a certain sense of domestic responsibility by being *too* free and independent. A May 5, 1916, column called "Folks Are 'Just Folks'" suggests that she believed, with the poet Longfellow, that "homekeeping hearts are happiest." Rose had a much more conflicted view of home keeping. She wished to mother her parents and look after them in retirement—and at the same time to be free of that responsibility. From the diaries and letters of long ago, it is almost impossible to know if Laura and Almanzo really needed their daughter's parenting skills. The only thing that is certain is that Rose resented the responsibility but found it impossible to ignore.

How much supervision did Rose provide during her mother's composition of the Little House books? Laura's columns provide some insight on this issue. It is clear that Mrs. Wilder knew how to use the telling anecdote, and she also had a good eye for revealing detail. In a September 20, 1916, column titled "All the World Is Queer," she tells of receiving a modern butter churn that lacks a motor and is too difficult to churn by hand in the fashion she is used to. She yearns for her old churn but can't convince the Man of the Place that she appreciates the kind thought behind the gift, though she can't stand the gift itself. Finally, Laura throws the abominable churn outside, "just as far as I could," she tells Almanzo with embarrassment. Then Almanzo moans: "I wish I had known that you did not want to use it. I would like to have the wheels and shaft, but they're ruined now." All the world is "queer," Mrs. Wilder notes, including herself.

But as one who admitted to her editor, John Case, "I never graduated from anything and only attended high school two terms," Wilder would have had difficulty organizing the sustained narrative that was one reason for the success of her books. Rose was a professional writer and would have been able to pull the anecdotes together. Thus, I believe, the mother's talent for anecdote *and* the daughter's talent for narrative were both necessary to create America's classic stories of the settling of the West.

For more information on how mother and daughter actually worked with or against each other in the making of this series, I recommend two books: *The Ghost in the Little House* by William Holtz and *Becoming Laura Ingalls Wilder* by John E. Miller.[6] Miller's chapter titled "Building a Writing Career" offers useful comments on Laura's journalistic work and development.

Laura wrote in an August 1, 1923, column that the picking of a single sunflower in a meadow brought back "memories of sweet words of counsel. . . . I realize that all my life the teachings of those early days have influenced me and the example set by father and mother has been something I have tried to follow. . . . The real things of life that are the common possession of us all are of the greatest value; worth far more than motor cars or radio outfits, more than lands or money; and our whole store of these wonderful riches

6. John E. Miller, *Becoming Laura Ingalls Wilder: The Woman behind the Legend* (Columbia: University of Missouri Press, 1998).

may be revealed to us by such a common, beautiful thing as a wild sunflower."

It is in this same spirit of remembrance that these columns are gathered here. They represent the work of a woman who was not frozen in the land of long ago but who was ever looking forward to the adventures that lay ahead. That is the essence of the pioneer heritage and of the heritage we have from Laura.

A NOTE ON THE TEXT

The columns have been reproduced here as they were originally published. Punctuation, spelling, and capitalization remain unchanged with the exception of obvious typos such as "teh" for "the" and the article titles, which have been altered only to standardize the capitalization.

Being a child of the prairie and catching such education as she could between the many little houses of her youth, Laura had an understanding of grammar and punctuation that was elementary at best. Her early columns for the *Ruralist* appear to have been more carefully edited than her later ones. In its spellings, the *Ruralist* appears to have adopted some of the reforms once proposed by President Theodore Roosevelt, himself a notoriously bad speller. At the time of the *Ruralist* columns, acceptable shortcuts were "tho" for "though," "altho" for "although," and "thru" for "through," among others the reader will notice.

The n-word appears in one column because that is the word Laura Ingalls Wilder heard when she was reporting on the San Francisco exhibition of 1915. So far as I know, it did not reflect her own thinking about blacks of the time but only what some sailors said.

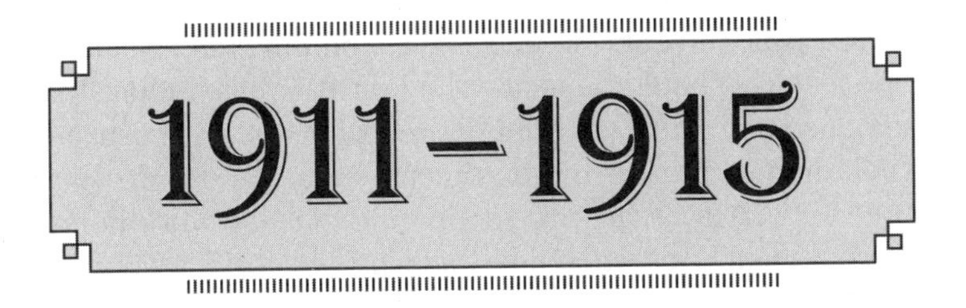

Favors the Small Farm Home

It Lessens the Investment, Improves Country Social Conditions, Makes the Owner More Independent of Poor Help, Promotes Better Farming Methods and Reduces the Labor of Housekeeping

February 18, 1911

There is a movement in the United States today, wide-spread and very far-reaching in its consequences. People are seeking after a freer, healthier, happier life. They are tired of the noise and dirt, bad air and crowds of the cities and are turning longing eyes toward the green slopes, wooded hills, pure running water and health giving breezes of the country.

A great many of these people are discouraged by the amount of capital required to buy a farm and hesitate at the thought of undertaking a new business. But there is no need to buy a large farm. A small farm will bring in a good living with less work and worry and the business is not hard to learn.

In a settlement of small farms the social life can be much pleasanter than on large farms, where the distance to the nearest neighbor is so great. Fifteen or twenty families on five-acre farms will be near enough together to have pleasant social gatherings in the evenings. The women can have their embroidery clubs, their reading club and even the children can have their little parties, without much trouble or loss of time. This could not be done if each family lived on a 100 or 200-acre farm. There is less hired help required on the small farm also, and this makes the work in the house lighter.

I am an advocate of the small farm and I want to tell you how an ideal home can be made on, and a good living made from, five acres of land.

Whenever a woman's home-making is spoken of, the man in the case is presupposed and the woman's home-making is expected to consist in keeping the house clean and serving good meals on time, etc. In short, that all of her home-making should be inside the house. It takes more than the inside of the house to make a pleasant home and women are capable of making the whole home, outside and in, if necessary. She can do so to perfection on a five-acre farm by hireing some of the outside work done.

However, our ideal home should be made by a man and a woman together. First, I want to say that a five-acre farm is large enough for the support of a family. From $75 to $150 a month, besides a great part of the living can be made on that size farm from poultry or fruit or a combination of poultry, fruit and dairy.

This has been proved by actual experience so that the financial part of this small home is provided for.

Conditions have changed so much in the country within the last few years that we country women have no need to envy our sisters in the city. We women on the farm no longer expect to work as our grandmothers did.

With the high prices to be had for all kinds of timber and wood we now do not have to burn wood to save the expense of fuel, but can have our oil stove, which makes the work so much cooler in the summer, so much lighter and cleaner. There need be no carrying in of wood and carrying out of ashes, with the attendant dirt, dust and disorder.

Our cream separator saves us hours formerly spent in setting and skimming milk and washing pans, besides saving the large amount of cream that was lost in the old way.

Then there is the gasoline engine. Bless it! Besides doing the work of a hired man outside, it can be made to do the pumping of the water and the churning, turn the washing machine and even run the sewing machine.[1]

On many farms running water can be supplied in the house from springs by means of rams or air pumps and I know of two places where water is piped into and through the house from springs farther up on the hills. This water is brought down by gravity alone and the only expense is the pipeing. There are many such places in the Ozark hills waiting to be taken advantage of.

This, you see, supplies water works for the kitchen and bath room simply for the initial cost of putting in the pipes. In one farm home I know, where there are no springs to pipe the water from, there is a deep well and a pump just outside the kitchen door. From this a pipe runs into a tank in the kitchen

1. During this era of newly developed labor-saving devices, the promise of work and time saved seemed to outweigh the dangers posed by gas fumes and the possibility of fire.

and from this tank there are two pipes. One runs into the cellar and the other underground to a tank in the barnyard, which is of course much lower than the one in the kitchen.

When water is wanted down cellar to keep the cream and butter cool a cork is pulled from the cellar pipe by means of a little chain and by simply pumping the pump out doors, cold water runs into the vat in the cellar. The water already there rises and runs out at the overflow pipe through the cellar and out at the cellar drain.

When the stock at the barn need watering, the cork is pulled from the other pipe and the water flows from the tank in the kitchen into the tank in the yard. And always the tank in the kitchen is full of fresh, cold water, because this other water all runs through it. This is a simple, inexpensive contrivance for use on a place where there is no running water.

It used to be that the woman on a farm was isolated and behind the times. A weekly paper was what the farmer read and he had to go to town to get that. All this is changed. Now the rural delivery brings us our daily papers and we keep up on the news of the world as well or better than though we lived in the city. The telephone gives us connection with the outside world at all times and we know what is going on in our nearest town by many a pleasant chat with our friends there.

Circulating libraries, thanks to our state university, are scattered through the rural districts and we are eagerly taking advantage of them.

The interurban trolly lines being built throughout our country will make it increasingly easy for us to run into town for an afternoon's shopping or any other pleasure. These trolly lines are and more will be, operated by electricity, furnished by our swift running streams, and in a few years our country homes will be lighted by this same electric power.

Yes indeed, things have changed in the country and we have the advantages of city life if we care to take them. Besides we have what it is impossible for the woman in the city to have. We have a whole five acres for our back yard and all out doors for our conservatory, filled not only with beautiful flowers, but with grand old trees as well, with running water and beautiful birds, with sunshine and fresh air and all wild, free, beautiful things.

The children, instead of playing with other children in some street or alley can go make friends with the birds, on their nests in the bushes, as my little girl used to do, until the birds are so tame they will not fly at their approach. They can gather berries in the garden and nuts in the woods and grow strong and healthy, with rosy cheeks and bright eyes. This little farm home is a delightful place for friends to come for afternoon tea under the trees. There is room for a tennis court for the young people. There are skating parties in the winter and the sewing and reading clubs of the nearby towns, as well as the neighbor women, are always anxious for an invitation to hold their meetings there.

In conclusion I must say if there are any country women who are wasting their time envying their sisters in the city—don't do it. Such an attitude is out of date. Wake up to your opportunities. Look your place over and if you have not kept up with the modern improvements and conveniences in your home, bring yourself up to date. Then take the time saved from bringing water from the spring, setting the milk in the old way and churning by hand, to build yourself a better social life. If you don't take a daily paper subscribe for one. They are not expensive and are well worth the price in the brightening they will give your mind and in the pleasant evenings you can have reading and discussing the news of the world. Take advantage of the circulating library. Make your little farm home noted for its hospitality and the social times you have there. Keep up with the march of progress for the time is coming when the cities will be the workshops of the world and abandoned to the workers, while the real cultured, social, and intellectual life will be in the country.

The People in God's Out-of-Doors

April 15, 1911

I love to listen to the bird songs every day
And hear the free winds whisper in their play,
Among the tall old trees and sweet wild flowers.
I love to watch the little brook
That gushes from its cool and rocky bed
Deep in the earth. The sky is blue o'er head
And sunbeams dance upon its tiny rivulete.
I love the timid things
That gather round the little watercourse,
To listen to the frogs with voices hoarse,
And see the squirrels leap and bound at play.
Then, too, I love to hear
The loud clear whistle of the pretty quail,
To see the chipmunk flirt his saucy tail,
Then peep from out his home within the tree.
I love to watch the busy bees,

To see the rabbit scurry in the brush,
Or sit when falls the dewy evening's hush
And listen to the sad-voiced whippoorwill.

From Mrs. Wilder's Nature Songs

The Story of Rocky Ridge Farm

How Mother Nature in the Ozarks Rewarded Well Directed Efforts after a Fruitless Struggle on the Plains of the Dakotas. The Blessings of Living Water and a Gentle Climate

July 22, 1911

Editor's Note:—Among the stories received in the course of our farm home story contest, the following came from Mr. Wilder,[2] with the request that it be published, if worthy, but that it be not considered an entrant for any prize. We certainly consider it worthy—one of the most helpful and interesting—and believe all contributors to this feature will approve of our giving it good position on this page since we cannot give it a prize. The list of winners will be found on page 5.

To appreciate fully the reason why we named our place Rocky Ridge Farm, it should have been seen at the time of the christening. To begin with it was not bottom land nor by any stretch of the imagination could it have been called second bottom. It was, and is, uncompromisingly ridge land, on the very tip top of the ridge at that, within a very few miles of the highest point in the Ozarks. And rocky—it certainly was rocky when it was named, although strangers coming to the place now, say "but why do you call it Rocky Ridge?"

The place looked unpromising enough when we first saw it, not only one but several ridges rolling in every direction and covered with rocks and brush and timber. Perhaps it looked worse to me because I had just left the prairies of South Dakota where the land is easily farmed. I had been ordered

2. Although this piece was bylined simply A. J. Wilder, what existing manuscript evidence there is of Almanzo's writing strongly suggests to scholars that Laura did all of the for-publication writing in her household.

south because those prairies had robbed me of my health[3] and I was glad to leave them for they had also robbed me of nearly everything I owned, by continual crop failures. Still coming from such a smooth country the place looked so rough to me that I hesitated to buy it. But wife had taken a violent fancy to this particular piece of land, saying if she could not have it, she did not want any because it could be made into such a pretty place. It needed the eye of faith, however, to see that in time it could be made very beautiful.

So we bought Rocky Ridge Farm and went to work. We had to put a mortgage on it of $200, and had very little except our bare hands with which to pay it off, improve the farm and make our living while we did it. It speaks well for the farm, rough and rocky as it was that my wife and myself with my broken health were able to do all this.

A flock of hens—by the way, there is no better place in the country for raising poultry than right here—a flock of hens and the wood we cleared from the land bought our groceries and clothing. The timber on the place also made rails to fence it and furnished the materials for a large log barn.

At the time I bought it there were on the place four acres cleared and a small log house with a fire place and no windows. These were practically all the improvements and there was not grass enough growing on the whole forty acres to keep a cow. The four acres cleared had been set out to apple trees and enough trees to set twenty acres more were in nursery rows near the house. The land on which to set them was not even cleared of the timber. Luckily I had bought the place before any serious damage had been done to the fine timber around the building site, although the start had been made to cut it down.

It was hard work and sometimes short rations at the first, but gradually the difficulties were overcome. Land was cleared and prepared, by heroic effort, in time to set out all the apple trees and in a few years the orchard came into bearing. Fields were cleared and brought to a good state of fertility. The timber around the buildings was thinned out enough so that grass would grow between the trees, and each tree would grow in good shape, which has made a beautiful park of the grounds. The rocks have been picked up and grass seed sown so that the pastures and meadows are in fine condition and support quite a little herd of cows, for grass grows remarkably well on "Rocky Ridge" when the timber is cleared away to give it a chance. This good grass and clear spring water make it an ideal dairy farm.

3. Almanzo had suffered a paralysis of his leg while in the Dakotas. None of those I interviewed forty years after his death could tell me which leg he favored.

Sixty acres more have been bought and paid for, which added to the original forty makes a farm of one hundred acres. There is no waste land on the farm except a wood lot which we have decided to leave permanently for the timber. Perhaps we have not made so much money as farmers in a more level country, but neither have we been obliged to spend so much for expenses and as the net profit is what counts at the end of the year, I am not afraid to compare the results for a term of years with farms of the same size in a more level country.

Our little Rocky Ridge Farm has supplied everything necessary for a good living and given us good interest on all the money invested every year since the first two. No year has it fallen below ten per cent and one extra good year it paid 100 per cent. Besides this it has doubled in value, and $3,000 more, since it was bought.

We are not by any means through with making improvements on Rocky Ridge Farm. There are on the place five springs of running water which never fail even in the dryest season. Some of these springs are so situated that by building a dam below them, a lake of three acres, twenty feet deep in places will be near the house. Another small lake can be made in the same way in the duck pasture and these are planned for the near future. But the first thing on the improvement program is building a cement tank as a reservoir around a spring which is higher than the buildings. Water from this tank will be piped down and supply water in the house and barn and in the poultry yards.

When I look around the farm now and see the smooth, green, rolling meadows and pastures, the good fields of corn and wheat and oats; when I see the orchard and strawberry field like huge bouquets in the spring or full of fruit later in the season; when I see the grape vines hanging full of lucious grapes, I can hardly bring back to my mind the rough, rocky, brushy, ugly place that we first called Rocky Ridge Farm. The name given it then serves to remind us of the battles we have fought and won and gives a touch of sentiment and an added value to the place.

In conclusion, I am going to quote from a little gift book which my wife sent out to a few friends last Christmas:

> "Just come and visit Rocky Ridge,
>   Please grant us our request,
> We'll give you all a jolly time—
>   Welcome the coming; speed the parting guest."

My Apple Orchard

How a "Tenderfoot" Knowing Nothing about Orcharding Learned the Business in Missouri—Quail as Insect Destroyers

June 1, 1912

This week the Ruralist's front cover illustration shows a 12-year-old apple tree with Mr. Wilder, the writer of this article, standing beside it. There was gathered from this tree at one time 5 barrels of No. 1 and 3 barrels of No. 2 apples as a result of his cultural methods.—Editor

When I bought my farm in the fall, some years ago, there were 800 apple trees on it growing in nursery rows. Two hundred had been set out the spring before, in an old wornout field, where the land was so poor it would not raise a stalk of corn over 4 feet high. This field was all the land cleared on the place; the rest of the farm was covered with oak timber.

I have always thought it must have been a good agent who persuaded the man of whom I bought the place to mortgage it for 1,000 apple trees when the ground was not even cleared on which to set them. However he unloaded his blunder onto me and I knew nothing about an orchard; did not even know one apple from another. I did know though that apple trees, or indeed trees of any kind, could not be expected to thrive in land too poor to raise corn-fodder, so whenever I made a trip to town, I brought back a load of wood ashes from the mill or a load of manure from the livery barn and put it around those trees that were already set out in the field.

I cleared enough land that winter on which to set out the trees from the nursery, broke it the next spring and put in the trees after I had worked it as smooth as I could. The trees already set out were 25 feet apart in the rows and 32 feet between the rows so I set the others the same way. I dug the holes for the trees large and deep, making the dirt fine in the bottom and mixing some wood ashes with it.

The trees I handled very carefully not to injure the roots and spread the roots out as nearly as possible in a natural manner, when setting the trees. Fine dirt was put over the roots at first and pressed down firmly, then the dirt was shoveled in to fill the hole. Some more wood ashes was mixed with the dirt when it was being shoveled in. I did not hill the dirt up around the tree, but left it a little cupping for conserving moisture. All trash was raked away, leaving it clean and smooth, and again I used some wood ashes, scattering them around the tree, but being careful that none touched it to injure the bark. The ashes were used altogether with the idea of fertilizing the soil and with no idea of any other benefit, but I think they may have saved my orchard.

It is confessing to a colossal ignorance, but I found out later that I planted woolly aphis on nearly every one of my apple tree roots. At the time I thought that for some reason they were a little moldy. I read afterward in an orchard paper that the lye from wood ashes would destroy the woolly aphis and save the tree and as the use of wood ashes around the trees was kept up for several years I give them the credit for saving my trees.

As I never allowed hunting on the farm, the quail were thick in the orchard and used to wallow and dust themselves like chickens in this fine dirt close to the tree. I wish this fact to be particularly noted in connection with the other fact that I had no borers in my trees for years.

A near neighbor set out 2,000 trees about the same time and lost seven-eighths of them because of borers. He used every possible means to rid his trees of them except the simple one of letting the quail and other birds live in his orchard. Instead he allowed his boys to kill every bird they saw.

My apples were sound and smooth, not wormy, which I also credit to the birds for catching insects of all kinds, as I never sprayed the trees. Within the last few years the hunters, both boys and men, have been so active that it has been impossible to save my quail and so I have had to begin the eternal round of spraying, and cutting the trees to get the borers out.

When I set the trees I trimmed them back a good deal. While I knew nothing of the science of trimming I knew that I did not want a forked tree, so I trimmed to one stem with a few little branches left at the top. I watched the trees as they grew and trimmed away while they were very small all the branches that would interlock or rub against another branch.

In the fall I always whitewashed the trees to keep the rabbits from gnawing the bark and if the storms washed it off I whitewashed them again. Every spring they were whitewashed in April as a sort of house-cleaning and to make the bark smooth, so it would not harbor insects, for I found that if there was a rough place that was where the eggs of insects were deposited.

Between the trees I raised corn, potatoes and garden until the trees were 8 years old, when I seeded the land down to timothy and clover. Of course when I raised crops I fertilized them enough to make them grow and the trees always got their share. As a result I get a good hay crop out of the orchard making two good crops from the land. I think that one thing that has made my orchard a success is that I took individual care of each tree. What that particular tree needed it got. Wife and I were so well acquainted with the trees that if I wished to mention one to her, I would say "that tree with the large branch to the south," or "the tree that leans to the north," etc. The tree that leaned was gently taught to stand straight so that the sun would not burn the bark. This was done by tying it to a stake, firmly driven into the ground on the south side of the tree and from time to time shortening the string which held it.

The trees came into bearing at 7 years old and the apples were extra well colored and smooth skinned. I have had apple buyers and nursery men tell me that my orchard was the prettiest they ever saw, and my Ben Davis are different from any I have ever seen in being better colored and flavored and in the texture of the flesh. People even refuse to believe that they are Ben Davis, at times. My orchard is mostly Ben Davis and the rest is Missouri Pippin.

If I were to start another orchard I would plow and cultivate the land for several seasons to prepare it for the trees. The wildness and roughness should be worked out in order to give the little trees a fair chance. Then I should plant apple seed where I wanted the trees to stand, and then bud, onto the sprout, the variety I wished to raise. In this way the tap root would not be disturbed as it is by moving the tree but would run straight down. This makes a longer-lived, stronger tree.

Shorter Hours for Farm Women

The Woman Who Manages the Farm Home Should Have Every Means of Saving Labor Placed at Her Disposal. Simple Conveniences within Reach of All

June 28, 1913

Editor's Note.—At a time when women across the seas are marching the streets and demanding votes for women, when the law gives the woman in shop or factory a nine hour day it is interesting to note that the Missouri farm woman is making no demands. Her lot is a fairly happy one and she wisely realizes it. Yet it can and must be improved, and Mrs. Wilder who is herself a farm woman here makes some suggestions which should be helpful even to the wife of the tenant who has but little to call her own.

When so much is being done to better the condition of the laboring man all over the world, it is good to know that the work of farm women is receiving its share of attention. Thinking persons realize that the woman, on the farm, is a most important factor in the success or failure of the whole farm business and that, aside from any kindly feeling toward her, it pays in dollars and cents to conserve her health and strength. Women on the farm have not as a rule the conveniences that city housekeepers have and their work includes much outside work, such as gardening, caring for chickens and gathering as well as putting up fruits and vegetables.

Farm women have been patient and worked very hard. It has seemed sometimes as though they and their work were overlooked in the march of progress. Yet improvement has found them out and a great many helps in their work have been put into use in the last few years. Farm homes with modern heating, lighting and water equipments are increasing in number and, although the majority have not yet advanced so far as that, a great number have passed the stage of the bucket brigade from the spring, or the hand over hand hauling of water from deep wells. It is getting to be quite the common thing to have the water piped down from the spring, raised up from the spring with a ram, or forced up from the bottom of deep wells by the compressed air pump. So, many steps have been saved the women folks, for they did most of the water carrying. It is so much easier to turn a faucet when one wants a bucket of water and the time and strength saved can be used to so much better advantage in other ways.

Cream separators are taking the place of the troublesome setting of milk; gardens are being planted in rows so that a horse will do in a few minutes what would be a work of hours by hand; home canning outfits are lessening the labor of canning fruits and vegetables; kitchen cabinets are saving steps in the kitchen and bread and cake mixers save tired hands and arms. Just the change from heavy iron ware utensils to granite ware and tin has made more difference than one would think at first. Vacuum cleaners have almost done away with house cleaning time, for many farm women. In place of the above-ground cellar there is the simple little hanging cellarette. Several shelves of convenient size, either round or square are fastened together the required distance apart. A close fitting case or cover, of two thicknesses of burlap or bran sack is made which completely encloses all the shelves and is closely buttoned down one side, for the door. The "cellar" is then hung from the ceiling in some convenient place; a leaky bucket full of water is hung above it so that the water will drip on it, keeping all the burlap wet; a pan is set under it to catch the drips and there you have a handy cellar for keeping cool the butter and milk. One will save many a trip up and down cellar stairs or perhaps down to the spring. This hanging cellar is kept cool by the evaporation of the water from its surface.

A friend of mine was unable to stand the heat of the cook stove in summer, so she bought an inexpensive oil stove and a fireless cooker. Anything which required long cooking she started on the oil stove, then placed in the fireless cooker, finishing off, if necessary, when the time came, by a few minutes browning on the oil stove. The combination worked perfectly. There was only a little heat from the oil stove; none at all from the fireless cooker; time and labor of carrying in fuel and keeping up fires; of taking up ashes and cleaning up the dust and dirt all saved and no increase in the running expenses, for the wood, on the farm, sold and bought the coal oil for the oil stove.

Another labor-saving idea is the use of a small work table on casters, which can be easily moved from place to place. If cupboards, stove and table are some distance apart this is a great step saver. At one trip it can take from the cupboard to the stove all the things necessary in the getting of a meal. The meal can be dished up on it and all taken to the dining table at once. The dishes can be taken away to wash upon it.

It was while recovering from a serious illness that I discovered the uses and value of a high stool. It is surprising how much of the house work can be done while sitting,—ironing, washing dishes, preparing vegetables and dishes to cook or bake and even such cooking as frying griddle cakes can be accomplished while sitting. There should be a foot rest on the stool so the feet will not hang and it should be light so it can be easily moved. The movable table and the high stool form a combination for saving steps and tiresome standing that is hard to beat.

Ideas for using the things at hand to make our work easier will come to us if we notice a little. For instance if we keep some old newspapers on hand in the kitchen the uses we find for them will multiply. Rub the stove over with one when washing the dishes and the disagreeable task of blacking the stove can be delayed much longer. The paper can be burned and our hands remain clean. Put papers on the work table to set the pots and pans on while working and the table will not have to be scoured. When the men come to a meal, with their work clothes on, from some particularly dirty job, newspapers spread over the tablecloth will save a hard job of washing and ironing.

Time and strength saved by the use of one help makes it easier to get the next and the time saved gives leisure to meet with the neighborhood club or to talk with a neighbor and find still other ways of doing the work more easily. Talking things over is a great help as is also the planning of the work so that the whole family can work together to advantage and without friction. As in any other business each one must do his work well and on time so as not to hinder the others in what they are trying to accomplish.

The combination of capital or business interests forms a trust, the joining together of union forces makes a labor trust and each does much better for his own interests than though everyone worked alone. Why not join the household forces and make a family trust all working together for the same objects? In order to do this successfully there must be system in the work and each one must know what is expected of him. In this way more and better work can be accomplished. It takes careful thought and planning to have the household machinery run smoothly and to the minute, with meals on time so that the farm work will not be hindered and the woman who can do this and the outside work connected with the house has proven her executive ability and business talent.

While system is a great help in the work it is best to get a new light on it once in a while, so we will not get in a rut and do things a certain way because we are in the habit, when we might make some improvement. It helps in finding the little kinks that need straightening out in our work, to notice if there is any of it that we dread to do and if there is, then study that thing and find some way to do it differently. Perhaps just some little change will be a great help. A woman's work on the farm is very interesting if thought and study are given it and in no other business can a woman so well keep up with her husband in his work. The more the farm is studied with the help of good farm papers and the Experiment stations, the more interesting it becomes and the woman on a farm may, if she wishes, become such an expert as to take the place of a farm adviser. Work in which we are interested can never become drudgery so long as we keep up that interest.

One thing is most important if we expect to keep rested and fit to do our best and that is not to worry over the work nor to try to do it before the time comes. The feeling of worry and strain caused by trying to carry the whole week's work at once is very tiring. It doesn't pay to be like the woman of years ago, in old Vermont, who opened the stairway door at 5 o'clock on Monday morning and called to the hired girl: "Liza! Liza! Hurry up and come down! Today is wash day and the washing not started; tomorrow is ironing day and the ironing not begun; and the next day is Wednesday and here's the week half gone and nothing done yet."

Better for a little while each day to be like the tramp who was not at all afraid of work, yet could lie down right beside it and go to sleep. Slipping away to some quiet place to lie down and relax for 15 minutes, if no longer, each day rests both mind and body surprisingly. This rest does more good if taken at a regular time and the work goes along so much better when we are rested and bright that there is no time lost.

Change is rest! How often we have proved this by going away from our work for a day or even part of a day, thinking of other things and forgetting the daily round for a little while. On coming back the work is taken up with new interest and seems much easier.

If it is not possible to go away, why not let the mind wander a little when the hands can do the task without our strict attention? I have always found that I did not get so tired, and my day seemed shorter when I listened to the birds singing or noticed, from the window, the beauties of the trees or clouds. This is a part of the farm equipment that cannot be improved upon, though it might be increased with advantage. Perhaps some day we will all have kitchens like the club kitchen lately installed in New York, where everything from peeling the potatoes to cooking the dinner and washing the dishes is done by electricity, but the birds' songs will never be any sweeter nor the beauties of field and forest, of cloud and stream, be any more full of delight, and these are already ours.

Good Times on the Farm

It's Easy to Have Fun if You Plan for It

February 5, 1914

Distances are long in the country, and although it is very pleasant to go and spend the day with a friend it takes a good while to see many people in that way. Women who have been rather isolated all summer need to be enlivened by seeing people, the more the better. There is something brightening to the wits and cheering to the spirits in congenial crowds that is found in nothing else. Why not form a neighborhood club and combine the pleasure of going "a visiting" with the excitement of a little crowd and the joy of entertaining our friends all together when our turn comes? It is less trouble to entertain several at once than to entertain several times; besides there is a great saving of time, and as the club meets at first one house and then another, the neighborhood visiting is done with less of work and worry and more of pleasure than in any other way.

NEEDED BY COUNTRY WOMEN

It used to be that only the women in town could have the advantages of women's clubs, but now the woman in the country can be just as cultured a club woman as though she lived in town. The Neighborhood club can take up any line of work or study the members wish. Courses of reading can be obtained from the state university or the International Congress of Farm Women, and either organization will be glad to help with plans, advice and instruction. Bits of fancy work or sewing may be taken to the meetings and the latest stitch or the short cut in plain sewing can be learned by all. Recipes may be exchanged, good stories told, songs sung and jokes enjoyed.

The serving of some dainty refreshments would add to the pleasure of the afternoon and keep the social graces in good practice. Women in the country as well as those in town need these occasions to show what charming hostesses and pleasant guests they can be. If the men folks want to go along, by all means let them do so. They might gather by themselves and discuss farm matters. They might even organize and have a little farmers' club of their own, if they have not done so already; then they would be even more willing to hitch up and drive to the meeting place.

NO TIRESOME MEETINGS

There are so many ways to vary the meetings and programs they need never become tiresome or dull. Now and then the meeting may be held in the evening and an entertainment given by home talent. Sometimes the club might go in a body to a lecture or some amusement in town, or for a little excursion to the nearest city. A regular organization with the proper officers, a motto, and membership badges will add to the interest, as will also being an auxiliary of some larger organization such as the International Congress of Farm Women.

Although the fall with its greater amount of leisure may be the best time to start a club of this kind, it need not be given up at the coming of spring. The long, bright days of summer, when we all long to go picnicking and fishing, offer simply a different form of entertainment and social life and should be enjoyed to the full. Perhaps the meetings might best be farther apart while the rush of work is on, but a day off now and then will never be noticed in the work and will do the workers a world of good.

A Plain Beauty Talk

Women Can Afford to Spend Time on Their Looks

April 20, 1914

"Beauty is but skin deep" says the old adage, and most of us would be glad to know it was as deep as that. Why ugliness should have been made a virtue, in the teachings of our youth, is passing strange. We all admire beauty of character, but the possession of it is no excuse for neglecting our personal appearance. Indeed it seems to me there must be a fault in the character when one is satisfied with anything less than the best she can make of herself. It is not vanity to wish to appear pleasing to the eyes of our home folks and friends, nor is it a matter of small importance. To be well groomed and good to look at will give us an added self respect and a greater influence over others.

It is more difficult for country women than for those in the city to make a well-groomed appearance, for they usually do rougher work and they cannot go to a beauty parlor and have themselves put in trim as the city woman can. However many barber shops there may be in a country town, there is almost never a beauty parlor for the women. Until we can make a change in things, and have our beauty parlor in town where we can have the same attention that men do at theirs—oh yes, the barber shop is a man's beauty parlor! They have things put on their hair to prevent its falling and to make it grow, they have soothing lotions and astringents and powder put on their faces. Don't let any of them tell you a beauty parlor is foolish or unnecessary, or any of those things—until we can have our beauty parlor in town, we must do these things for ourselves.

We can make a very good job of it, too, with some good, pure soap, a bottle of dioxogen and some orange wood sticks, a bottle of glycerine and rosewater and a good tooth brush. With these aids, we can take care of our complexion, our hair, our hands and our teeth, and with these in good condition we shall have all the skin-deep beauty necessary for practical purposes; and this will help rather than hinder us in making a beautiful character.

There are a few simple things to remember in caring for the complexion. When washing the face it should first be thoroughly cleansed with warm water, using a good soap, then the soap should be well rinsed off with clear warm water. The warm water opens the pores of the skin and with the soap thoroughly cleanses them; the clear warm water rinses out the soap so it will not clog the pores. The face should then be well rinsed with cold water, the colder the better, to close the pores and tighten the skin to prevent flabbiness. Cold water is one of the best aids in keeping a good complexion if it is used in this way. It keeps the pores of the skin from becoming enlarged and brings the blood to the face, thus keeping up a good circulation in the minute blood vessels; and this makes the skin look fresh and youthful.

Cheap perfumed soaps are apt to be injurious to the skin and their use is risky. A good castile soap is always good and not expensive when bought a large bar at a time.

When washing the face the skin should always be rubbed up and outward, because it is the gradual sagging down of the muscles of the face that causes wrinkles. You can satisfy yourself of this by a few experiments before a glass. A good cold cream rubbed into the skin just before the cold water is used, and then wiped lightly off with a soft cloth, will help to keep the wrinkles away and make the skin softer.

Face and hands should always be well dried after washing. If it is not the skin will become rough. Keep the bottle of glycerine and rosewater close by the wash pan and after the hands are washed and dried, while they are still damp, rub a few drops of this over them. Do this as many times a day as the hands are washed and they will keep soft and white.

Wrap a little cotton around the point of one of the little orange wood sticks, dip it into the bottle of dioxygen and wipe out the dirt from under the finger nails. Then take a little dry cotton on the stick and dry under them. This will do away with the annoying black line, for it cleanses and bleaches and does not make the nail rough, to catch more dirt, as a knife or scissors will when used to clean the nails.

There are many simple things in daily use on a farm that are splendid beautifiers. Washing in buttermilk will whiten the hands and face. Fresh strawberries rubbed on the skin will bleach it, and rhubarb or tomatoes will remove stains from the fingers. None of these things will do the least harm. Common table salt is one of the best tooth powders, and with a good brush and water will keep the teeth clean and white.

The hair should not be washed too often, for this will cause it to fall. Still, the scalp should be kept clean. Wearing a little dust cap over the hair while doing the work will help greatly in this, and such frequent washings will not be necessary.

When washing the hair it is best to dissolve the soap in a little water, making a soft soap. Rub this into the hair with water until it lathers well, then wash it off. Repeat if necessary. When the hair is clean, rinse it well with clear warm water, until the soap is all out, then pour some cold water over the scalp to close the pores of the skin. This will prevent taking cold and also act as a tonic to the scalp. The addition of a little baking soda to the water will lighten the hair and help to make it fluffy.

A tea made from common garden sage will darken the hair and help it to grow.

A Homemaker of the Ozarks

Mrs. Durnell Reclaimed a Farm, Built a House in the Wilderness and Learned the Secret of Contentment

June 20, 1914

Women have always been the home makers, but it is not usually expected of them that they should also be the home builders from the ground up. Nevertheless they sometimes are and their success in this double capacity shows what women can do when they try. Among the women who have done both is Mrs. C. A. Durnell of Mansfield, Mo. She has not only made a home but she has put a farm in condition to support it.

Mansfield is on the very crest of the Ozarks and the land is rough and hilly, covered with timber, where it has not been cleared. Although one of the most beautiful places in the world to live, with a soil repaying bountifully the care given it, still it is no easy thing to make a farm out of a piece of rough land. Imagine then the task for a woman, especially one with no previous experience of farming.

Mrs. Durnell was a city woman and for twenty years after her marriage, lived in St. Louis where her husband worked in the railroad terminal yards. Here she raised her three children until the eldest, a son, was through college and established in his profession.

None of the children were strong and about this time the second, a daughter, was taken sick with consumption, while the youngest, also a daughter, was threatened with the same disease. Hoping to restore their health, Mrs. Durnell brought them into the Ozarks, but too late to save the sick daughter.

As the other daughter showed signs of improvement, Mrs. Durnell decided to stay and the thought came to her to go on a little farm and make a home for her own and her husband's old age.

Sickness and the expense of living had used up the most of Mr. Durnell's wages as they went along and all they had to show for their twenty years of work was a house with a mortgage on it. Mrs. Durnell saw what so many do not realize until too late, that when Mr. Durnell became too old to hold his position any longer they would have no business of their own and quite likely no home either. A small farm, if she could get one running in good shape, would be a business of their own and a home where they could be independent and need not fear the age limit.

Mr. Durnell stayed with his job in St. Louis, to be able to send what money he could spare to help in making the start.

They secured a farm of 23 acres a quarter of a mile from town. Ten acres was in an old, wornout field that to use a local expression has been "corned to death"; 5 acres was in an old orchard, unkempt, neglected and grown up to wild blackberries. In the Ozark hills, neglected ground will grow up to wild blackberry briars, loaded with fruit in season. As the shiftless farmer said, "anyone can raise blackberries if he aint too durned lazy." Aside from this old orchard and the wornout field, the place was covered with oak thicket where the land had been cleared and then allowed to go back. This second growth oak was about six feet high and as large around as a man's wrist. The fences were mostly down and such as were standing were the old worm, rail fence. The house was a log shack.

Mrs. Durnell and her daughter moved into the log house and went to work. They bought a cow to furnish them milk and butter, but the cow would not stay inside the tumble-down fences, so repairing the fence was the first job. Some of it they built higher with their own hands and some they hired rebuilt, but there was only a little money to go on, so the work moved slowly. When the fences were in order and the cow kept at home they felt that a great deal had been gained.

The property in St. Louis was sold and after paying the mortgage there was enough left to build a five room house, which Mrs. Durnell planned and the construction of which she superintended. It was a happy day for them when they moved from the log cabin into the comfortable new house, although it stood in a thick patch of the oak thicket that made them feel terribly alone in the wilderness.

The crop the first year was 154 gallon of wild blackberries which grew in the orchard. There were no apples.

In the spring, Mrs. Durnell hired the 10 acre field broken; then she and the daughter planted it to corn. When the corn was large enough to be cultivated, a neighbor boy was hired to plow it and when he said the job was done she paid him for plowing the 10 acres. What was her surprise, some time later when walking across the field, to find that only ten rows on the outside of the field had been plowed and the rest was standing waist high in weeds. Since then she has personally overseen the work on the place.

Mrs. Durnell was learning by experience, also she was studying farming with the help of good farm papers and the state university and experiment stations. By the second spring she had learned better than to continue planting corn on the old field, so that spring she sowed it to oats and in the fall put it in wheat with a generous allowance for fertilizer. With the wheat was sowed 8 pounds of timothy seed to the acre and the next February 6 pounds of clover seed to the acre was sown over the field. When the wheat was cut the next summer there was a good stand of clover and timothy. The field was so rocky and brushy however that no one would cut the hay so the grass was wasted. This naturally suggested the next thing to be done, and the brush was sprouted out and the stones picked up, so that the grass could be cut; and the crop of hay secured.

A good many men have failed to raise alfalfa, in the hills, but Mrs. Durnell has succeeded. She says that care in preparing a good seedbed and plenty of fertilizer does the trick. The ground must be rich and the weeds must be worked out of it before alfalfa seed is sown, she says. One piece was sown in April and another was sown in September; both are a success.

The whole place is now cleared and seeded to grass, except in a little draw, where the timber is left to shade and protect the spring; and where the garden and berries grow.

Mrs. Durnell and her daughter cleared away some of the oak thicket and set out blackberries, raspberries, strawberries and grapes for home use. The wild blackberries have been cleaned out of the orchard, the apple trees have been trimmed, the ground cultivated and seeded to grass. Now there are plenty of apples and good grass for hay instead of wild blackberries and briars.

Gardening has been carefully studied; and the garden is always planned to raise the greatest variety and amount possible on the ground, and with the least labor. It is planted in long rows so that it can be plowed and leave very little to hand work. A furrow is plowed the length of the garden to plant the Irish potatoes in. These are dropped and lightly covered. This leaves them a little lower than the rest of the ground. As they are cultivated the dirt is thrown toward them and when they are cultivated for the last time they are hilled up, and the weeds have been kept down, all without any hand work. At the last cultivation, kafir and milo are planted between the rows of potatoes and early garden stuff and there is plenty of time for it to mature and make fine large heads of grain for chicken feed.

Of all her farm Mrs. Durnell is most interested in her flock of beautiful Rhode Island Reds. "I love them because they are so bright," she says, and they certainly seem to appreciate her kindness. Although they all look alike to a stranger, she knows every one by sight and calls them pet names as they feed from her hand. She knows which pullets lay the earliest and saves their eggs for hatching, for she has made a study of poultry as well as the other branches of farming, and knows that in this way she improves the laying qualities of the flock. "When starting my flock," said Mrs. Durnell, "I determined to have the best and I still get the best stock obtainable." She selects her breeders very carefully both for their early laying qualities and for their color and so has a flock of which any fancier might be proud as well as one that returns a good profit.

Everything is very carefully looked after on this little farm, nothing is wasted. The cleanings from the poultry house are spread over the garden because there are no grass or weed seeds mixed with them to become a nuisance. The cleanings from the cow barn are spread over the meadows and if there is grass seed among them so much the better for the meadow.

Nor has the inside of the house been neglected because of the rush of work outside. Although this homemaker has learned to husband her strength and not do unnecessary things, still she has done the job thoroughly in the house also. Here are rare bits of old furniture brought from the old home, hand made, some of it, and hand carved. There is a fireplace, made according to Mrs. Durnell's own plan, with a chimney that draws even though she had to stand by the mason as he was building it and insist that he build it as she directed. There are pictures and bits of china and there are books and papers everywhere, the daily paper and the latest novel mingling in pleasant companionship with farm papers and bulletins.

Mrs. Durnell says she never has a dull moment, because farming is so interesting. And one can understand the reason why, after being with her in the house and going around with her over the farm.

The whole place is carefully planned for beauty, as well as profit. The house is set on a rise of ground which adds much to its appearance and at the same time will allow of the whole place being overlooked as it can all be seen from the front porch and windows. Just south of the house is the old spring, where marching bands of soldiers used to drink in war time.

Not far way is the sink hole, a place where the rock shell of the hills is crushed in, making a cup shaped hollow in the ground, which gathers the water from the surrounding hills when it rains. This water pours down through a crack in the rock, sometimes as large around as a barrel in volume, to flow through the crevices and caverns of the hills, emerging later, when purified by its journey; and flowing away in springs and creeks to join the waters of the Gasconade.

Mrs. Durnell has made a beautiful home out of a rough, wild piece of land and a wornout field and she now feels that it is established on a permanent paying basis. The fruits and garden with the cow and chickens more than furnish the living. The farm is growing in value every day, without any more very strenuous efforts on her part; and the home that she and Mr. Durnell planned for their old age is theirs, because of her determination and great good sense.

It has taken a great deal of hard work to accomplish this desired end, but it has been done without any worry. Mrs. Durnell early decided that the burden was heavy enough without adding to it a load of worry and so she chose as a motto for her life and work: "Just do your best and leave the rest"—and this she has lived up to through it all.

Her only regret is that she did not come to the farm when her children were small, for she says: "There is no place like a farm for raising children, where they can have in such abundance the fresh air and sunshine, with pure living water, good wholesome food and a happy outdoor life."

Economy in Egg Production

April 5, 1915

To economize in the feeding of our hens, we should try to get results with as little expenditure of time and acreage as possible. We cannot produce eggs more cheaply by feeding less. It works rather the other way, for it takes a certain amount of food to keep up the body of a hen and that naturally comes first with her. Whatever food of the right kind that she eats, over and above what is necessary for the upkeep of the body, goes to the making of eggs. If the wrong kind of food is given, the surplus goes to fat and unless we wish to market the hens this extra feed is wasted.

Some corn is necessary in the winter to keep up the bodily heat, but a little corn thrown to the hens is not enough for them to manufacture eggs from, nor is it better feeding to throw them a little more corn. Corn is a heating, fattening food and feeding of corn alone, or of too much corn, simply makes the hens fat and does not produce eggs.

Corn is also more expensive than some other feeds that are better for our purpose. The same ground with the same amount of work will produce much more feed if planted to milo. Milo is said to have produced 40 bushels of seed on ground that would not raise 10 bushels of corn and the seed contains 80 per cent of the feeding value of corn. Jerusalem corn, kafir, and cowpeas, are also fine for the hens and will grow more feed to the acre than corn.

Cowpeas especially are good. The hens will eat both the peas and the leaves and while feeding on them the hens will lay remarkably well. It is fine to have some planted near enough so that the hens can pasture on them and harvest whatever peas get ripe.

Some stock beets should be raised to feed the layers in winter. The hens are fond of them and they act as a relish and appetizer as well as save other feed.

Sunflowers can be raised in odd places. They will grow very good heads without cultivation and for this reason can be grown in fence corners and places where nothing else can be raised to advantage. The seeds are very rich and will make the plumage of the fowls bright as well as increase the number of eggs, and all they cost is the planting of the seed and the gathering of the heads.

Now, with the right crops planted to furnish our grain feed, let us see what can be done with the waste of the farm. Small vegetables, cabbages that have failed to head well and some turnips should be saved at gathering time to feed the hens in winter, when they will not be able to get green food. They like vegetables and the parings from vegetables either raw or cooked.

Let the hens help the hogs save the skimmilk. Meat scraps are rather expensive to buy and skimmilk will take their place to a certain extent. Meat in some form is necessary if the hens are to lay well so if possible give them what skimmilk they will drink.

When the butchering is done there are a good many scraps and waste pieces that should be fed to the hens. Not all at once, as too much at a time will make them sick, but a few each day until they are used up. The lights,[4] kidneys and livers should be cut up in small pieces before feeding. The scraps from pressing out the lard are also good. These will all help save the grain feed, besides being just what the hens need.

Another good plan is to save the wheat and oats in the bundle for feeding the hens. It saves the thresh bill and is much better for the hens to let them do their own threshing.

One very important thing in producing eggs cheaply is to produce the eggs. Otherwise what we do feed is wasted. To get the eggs we must feed a variety and if a part of this is what would be saved in no other way, we are turning this waste material into cash.

Making the Best of Things

June 20, 1915

We would all be delighted to have modern kitchens, with up-to-date utensils; but some of us must put up with the old things while we are helping to pay off that mortgage or to save toward buying that little place of our own. However, we need not always use the old things in just exactly the old way;

4. The lungs of a slaughtered animal.

and sometimes we can even do better with a skillful juggling of our old tools than we could with some new fashioned utensil.

For instance, the woman who wishes she had a roaster so she would not be obliged to baste the roasting meat, may take two iron dripping pans, bend the handles of one pan a little narrower so they will slip through the handles of the other, and join them in that way with the roast inside. If she has poured a cup of hot water over the meat as she put it in the pan, she will not need to baste it.

The same pans used in the same way make a covered baking pan for light bread. The loaves cannot run over nor crack along the sides as they often do if baked in an open pan, and the crust is more tender and a more even brown. These pans may be separated in a second's time and used for anything else, and still become a roaster or baking pan at any time.

This idea of covering things may be carried farther and do away with some of the standing over a hot stove. When frying meat cover the skillet with a close cover. It will keep the grease from spattering on the stove, the meat will only require turning once, and it will be more tender. Do the same when frying eggs and they will not need to be turned, nor to have the hot grease dipped on them. They will cook much quicker and on both top and bottom. Chicken can be fried in the roasting pans and will brown evenly all over, without turning, if there is plenty of lard or butter in the pan.

If you wish to make some cheese and have no press, the lard press will do exactly as well. If you need the little kitchen table with the large wheel which you often see described for carrying loads of things from stove to table and from table to pantry, remember that any small table with large casters will do equally as well and be much less expensive.

We may not be able to have electric lights, but we may have a much better light from our coal oil lamps and make the care of them easier by using them properly. The simple expedient of turning a lamp down before blowing it out will make the difference between a bright, clean burner with a good light and a burner that is dark and greasy, so causing a poor light with a bad odor. The wick acts as a pump to bring the oil to the blaze. As long as it is warm it keeps right on pumping. If the blaze is not there to burn it the oil overflows onto the outside of the burner, making a dirty lamp and a poor light.

Magic in Plain Foods

All the World Serves a Woman When She Telephones

November 20, 1915

The thought came to me, while I wandered among the exhibits in the Food Products building at the San Francisco exposition,[5] that Aladdin with his wonderful lamp had no more power than the modern woman in her kitchen. She takes down the receiver to telephone her grocery order, and immediately all over the world the monstrous genii of machinery are obedient to her command. All the nations of the world bring their offerings to her door—fruits from South America, Hawaii, Africa; tea and spices from India, China and Japan; olives and oil from Italy; coffee from strange tropical islands; sugar from Cuba and the Philippines.

This modern magic works both ways. The natives of all these far away places may eat the flour made from the wheat growing in the fields outside our kitchen windows. I never shall look at Missouri wheat fields again without thinking of the "Breads of All Nations" exhibit, where natives of eight foreign nations, in the national costumes were busy making the breads of their countries from our own American flour.

We use raisins, flour, tea, breakfast food, and a score of other common things without a thought of the modern miracles that make it possible for us to have them. For instance, who would have thought that different varieties of wheat are blended to make fine flour, just as a blend of coffee is used to make a perfect beverage? An entire flour mill, running and producing flour for the market, in the Food Products building, illustrates this fact. In California mills California, Washington, Idaho, and Kansas wheat is blended according to scientific tests for the proper amount of gluten and starch. It is interesting to note that although this flour is not shipped east of the Rockies, because of the high freight rate, Kansas wheat is shipped west to make it.

One has a greater feeling of respect for the flour used daily, after seeing the infinite pains taken to turn out the perfect article. Every shipment of wheat to these mills, after being tested in the laboratories, is cleaned by a vacuum cleaner, ground through rollers and sifted, and then re-ground and

5. The occasion of the 1915 San Francisco Exhibition gave Laura an excuse to go west to visit her daughter and to seek Rose's advice on how to write for better-paying markets than the *Ruralist*.

re-shifted four times. During this process the finest, first grade flour is taken out, being sifted through 14 screens of fine, sheer silk. This first grade flour is kept for home use, the second grade being shipped to the Orient, where some of our middle-western wheat makes its final appearance in Chinese noodles.

From the time the wheat is poured into the hoppers until, in our kitchens, we cut the string that ties the sack, the flour is not exposed to the outer air. It is not touched by human hands until we dip the flour sifter into it. After the siftings the flour, still enclosed, passes through a machine which automatically removes a small sample every half hour, to be inspected by the miller. From this machine it goes into a compartment where it is purified by a current of filtered air, then it enters the chute which fills the sacks.

The output of this modern machine, handled by one man, is 400 sacks of flour and 125 sacks of bran, shorts and middlings every 24 hours. With the machinery in use 10 years ago, 10 or 12 men were required to produce the same amount.

Ten years ago, too, we seeded our raisins by hand ourselves, or bribed the children to the task by giving them a share to eat. Today we buy seeded raisins in boxes, without giving a thought to how the seeding is done. You may be sure of this—these packaged raisins are clean. They are scientifically clean, sterilized by steam and packed hot. In the Food Products building I saw these machines at work. This is the process:

Sun-dried Muscat grapes are stemmed by machinery, then sent through 26 feet of live steam, at 212 pounds pressure. From this they fall onto a steel, saw-tooth cylinder, and pass under three soft rubber rolls, which crush the raisin and loosen the seeds. They then strike a corrugated steel roll, which throws out the seeds. The raisin passes on, is lifted from the cylinder by a steel rake and dropped into paraffin-paper-lined boxes, which are closed while the raisins are still hot from the steam sterilizing.

Steam is one of the commonest things in our kitchens. Until I went through the Food Products building I never realized how much it is used in the preparation of foods before they come to us. It sterilizes the raisins, cooks the oats before they are crushed into flakes for our breakfast oatmeal, puffs the rice, and cooks the wheat for the making of a well known wheat biscuit.

A full sized unit of the factory which makes these biscuit is in operation near the raisin machine. In the preparation of this biscuit, after the wheat is screened and cleaned it is steam-cooked for 30 minutes, which softens the grain. It is then put into hoppers, which pour onto a corrugated steel cone, where the wheat is crushed into shreds. Each wheat berry makes a shred about 2 inches in length. These shreds fall from the cone into a narrow tray, which slowly moves back and forth on a carrier under the cone until it is full. Thirty-six layers of the shreds make the proper thickness. They are then cut into biscuit by steel knives, put on trays, and baked on revolving shelves in the oven. During all this process they are not touched by human hands. The moisture of the wheat and the heat of the baking combine to puff the biscuit to twice their former size.

Space forbids that I should describe the scores of exhibits in this enormous building devoted to the preparation of different foods, a task which always has been considered woman's work. I will only briefly mention the Japanese rice cakes—tiny bits of paste half an inch long and no thicker than paper. The smiling Oriental in charge drops them in to boiling olive oil, and they puff into delicious looking brown rolls 3 inches long. They look as toothsome as a homemade doughnut, but to your wild amazement, when you bite them there is nothing there.

I must say one word about the rose cakes, delicious cakes baked in the form of a rose, and as good as they are beautiful. And I am sure nobody leaves the exposition without speaking of the Scotch scones; everybody eats them who can reach them. They are baked by a Scotchman from Edinburg, who turns out more than 4,000 of them daily. They are buttered, spread with jam, and handed over the counter as fast as four girls can do it. And the counter is surrounded by a surging mob all day long.

As I went from booth to booth they gave me samples of the breads they had made with our American flour—the little, bland Chinese girl in her bright blue pajama costume, the smiling, high-cheeked Russian peasant girl, the Hindoo in his gay turban, the swarthy, black-eyed Mexican—all of them eager to have me like their national foods. And I must say I did like most of it so well that I brought the recipes away with me, and pass them on to you:

RUSSIAN FORREST

One pound flour, yolks of 3 eggs, 1 whole egg, ½ cup milk. Mix well and knead very thoroughly. Cut in pieces size of walnuts; roll very, very thin. Cut the center in strips, braid together and fry in deep fat. Drain, and sprinkle with powdered sugar.

MEXICAN TAMALE LOAF

One pound veal, 1 onion, 2 cloves of garlic, 1 tablespoon chili powder, 1 can tomatoes (strained), 24 green olives (chopped). Boil the meat until very tender, take from the broth, cool and chop. Return to the broth, add salt to taste, add the onion and garlic chopped fine, then the tomatoes, garlic[6] and

6. This second listing of "garlic" is likely a mistake that should read "olives."

chili powder. Let all come to the boiling point, then add enough yellow cornmeal to make as thick as mush, turn into molds and set aside to cool. The loaf may be served either cold or sliced and fried.

GERMAN HONEY CAKE

One cup honey, molasses or sirup; ½ cup sugar, 2 cups flour, 1 teaspoon cinnamon, 1 teaspoon cloves, 1 teaspoon ginger, 2 teaspoons baking powder. Beat honey and sugar 20 minutes, then add the spices, the baking powder, and lastly the flour. Pour into well buttered baking sheets and bake 15 minutes in a moderate oven. Cover with chocolate icing and cut in squares.

ITALIAN WHITE TAGLIARINI

Three cups flour, ½ cup hot water, 2 eggs, 1 teaspoon salt. Mix and knead thoroughly, roll very thin as for noodles, and cut in any desired shape. Allow to dry 1 hour and cook in boiling water for 10 minutes, drain, and serve with sauce.

SAUCE FOR TAGLIARINI

One-half cup olive oil, 1 large pod garlic, 1 large carrot, 1 large can tomatoes, salt and pepper, 2 large onions, 5 stalks celery, 1 cup parsley, ½ pound hamburg steak, ⅛ teaspoon cloves, ½ cup butter. Heat the oil in an iron skillet or kettle, then add onions and garlic chopped fine. Cook until transparent but not brown, then add the rest of the ingredients chopped fine. Cook slowly for 2 hours.

CROISSONTS (FRENCH CRESCENTS)

Four cups flour, 1 cup warm water, 1 cake compressed yeast, ½ teaspoon salt, 1 cup butter. Sift and measure the flour into a bowl, add the yeast which has been dissolved in the water, then the salt. Mix and knead thoroughly. Let rise 2 or 3 hours, then roll out 1 inch thick and lay the butter on the center. Fold the dough over and roll out four times as for puff paste, then cut in pieces as for finger rolls, having the ends thinner than the middles. Form in crescent shape, brush with egg, and bake in a moderate oven.

CHINESE ALMOND CAKES

Four cups flour, 1 cup lard, 1¼ cups sugar, 1 egg, ½ teaspoon baking powder. Mix and knead thoroughly. Take off pieces of dough the size of an English walnut, roll in a smooth round ball, then flatten about half. Make a depression on the top and place in it 1 almond. Place on pans, 2 inches apart, and bake a golden brown.

UNLEAVENED BREAD, OR MATZAS

From the earliest Bible times to the present, the Hebrew people have observed the feast of the Passover by eating unleavened bread. This bread is a hard cracker made from unfermented dough. The process of making is very simple. Mix flour and water to a very stiff dough. Roll this into a thin sheet, cut into round or square pieces, and bake in a hot oven.

POORI

This bread is considered by the Hindus as a luxury and usually is eaten on feast days. A rather stiff dough is made from flour, water and salt. Small cakes are cut from this dough and cooked in boiling butter.

And Missouri "Showed" Them

From A To Z—Alfalfa to Zinc—the "Show Me State" Won Honors at 'Frisco's Exposition

December 5, 1915

Missouri has taken more prizes at the International Exposition than any other state in the Union except California, and Missouri's mines have beaten, on its own ground, the Golden State of the Forty-niners. We have "shown" them. Missouri has met all the states of the Union, all the countries of the world, in fair competition, and has made a proud record.

In agriculture alone Missouri has won the Grand Medal of Honor, 17 gold medals, 21 silver medals, 15 bronze medals, besides two honorable mentions, which go to Henry county. In education the state carried off the silver medal.

Missouri's mines won the Medal of Honor, 6 gold medals, 54 silver medals, and one bronze medal. Our livestock exhibitors received cash prizes amounting to $6,834 and eight ribbons. In processed fruit Missouri won the silver medal. Awards in horticulture were still to be made when this was written.

In hospitality, too, Missouri has been a charming example to many sister states. Our beautiful Colonial Home, on a grassy terrace overlooking the

Avenue of the States and the blue waters of San Francisco Bay, has won the reputation of being the most homelike and inviting at the great fair.

The portico with its pillars, and the broad flights of steps leading up to it, gives an impression both dignified and hospitable. From it, one steps through wide glass doors into a spacious reception hall, finished in white enamel and furnished in dull blue velvet. This great room, more than 80 feet long, with a high beamed ceiling, combines with its feeling of space an effect of cosiness and comfort, given by a huge fireplace, soft-toned velvet rugs and big inviting arm-chairs.

Large French doors of glass open from it on to a rear plaza, which fronts directly on the sparkling blue Bay, dotted with the white sails of innumerable tiny yachts. From this plaza, sheltered from the ocean winds by the wings of the building, one sees, across the expanse of water, the mountain ranges of Marin county, Tamalpais, Muir woods, and dozens of little towns. The view is inspiring and beautiful.

A feature of the building which has been a revelation to thousands of visitors is the library in one of the wings. Its bookshelves contain more than 1,500 volumes, all written by Missouri authors. Hundreds of persons have been surprised to learn here for the first time the fact that our state has produced more successful authors than any other in the Union.

On the lower floor of the building, besides the rooms already mentioned, are the rest-rooms, a large board-room, and offices for the commission. At the second-floor level a balcony overhangs the reception hall, and opening from it are the bedrooms for the members of the commission and their families. The advantages of architectural arrangement, as well as its beauty, have been widely praised, and it is a credit to the artistic skill of the Missourian who designed it, Senator H.H. Hohenschild of Rolla. Within a few weeks of its completion, by the McCarthy construction company of Farmington, dozens of local and national societies had requested to be allowed to hold meetings or give social affairs there. Hon. D. S. Smith, vice-chairman of the commission, who has been in charge of all Missouri's activities at the fair, found time somehow in his crowded days to uphold the reputation of our state for hospitality.

The popularity of the building grew, and every week since the fair began it has been the scene of at least one brilliant social or philanthropic gathering. Mrs. D. S. Smith has been a charming hostess at these affairs, acting with the official hostess, Mrs. James B. Gantt, of Jefferson City, and their popularity with the best people of the Pacific Coast has reflected no little credit upon Missouri's social ability.

Our showing in horticulture is very good indeed. In this department Missouri processed fruits have already taken the silver medal, and the whole exhibit is very attractive. No Missourian, I am sure, has gone through the Palace of Horticulture without feeling justifiable pride in that array of apples, nuts, vegetables, watermelons and flowers, beautifully displayed under green-latticed archways. I noticed especially the apples, which were not surpassed in size, coloring, or flavor by any shown at the fair.

It is a pity that the ruling of the Exposition directors has prevented all states east of the Rockies from entering into competition for the awards on apples. These awards will be made only on five boxes of orchard-packed fruit, and the shipping distance makes it impossible for any but near-by states to get them to the fair in good condition. However, the people at the fair do not see the prizes, they see the fruit, and not a state in the Union has sent better fruit to the fair than Missouri.

Their keeping qualities, too, are proved by the fact that a great many of the apples on the tables were shown last fall at the Sedalia State Fair.

I was glad to see, also, that our watermelons were the best in the entire building, not even excepting the Burbank display, or the exhibit of the Turlock district, which is California's great melon-growing region. Scarcely anyone who passed through our exhibit while I was there failed to notice and comment on this.

While our native-grown black walnut is perhaps not quite so aristocratic as the California English walnut, still no nut that grows equals it in richness and flavor. In our state Nature bountifully supplies this delicious nut, with no trouble or expense to us, while the Californians must plant, graft, cultivate, irrigate and spray their English variety. The jars of walnuts, hickory nuts, and hazel nuts displayed in our horticultural exhibit were for this reason a striking illustration of Missouri's natural advantages.

The whole display was very ably handled by Director Charles W. Steinman, of Dalton, and his assistant, John McDemott of Montgomery county, and the horticulturists of Missouri can feel that they have done the state full justice.

Nearly 20,000 Missourians had already registered at our agricultural booth, under the great tower with its electric sign, "Missouri," which is conspicuous from any part of the Palace of Agriculture, when this was written in November. This tower, 65 feet in height, stands in one corner of the space allotted to our state, and is the principal feature of the display. It is literally covered with Missouri corn, from the arches up to the top, an impressive spectacle which is given added point by a sign stating, "Missouri produces one-tenth of the world's corn." The archways themselves, through which one passes in going under the tower, are decorated with excellent specimens of oats, wheat, kafir, maize, timothy, alfalfa, tobacco and cotton, arranged attractively on a background of dull blue cloth.

It was distinctly a pleasure to me to observe how excellently well these products compare with those grown in other states. Indeed, with the exception of the alfalfa, which of course competed with that grown under irrigation in the intensely hot California interior valleys, I saw no specimens exhibited anywhere, and even in alfalfa Missouri won a bronze medal awarded to Scott county.

When I came through the archways under the tower and stood in the main exhibit space, I fairly jumped with surprise. There on the wall was a picture of Governor Major, more than life-size and more than life-like, made entirely of corn. I would have recognized it anywhere for Missouri's governor, and almost anywhere for Missouri corn, so the artist who designed and worked it out may feel he has done full justice to both his subjects. Above the governor's pictured head an American eagle, made of corn husks, oats and kafir, stood proudly out on the blue cloth background, while above the eagle the state seal was displayed, also made of grains.

Other Missouri products were shown in glass cases, arranged in the main floor space. Except the tower with its decorations, and a skillful use of cotton, grain and grasses in trimming the rest of the exhibit, no attempt was made to produce a spectacular effect. Missouri went to the fair to show, in a business-like way, what she could do in agriculture at home, and she did it. She is bringing home the Grand Medal of Honor.

We surprised our fellow exhibitors in the livestock section, but it was a surprise that re-acted upon the Missouri commission itself. The commission, to encourage our local livestock breeders, had offered to double the amounts won by them at the Exposition. Now the members of the commission are all enthusiastic boosters for Missouri. They expected to make a good showing in livestock; indeed, they expected to make a very good showing. But, sanguine as their expectations were, they had not supposed they would be called upon to double $3,200 in prizes, as they had to do when the Exposition awards were announced. Goodness knows what would have happened to the pocketbook of the commission if the whole of our livestock had reached the fair. Five hundred thousand dollars' worth of Missouri cattle, gathered, inspected, and ready to ship West from Kansas City, was refused by the Exposition directors, on account of a ruling quarantining the Exposition against all cattle from the Middle West. There is no doubt that if that exhibit had gone through we would have a much larger share of the livestock prizes, but as it was our breeders won enough to startle the commission, and to flatten its purse considerably.

Our jennets[7] carried off every prize offered in their class. Sixteen little

7. Female donkeys.

beauties, exhibited by Monsees & Son, won $1,790 in prizes. It is interesting to note that the jennet who carried off all honors at the St. Louis Exposition was beaten here only by her daughter, who is now champion.

Our saddle horses—beauties, every one of them, with their slim dainty legs, heads held high, and bright, intelligent eyes—were one of the most popular exhibits in the livestock section, and they won substantial proof of their fine qualities, $1,410 in cash prizes, and a number of ribbons.

EDUCATIONAL EXHIBITS WERE FINE

The increased interest in educational methods, and systems of child-training, which has grown so rapidly in the last few years, made the Palace of Education one of the most popular buildings at the grounds. Here were shown school work, educational methods, and handicraft of children from New York state to the Philippines, China and Japan. Madame Montessori herself came from Italy to take charge of a class of tiny children in this building. Entered thus in competition against the whole world, Missouri won the silver medal. I must admit that this was a surprise to me. We are so likely to see the defects in institutions close at hand and imagine that farther away conditions are so much better.

When I realized the place Missouri takes in education I felt greater interest in our school problems, and while there are still many improvements possible, I am sure we should all be very much pleased, and proud of this award.

Our commissioner of education, Norman Vaughan, and his assistant, W. N. Laidlaw deserve great credit for the demonstration they have given of Missouri's school system. Our decentralized method is shown by a system of tiny electric lights, representing children, which flash on and off, showing the pupil's progress from grade to grade and from school to school, without any unnecessary loss of time.

A mammoth map of the state, also dotted with electric lights, shows our high school growth from 1894 to the present day. At a glance, while the groups of lights flash on and off; one literally sees the high schools multiply, and multiply again. The sight shows quickly, and in a very impressive manner, the really extraordinary growth in the number of our high schools.

Views of the Missouri University, the five state normal schools, and other colleges and high schools, are shown on an illuminated screen, the pictures changing automatically every 20 seconds. The whole exhibit has attracted the interested attention of educators from all over the world, and it is a pleasure to wander about it and listen to their comments.

When Otto Ruhl of Joplin took charge of our mining exhibit at the fair he intended to show Missouri mines to the best possible advantage. Without intending it he has also shown another Missouri characteristic of which we should be as proud as we are of any product of our state. He has given an exhibition of thrift. With only $6,500 to spend, he arranged a display which is more attractive to the eye, more instructive and interesting, than Nevada was able to show with $27,000. He also has won for us a Medal of Honor, seven gold medals, 54 silver medals, and one bronze, standing second only to Nevada among all the states, and leaving California, with her great mining industries, far behind.

Beginning with the mine itself, every process in handling the ore is shown, from the raw quartz in the ground to the finished product. The idea is good, and the way it is carried out is perfect. The display occupies 3,000 feet of floor space, in a long strip down one side of the Palace of Mines and Metallurgy. It is surrounded by a low wall, built up to give the exact appearance of a mine—all the ores showing among the native rock and flint exactly as they are found in our hills. Above this wall great columns covered with zinc and lead concentrates, support cornices of zinc metal. Thus, from first sight of the place, the eye follows the progress of the metal from the mines to the finished product.

The entrances are three great arches, one of zinc, one of lead, and one of our Carthage marble. Inside, one sees first a model Joplin mine, showing in detail the tunnels, the little cars and railways used underground, the exact rock formation of the mine, and the buildings on the surface. Following this are the crushers, and a concentrating plant, which show the method of bringing our low-grade 2 per cent ore, ready for smelting. After this, one comes to the finished product, shown in wash boards and fruit jar covers.

Beside the cases, displaying the zinc as it enters our kitchens, were cases containing specimens of lead and zinc ores, which were beautiful enough to hold the attention of everyone who saw them. Several specimens of lead ore here contain 68 per cent of pure lead, an impossible proportion according to all the books, for theoretically, a 67 per cent lead ore is the highest possible. However, here are the actual specimens, with 68 per cent. What does Missouri care for theories, when she beats them in actual facts? On the outside of these blocks of almost pure lead, are iron pyrites and pure lead crystals.

Missouri's Crystal Springs, too, are represented here by a beautiful display of mineral waters, shining through dozens of bottles, and accompanied by pictures of the springs.

Another unique exhibit to our credit are the clays, which no other state had shown. Here, too, the whole process from the raw earth dug from the St. Louis quarries, to its final appearance in roofing tiles, sewer pipe, garden ornaments and statuary. It might have taxed almost any brain to devise an attractive display of sewer pipe and roofing tile, but Mr. Ruhl has solved the difficulty. He built up the sewer pipe into a tall flagpole, and designed the American flag from the roofing tile, in red, white and blue.

Beside the clays are the coal, supplied by Macon, Randolph, and Barton counties, and the iron, which comes from Crawford county. Specimens of Missouri granite appear here also, the red granite being perfect in texture and coloring. Nor are these the only products of Missouri's mines. Hannibal has represented her cement industry by samples showing every step of its production from shale and limestone to cement blocks, brick and tile.

AMAZING AND UNEXPECTED THINGS

Huge slabs of tripoli, that stone of so many amazing uses, have been the center of a great deal of attention. It is a fine, smooth rock, looking with its colored veinings, something like a cake of Castile soap, and I was amazed to find it the parent of dozens of familiar things. Sapolio, Gold Dust, Bon Ami, Old Dutch Cleanser, and practically all other scouring soaps, are made from it.

Another display was startling to me. I have been a Missourian for nearly 30 years, but I had to travel to the Exposition to find out that there is in my state a mining industry entirely controlled by farmers. A mining industry, moreover, which brings in an income of $250,000 to $300,000 a year. This tremendous sum goes to the farmers of Washington county, in payment for their mining of barytes.

The depth of their mines is little more than the depth of a plow-furrow. Barytes, a valuable stone, the use of which has made possible our fine magazine pictures, is found on Washington county farms, on or near the surface. In the fall the farmers plow and dig out the rock, pile it up until the rains have washed it clean of clay and gravel, and then haul it to town, like so much cord wood.

1916

All in the Day's Work

Just a Neighborly Visit with Folks at Rocky Ridge Farm

February 5, 1916

One hundred and seventeen thousand dollars was paid for poultry, eggs and cream, in the town of Mansfield during 1915. Of this amount $58,000 was paid for eggs alone, $39,000 for poultry and $20,000 for cream.

During the time of the turkey drives $10,000 in 10 days was paid for these farm products by the produce men of Mansfield.

A big turkey drive is quite a sight to see. There were several came to Mansfield just before the holiday. In one drive alone there were 650 turkeys. Six hundred and fifty Christmas dinners for somebody walked into town in a drove.

These figures on poultry products speak well for the industry and capability of the women in the section tributary to Mansfield for we all know who raises the poultry.

- - - - - -

I wonder if Missouri farm women realize the value in dollars and cents of the work they do from day to day in raising farm products for the market? How many persons when reading the astonishing amount received in a year for Missouri poultry and eggs think of the fact that it is practically all produced by the women, and as a sideline at that! For of course a woman's real business is the keeping of the house and caring for the family. Not only the care of the poultry, but the raising of garden products and small fruits is largely women's work; and in many instances the greater part of the labor of producing cream and butter. The fact is that while there has been a good deal of discussion for and against women in business, farm women have always been business women and I have never heard a protest.

- - - - - -

A friend of mine has a large tree in her back yard that she calls her turkey tree. Out of this tree every fall she gathers $100 worth of turkeys. If one could only have unlimited numbers of trees like that! But, unfortunately, there are a great many like another friend of mine who lost all the chicks she hatched last summer. The rats took them, sometimes a whole flock in a night. I raised 300 chicks myself by keeping the coops as far away from the buildings as possible. But every morning I wondered whether I should find them alive or stacked up in a pile somewhere.

- - - - - -

When one thinks of the difficulties under which poultry and eggs are brought to the market, the wonder is that the amount is one-tenth as great. There are all the diseases to which chicks are heir to be contended with and besides there is a hawk in every treetop and a rat in every corner waiting for them as soon as they come out of the shell. I feel sure if Governor Major had ever tried to raise chickens on a farm he would not have vetoed that bill placing a bounty on hawks. And why not a bounty on rats? They are a perfect nuisance around the buildings and frightfully expensive to feed, besides the loss of the young chicks they kill. And I'm sure no one could say a word in their favor.

Learning how to build rat-proof buildings does not help much with the old buildings. We keep up a continual war on rats with traps and poison and cats. Once in a while we get the place well cleared, but soon they swarm in again. If everyone would take care of their own rats it would simplify matters. But they do not and so the rats increase and multiply and spread to other places, carrying disease and destruction.

- - - - - -

I find that it adds greatly to the interest of life to keep careful accounts of the business of housekeeping with its sidelines of poultry and small fruits.

Especially do the account books add a spice when the Man Of The Place gets angry because the hens get into the barn and scratch things around, or when the grain is getting low in the bins in the spring and he comes to you and says: "Those durn hens are eating their heads off!"

Then, if you can bring your little account book and show him that the feed for the hens cost so much, and the eggs and poultry sold brought so much, leaving a good little profit besides the eggs and poultry used in the house, he will feel better about things in general and especially the hens.

- - - - - -

A woman I know kept for one year the accounts of the household and her own especial little extra work and surprised herself by finding that by her own efforts she had made a clear profit of $395 during the year, and this without neglecting in any way her household or home duties.

The total for household expenses and her own personal expenses for the same time was $122.29. There is after all, you see, some excuse for the man who told a friend he was going to be married. "Be married!" the friend exclaimed, in surprise. "Why, you can't make a living for yourself!" To which the first man replied, sulkily: "Well, it's a pity if she can't help a little."

My friend proved that she could "help a little." Her books made such a good showing that her husband asked her to keep books for the farm, and so she was promoted to the position of farm accountant (without salary).

- - - - - -

Considering the amount of time, labor and capital invested, the farm books did not balance out so well as her own and she became interested in hunting the reason why. So now she has become a sort of farm adviser with whom her husband consults on all matters of farm business.

- - - - - -

We are told that the life of a woman on a farm is narrow and that the monotony of it drives many farm women insane. That life on a farm as elsewhere is just what we make it, that much and no more, is being proved every day by women who, like this one, pick up a thread connecting farm life with the whole, great outside world.

- - - - - -

In the study of soils, of crops, their origin and proper cultivation and rotation; in the study of the livestock on the place, their proper selection and care; with the care of her house and poultry, always looking for a short cut in the work to gain time for some other interesting thing, there does not seem to be much chance for monotony to drive her insane.

That "all work and no play makes Jack a dull boy" is very true, I think. It is just as dull for Jill as it is for Jack and so they formed a "Neighborhood

Crochet club" down in "Happy Hollow." The women met and learned the new crochet patterns and visited—?—Well, gossiped, then—as the men do when they go to town on Saturday and have so much business (?) to attend to that they cannot get home until late chore time.

By the way, did you ever think that as much good can be done by the right kind of gossip as harm by the unkind sort? The Crochet club made a little play time mixed with the work all summer, until bad weather and the grippe interfered in the fall. Jill was not so dull and the plans are made for the club to meet again soon.

We do enjoy sitting around the fireplace in the evening and on stormy days in the winter.

When we planned our new house we determined that we would build the fireplace first and the rest of the house if we could afford it—not a grate, but a good old-fashioned fireplace that will burn a stick of wood as large as a man can carry. We have seen to it besides that there is a wood lot left on the farm to provide those sticks. So far we have escaped having the grippe while all the neighborhood has been suffering with it. We attribute our good fortune to this same big fireplace and the two open stairs in the house. The fresh air they furnish has been much cheaper as well as pleasanter to take than the doctor's medicine.

Some old-fashioned things like fresh air and sunshine are hard to beat. In our mad rush for progress and modern improvements let's be sure we take along with us all the old-fashioned things worth while.

The magazines say that the spring fashions will return to the styles of our grandmothers, ruffles, pantalettes, ribbon armlets and all. It will surely be delightful to have women's clothes soft and fluffy again and we need not follow the freak styles, you know. There is a distinct advantage in choosing the rather moderate, quiet styles for the up-to-the-minute freaks soon go out and then they call attention to their out-of-date-ness by their striking appearance, while others equally as good style but not so pronounced will be a pleasure for more than one season.

Sometimes Misdirected Energy May Cease to Be a Virtue

February 20, 1916

A stranger once went to a small inland town, in the Ozarks, to look over the country. As he left the little hotel, in the morning, for his day's wandering among the hills, he noticed several men sitting comfortably in the shade of the "gallery," gazing out into the street.

- - - - - -

When the stranger returned late in the afternoon, the "gallery" was still occupied by the same men, looking as though they had not stirred from their places since he left them there in the early morning.

This happened for three days, and then as the stranger was coming in from his day's jaunt, in the evening he stopped and spoke to one of the men. "Say," he asked, "how do you fellows pass the time here all day? What do you do to amuse yourselves?"

The man emptied his mouth of its accumulation of tobacco juice and replied in a lazy drawl, "Oh, we jest set and—think—and—sometimes—we—jest—set."

- - - - - -

I have laughed many times over this story, which I know to be true, with never a thought, except for the humor of the tale, beyond the hackneyed ones on the value of wasted time; the vice of idleness.

- - - - - -

We are told continually by every one interested in our welfare or in "making the wheels go round" how to employ our spare moments to the best advantage, until, if we followed their advice, there would be no spare moments.

It is rank heresy, I know, to detract from these precepts, but lately I have been wondering whether perhaps it is not as great a fault to be too energetic as it is to be too idle.

Perhaps it would be better all around if we were to "jest set and think" a little more, or even sometimes "jest set."

- - - - - -

Vices are simply overworked virtues, anyway. Economy and frugality are to be commended but follow them on in an increasing ratio and what do we find at the other end? A miser! If we overdo the using of spare moments we may find an invalid at the end, while perhaps if we allowed ourselves more idle time we would conserve our nervous strength and health to more than the value of the work we could accomplish by emulating at all times the little busy bee.

- - - - - -

I once knew a woman, not very strong, who to the wonder of her friends, went through a time of extraordinary hard work without any ill effects.

I asked her for her secret and she told me that she was able to keep her health, under the strain, because she took 20 minutes, of each day, in which to absolutely relax both mind and body. She did not even "set and think." She lay at full length, every muscle and nerve relaxed and her mind as quiet as her body. This always relieved the strain and renewed her strength.

I spent a delightful day not long ago, visiting in a home where there are several children and the little mother not over strong. She is doing nothing to add to the family income; has no special work of her own to earn some pin money, but the way she has that little family organized would be a lesson in efficiency to many a business man. The training she is giving the children and the work she is doing in preparing them to meet the problems of life and become self-supporting, self-respecting citizens could not be paid for in money.

The children all help and the work for the day goes forward with no confusion. There is nothing left undone because one person thought another was to do it. There are no whines such as "I did that yesterday; let sister (or brother) do it this time." Each child has a particular part of the work to do. Each knows what their work is and that he is responsible for that work being done as it should be.

One of the girls does the upstairs work; another has the care of the parlor, dining room and library. The two smaller girls must keep their playthings in order and not leave their belongings scattered around the house. The mother does the cooking and washing the dishes. The places of each are changed from time to time that there may be no unfairness and that each may learn to do the different kinds of work. One boy keeps water in the house, milks the cow and keeps the motor car clean. Another boy brings in the wood and runs errands. Each receives, for the work done, a few cents a week and this is their spending money to do with as they please. When it is spent there is no teasing for a few cents to spend for this or that. They know the amount of their income and plan and spend accordingly. In this way they are learning the value of money; to work for what they want instead of begging for it and to live within their income. If their work is not well done, a fine of a few cents is a better punishment than a scolding or a whipping, leaving both parties with their self respect uninjured, while the child can see the punishment fits the crime.

- - - - - -

"I don't know what to do with Edith," said a mother to me. "I've no idea where she learned it, but she is a regular little liar. I can't depend on a thing she says."

Edith was a very bright, attractive child about three years old. Just then she started to go into another room. "Oh! Don't go in there!" her mother exclaimed. "It's dark in there and there is a big dog behind the door." The child opened the door a crack, peeped around it, smiled a knowing smile and went on in. Evidently she knew her mother and that she "could not depend on a thing she said," that she was "a regular little—." Sounds ugly, doesn't it? Perhaps I would better not quote it at all, but where do you suppose Edith learned to be untruthful?

- - - - - -

When I went to San Francisco last summer, I left The Man Of The Place and his hired man to "batch it." There were no women relatives near, no near neighbors with whom they could board and of course it was out of the question to hire a girl to stay with two lone men.

I was sorry for them, but our only child lives in San Francisco and I had not seen her for four years. Besides, there was the fair, so I left them and went.

Now the man of the place says, "If any man thinks housekeeping is easy work and not all a woman ought to do, just let him roll up his sleeves and tackle the job."

- - - - - -

More than any other business, that of farming depends upon the home and it is almost impossible for any farmer to succeed without the help of the house. In the country the home is still depended upon to furnish bed and board and the comforts of life.

- - - - - -

It is a good idea sometimes to think of the importance and dignity of our every-day duties. It keeps them from being so tiresome; besides, others are apt to take us at our own valuation.

Life Is an Adventure

Voyages of Discovery Can Be Made in Your Rocking-chair

March 5, 1916

As I was passing through the Missouri building, at the exposition last summer, I overheard a scrap of conversation between two women. Said the first woman, "How do you like San Francisco?" The other replied, "I don't like San Francisco at all! Everywhere I go there is a Chinaman on one side, a Jap on the other and a nigger behind."

- - - - - -

These women were missing a great deal, for the foreign life of San Francisco is very interesting and the strange vari-colored peoples on the streets give a touch of color and picturesqueness that adds much to the charm of the city. A morning's walk from the top of Russian Hill, where I lived when there, would take me thru "Little Italy" where one hears Italian spoken on all sides; where the people are black-eyed and handsome with a foreign beauty and where, I am sure, the children are the most beautiful in the world.

From here I passed directly into "Chinatown" where the quaint babies look exactly like Chinese dolls and the older people look exactly as if they had stepped out of a Chinese picture. The women, in their comfortable loose garments made of black or soft colored silks, with their shiny, smoothly combed black hair full of bright ornaments, were, some of them, very pretty. Only the older men seemed to be wearing the Chinese dress. The younger men were dressed like any American business man. It is a curious fact that the second generation of Chinese born in San Francisco are much larger than their parents and look a great deal more like our own people, while the third generation can scarcely be distinguished from Americans. And oh, the shops of Chinatown! I do not understand how any woman could resist their fascination. Such quaint and beautiful jewelry, such wonderful pieces of carved ivory, such fine pottery, and silks and embroideries as one finds there!

Wandering on from Chinatown, I would soon be at Market Street, which is the main business street of San Francisco, and everywhere, as the women in the Missouri building had said, there was "a Chinaman on one side, a Jap on the other and a nigger behind."

It gives a stay-at-home Middle Westerner something of a shock to meet a group of turbaned Hindoos on the street, or a Samoan, a Filipino or even a Mexican. People in happier times spent hundreds of dollars and months of time in traveling to see these foreign people and their manner of living. It is all to be seen, on a smaller scale, in this city of our own country.

Walking on the Zone one day at the fair, Daughter and I noticed ahead of us five sailormen. They were walking along discussing which one of the attractions they should visit. They were evidently on shore for a frolic. Tired of "rocking in the cradle of the deep," they were going to enjoy something different on shore. Should they see the wonderful educated horse? "No! Who cared anything about an old horse?" Should they see Creation, the marvelous electrical display? "No! Not that! We're here for a good time, aren't we?" Perhaps by now you suspect that Daughter and I had become so interested we determined to know which of the attractions they decided was worth while. We followed with the crowd at their heels. The sailors passed the places of amusement one after another until they came to a mimic river, with a wharf and row boats, oars and all. Immediately they made a rush for the wharf and the last we saw of them they were tumbling hilariously into one of the boats, for a good old row on the pleasant, familiar water.

Do you know, they reminded me someway, of the women in the Missouri building who did not like San Francisco.

A friend of mine used to sympathize with a woman for being "tied down" to a farm with no opportunity to travel or study; and with none of the advantages of town or city life. To her surprise she found that her sympathy was not needed. "My body may be tied here," her friend said, "but my mind is free. Books and papers are cheap and what I cannot buy I can borrow. I have traveled all over the world."

- - - - - -

The daughter of this woman was raised with a varied assortment of these same books and papers, pictures and magazines. When later she traveled over the United States, becoming familiar with the larger cities as well as the country, from Canada to the Gulf and from San Francisco to New York City, she said there was a great disappointment to her in traveling. She seemed to have seen it all before and thus had no "thrills" from viewing strange things. "I have read about foreign countries just as much" she said "and I don't suppose I'll find anything in the world that will be entirely new to me." Which shows that a very good travel education can be had from books and papers and also proves once more the old saying that, "As the twig is bent the tree inclines."

- - - - - -

Over at a neighbor's, the other day, I learned something new, as by the way quite often happens. She has little soft home-made mattresses as thick as a good comfort to lay over the top of the large mattresses on her beds. Over these small mattresses she slips a cover as one does a case on a pillow. They are easily removed for washing and protect the mattress from soil, making it a simple matter to keep the beds clean and sweet.

- - - - - -

This neighbor also makes her sheets last twice as long, by a little trick she has. When the sheets begin to wear thin in the middle she tears them down the center and sews the outsides together. Then she hems the outer edges down the sides. This throws the thin part to the outside and the center, where the wear comes, is as good as new. Of course the sheet has a seam down the middle, but it is not so very many years ago that all our sheets were that way, before we had sheeting and pillow tubing.

- - - - - -

It is no use trying! I seem unable today to get away from the idea of travel, perhaps because I read the "National Geographic Magazine" last night. A sentence in one of the articles keeps recurring to me and I am going to quote it to you for you may not have noticed it. "It is not a figure of speech to say that every American has it in his heart that he is in a small sense a discover; that he is joining in the revelation to the world of something that it was not before aware of and of which it may some day make use."

We have the right, you know, to take a thought and appropriate it to our own uses, and so I have been turning this one over and over in my mind with all sorts of strange ramifications. The greater number of us cannot be discoverers of the kind referred to in the article quoted, for like the woman before mentioned, our bodies are tied more or less securely to our home habitat, but I am sure we are all discoverers at heart. Life is often called a journey, "the journey of life." Usually when referred to in these terms it is also understood that it is "a weary pilgrimage." Why not call it a voyage of discovery and take it in the spirit of happy adventure?

- - - - - -

Adventurers and travelers worthy the name always make nothing of the difficulties they meet; nor are they so intent on the goal that they do not make discoveries on the way. Has anyone ever said to you, as a warning, "No man knoweth what a day may bring forth?" I have heard it often and it is always quoted with a melancholy droop at the corners of the mouth. But why! Suppose we do not know what will happen tomorrow. May it not just as well be a happy surprise as something unpleasant? To me it is a joy that "no man knoweth what a day may bring forth"[1] and that life is a journey from one discovery to another. It makes of every day a real adventure; and if things are not to my liking today, why, "There's a whole day tomorrer that ain't teched yet," as the old darkey said, "No man knoweth" what the day will be like. It is absolutely undiscovered country. I'll just travel along and find out for myself. Did you ever take a little trip anywhere with your conscience easy about things at home, your mind free from worry, and with all care cast aside and eyes wide open, give yourself to the joy of every passing incident; looking for interesting things which happen every moment? If you have, you will understand. If not, you should try it and you will be surprised how much of adventure can enter into ordinary things.

Join "Don't Worry" Club

Conservation of a Woman's Strength Is True Preparedness

March 20, 1916

"Eliminate—To thrust out." Did you never hear of the science of elimination? Didn't know there was such a science! Well, just try to eliminate, or to thrust out, from your everyday life the unnecessary, hindering things and if you do not decide that it takes a great deal of knowledge to do so successfully then I will admit that it was my mistake.

- - - - - -

The spring rush is almost upon us. The little chickens, the garden, the spring sewing and house-cleaning will be on our hands soon, and the worst of it is they will all come together, unless we have been very wise in our planning.

It almost makes one feel like the farmer's wife who called up the stairs to awaken the hired girl on a Monday morning. "Liza Jane," she called, "come hurry and get up and get the breakfast. This is wash day and here it is almost 6 o'clock and the washing not done yet. Tomorrow is ironing day and the ironing not touched, next day is churning day and it not begun, and here the week is half gone and nothing done yet."

1. Proverbs 27:1.

You'd hardly believe it, but it's true. And it's funny, of course, but one can just feel the worry and strain under which she was suffering. All without reason, too, as the greater part of our worry usually is.

It seems to me that the first thing that should be "thrust out" from our household arrangements is that same worry and feeling of hurry. I do not mean to eliminate haste, for sometimes, usually in fact, that is necessary, but there is a wide difference between haste and hurry. We may make haste with our hands and feet and still keep our minds unhurried. If our minds are cool and collected, our "heads" will be able to "save our heels" a great deal.

An engineer friend once remarked of the housekeeping of a capable woman, "There is no lost motion there." She never worried over her work. She appeared to have no feeling of hurry. Her mind, calm and quiet, directed the work of her hands and there was no bungling, no fruitless running here and there. Every motion and every step counted so that there was "no lost motion."

Household help is so very hard to get especially on the farm, that, with the housekeeper, it has become a question of what to leave undone or cut out altogether from her scheme of things as well as how to do in an easier manner what must be done.

The Man of the Place loved good things to eat. Does yet, for that matter, as, indeed, I think the men of all other places do. Trying to make him think I was a wonder of a wife I gratified this appetite, until at last, when planning the dinner for a feast day, I discovered to my horror that there was nothing extra I could cook to mark the day as being distinct and better than any other day. Pies, the best I could make, were common every-day affairs. Cakes, ditto. Puddings, preserves and jellies were ordinary things. Fried, roasted, broiled and boiled poultry of all kinds was no treat, we had so much of it as well as other kinds of meat raised on the farm. By canning and pickling and preserving all kinds of vegetables and fruits we had each and every kind the year around. In fact, we were surfeited with good things to eat all the time.

As I studied the subject it was impressed upon me, that in order to thoroly enjoy anything, one must feel the absence of it at times and I acted upon that theory. We have fresh fruit the year around; our apples bridging the gap from blackberries and plums in the summer to the first strawberries in the spring, and these fresh fruits are usually our desserts. Fresh fruits are better, more healthful, more economical, and so much less work to serve than pies, puddings and preserves. These things we have on our feast days, for Sunday treats and for company. They are relished so much more because they are something different.

I stopped canning vegetables altogether. There is enough variety in winter vegetables, if rightly used, and we enjoy the green garden truck all the more for having been without it for a few months. The family is just as well if not better satisfied under this treatment and a great deal of hard work is left out.

- - - - - -

Some time ago the semi-annual house-cleaning was dropped from my program, very much to everyone's advantage. If a room needed cleaning out of season, I used to think "Oh well, it will soon be house-cleaning time" and let it wait until then. I found that I was becoming like the man who did "wish Saturday would hurry and come so that he could take a bath." Then I decided I would have no more house-cleaning in the accepted meaning of that word.

- - - - - -

The first step in the new order of things was to dispense with carpets and use rugs instead. When a rug needs shaking and airing it gets it then, or as soon as possible, instead of waiting until house-cleaning time. If the windows need washing they are washed the first day I feel energetic enough. The house is gone over in this way a little at a time when it is needed and as suits my convenience and about all that is left of the bugaboo of housecleaning is the putting up of the heater in the fall and taking it out in the spring.

Never do I have the house in a turmoil and myself exhausted as it used to be when I house-cleaned twice a year.

- - - - - -

To be sure there are limits to the lessening of work. I could hardly go so far as a friend who said, "Why sweep? If I let it go today and tomorrow and the next day there will be just so much gained, for the floor will be just as clean when I do sweep, as it would be if I swept every day from now until then." Still after all there is something to be said for that viewpoint. The applied science of the elimination of work can best be studied by each housekeeper for herself, but believe me, it is well worth studying.

- - - - - -

During the first years of his married life, a man of my acquaintance, used to complain bitterly to his wife, because she did not make enough slop in the kitchen to keep a hog. "At home," he said, "they always kept a couple of hogs and they did not cost a cent for there was always enough waste and slop from the kitchen to feed them." How ridiculous we all are at times! This man actually thought that something was wrong instead of being thankful that there was no waste from his kitchen. The young wife was grieved, but said she did not "like to cook well enough to cook things and throw them to the hogs, for the sake of cooking more." The food on her table was always good even if some of it was made over dishes, and after a time her husband realized that he had a treasure in the kitchen and that it was much cheaper to feed the hogs their proper food than to give them what had been prepared for human consumption.

- - - - - -

There are so many little heedless ways in which a few cents are wasted here and a few more there. The total would be truly surprising if we should sum them up. I illustrated this to myself in an odd way lately. While looking over the pages of a catalog advertising articles from 2 cents to 10 cents the Man of the Place said, "There are a good many little tricks you'd like to have. Get what you want; they will only cost a few cents." So I made out a list of what I wanted, things I decided I could not get along without, as I found them, one by one, on those alluring pages. I was surprised when I added up the cost to find that it amounted to $5. I put the list away intending to go over it and cut out some things to make the total less. That was several months ago and I have not yet missed any of the things I would have ordered. I have decided to let the list wait until I do.

- - - - - -

Matches are small things to economize in, but why throw away even a match when it is just as easy to save it? In using an oil stove with several burners, I found that full half or more of the expense for matches could be saved by using the same match more than once. It was just as easy to touch the end of a used match to the flame already burning as it was to strike a new one. The only trouble necessary was to have an extra match safe in which to drop the match the first time it was used. When lighting the next burner it was just as easy to take the match from there as from the first match safe. A small thing, if you please, but small things have such a way of counting up. Everyone has heard the old saying that "a woman can throw more out of the window with a teaspoon than a man can throw in at the door with a shovel." Of course, that is an exaggeration. I'm sure it couldn't be done, anyway not if the man shoveled right hard!

\- - - - - -

We are told that in the struggle of the nations for existence, and in our own if it should be drawn into the vortex, a great deal depends upon the organization of the economic resources; that in the last analysis the strength of nations as of individuals rests upon the kitchens of the country.

If economy is so essential in war time why is it not a good thing in time of peace? If it so strengthens a nation in time of stress, would it not make a nation more powerful if practiced at other times? Thing cannot be considered small that have so great an effect!

\- - - - - -

With worry, waste and unnecessary work eliminated from our households we would be in a state of "preparedness" to which no one could possibly have any objection. And the beauty of it is that such a state of preparedness in our homes is good in war or peace, for both nations and individuals.

Look for Fairies Now

The "Little People" Still Appear to Those with Seeing Eyes

April 5, 1916

Have you seen any fairies lately? I asked the question of a little girl not long ago. "Huh! There's no such thing as fairies," she replied. Some way the answer hurt me and I have been vaguely disquieted when I have thought of it ever since. By the way. Have you seen any fairies lately? Please do not answer as the little girl did, for I'm sure there are fairies and that you at least have seen their work.

In the long, long ago days, when the farmers gathered their crops they always used to leave a part of whatever crop they were harvesting in or on the ground for the use of the "Little People." This was only fair for the "Little People" worked hard in the ground to help the farmer grow his crops and if a share were not left for them they became angry and the crops would not be good the next year. You may laugh at this as an old superstition but

I leave it to you if it has not been proved true that where the "Little People" of the soil are not fed the crops are poor. We call them different names now, nitrogen and humus and all the rest of it, but I always have preferred to think of them as fairy folk who must be treated right. Our agricultural schools and farm papers spend much time and energy telling us to put back into the soil the elements of which we rob it. Only another way of saying, "Don't rob the 'Little People'; feed them!"

\- - - - - -

Dryads used to live in the trees, you know, beautiful, fairy creatures who now and then were glimpsed beside the tree into which they vanished. There have been long years during which we have heard nothing of them, but now scientists have discovered that the leaves of trees have eyes, actual eyes that mirror surrounding objects. Of what use are eyes to a tree, I wonder? Would it not be fine if the men of science gave us back all our fairies under different names?

\- - - - - -

There is the old myth of Santa Claus! What child in these deadly, matter-of-fact times believes in Santa Claus; yet who can deny that at Christmas time there is a spirit, bringing gifts, abroad in the world, who can come down the chimney, or through the keyhole for that matter, and travel in the same night from the north pole to the south? Why not let the children believe in Santa Claus? Later they will understand that it is only a beautiful imagery. It is surely no harm to idealize things and make them more real by investing them with personalities and it might do away with some of the sordid estimating of the price of gifts, which children learn so surprisingly young.

I have a feeling that childhood has been robbed of a great deal of its joys by taking away its belief in wonderful, mystic things, in fairies and all their kin. It is not surprising that when children are grown they have so little idealism or imagination nor that so many of them are like the infidel who asserted that he would not believe anything he could not see. It was a good retort the Quaker made, "Friend! Does thee believe thee has any brains?"

\- - - - - -

It is astonishing what an effect a child's early training has upon its whole life. When one reflects upon the subject one is inclined to agree with the noted clergyman who said, "Give me the child for the first seven years of his life and you may have him all the rest of the time." What a wonderful power mothers have in their hands! They shape the lives of the children today, thru them the lives of the men and women of tomorrow, and thru them the nations and the world.

- - - - - -

I see by the papers that one of the suffrage leaders of the state will tour the Ozarks this spring in the interest of woman suffrage, bringing light into the dark places, as it were.

A great many seem to regard the securing of the ballot as the supreme attainment and think that with women allowed to vote, everything good will follow as a matter of course. To my mind the ballot is incidental, only a small thing in the work that is before the women of the nation. If politics are not what they should be, if there is graft in places of trust and if there are unjust laws, the men who are responsible are largely what their mothers have made them and their wives usually have finished the job. Perhaps that sounds as if I were claiming for the women a great deal of influence, but trace out a few instances for yourself, without being deceived by appearances, and see if you do not agree with me.

- - - - - -

During the controversy between Dr. Cook and Commodore Perry over the discovery of the north pole, the subject was being discussed in a home where I happened to be. It was when Cook was being paid such a high price for his lectures and the mother of two young men present exclaimed, "It makes no difference whether Cook is faking or not! He is getting the money, isn't he, and that's what counts!"[2] She was a woman of whom one expected better things, a refined, educated woman and a devout church member, but her influence on her boys would teach them that money was what counted, regardless of truth or honor.

- - - - - -

A young friend with whom I talked the other day said that life was so "much more interesting" to her since she "began to look below the surface of things and see what was beneath." There are deeps beyond deeps in the

2. The controversy over who really discovered the North Pole has never quite ended. Robert E. Peary and Dr. Frederick A. Cook vied for the claim of first place until Dr. Cook's lack of evidence put an end to his claim. As for Peary, although there have always been strong reservations, *National Geographic Magazine* continues to support him.

life of this wonderful world of ours. Let's help the children to see them instead of letting them grow up like the man of whom the poet wrote,

> A primrose by the river's brim
> A yellow primrose was to him and nothing more.

Let's train them, instead, to find "books in the running brooks, sermons in stones and good in everything."[3]

- - - - - -

But have you seen any fairies lately, or have you allowed the harsher facts of life to dull your "seeing eye"?

- - - - - -

The sunshine fairies cannot rest
When evening bells are rung;
Nor can they sleep in flowers
When bedtime songs are sung.

They are such busy fairies,
Their work is never done,
For all around and round the world
They travel with the sun.

And while you're soundly sleeping,
They do the best they can
A-painting cherry blossoms
In far away Japan.

The poppy fields of China,
With blossoms bright and gay,
They color on their journey—
And then pass on their way.

And all the happy children,
In islands of the sea,
Know little Ray O'Sunshine,
Who plays with you and me.

3. William Shakespeare, *As You Like It,* 2.1.

So We Moved the Spring

How Running Water Was Provided in the Rocky Ridge Farm Home

April 20, 1916

There once was a farmer, so the story goes, who hauled water in barrels from a distant creek. A neighbor remonstrated with him for not digging a well and having his water supply handier. The farmer contended that he did not have time.

"But," said the neighbor, "the time you would save by not having to haul water would be more than enough to do the work."

"Yes, I know," replied the farmer, "but you see, I am so busy hauling water that I can't get time to dig the well."

- - - - - -

There is a story of another man who also had trouble in supplying his place with water. This man hauled water for half a mile.

"Why don't you dig a well," asked a stranger, "and not haul water so far?"

"Well," said the farmer, "it's about as fur to water one way as 'tis t'other."

I do not pretend to be the original discoverer of these stories, neither do I vouch for their truthfulness, but I do know that they correctly picture the fix we were in before we moved the spring.

- - - - - -

We "packed water from the spring" for years at Rocky Ridge Farm. Now and then, when we were tired or in a special hurry, we would declare that something must be done about it. We would dig a well or build a cistern or something, the something being rather vague. At last the "something" was what we did. Like the men in the stories, we were too busy "packing water" to dig a well, and anyway it was "about as fur to water one way as t'other," so we decided to make an extra effort and move a spring. There were several never-failing springs on the farm but none of them were right at the house. We did not wish to move the house and besides it is very easy to move a spring, if one knows how, much easier than to move a house.

- - - - - -

Our trouble was to decide which spring. The one from which we carried water was nearest but it would require a ram to raise the water up to the house as the spring was in a gulch much lower than the buildings. Then, too, altho it never went dry, it did run a little low during a dry spell. There were the three springs in the "Little Pasture." They ran strong enough but they also would require a ram to lift the water. We wished our water supply to be permanent and as little trouble to us as possible when once arranged, so we looked further. Up on a hill in the pasture about 1,400 feet from the buildings, was a spring which we had been watching for a year. The flow of water was steady, not seeming to be much affected by dry weather.

We found by using a level that this spring, at the head of a hollow in the hill, was enough higher than the hill where the buildings were situated to give the water a fall of 60 feet. We decided to move this spring and The Man Of The Place would do it with only common labor to help. The spring was dug out down to solid rock in the shape of a well, and a basin made in this a foot deep. In this well was built a cement reservoir 8 feet in diameter, the walls of which were 11 feet high, extending 3 feet above the surface of the ground. It holds about 30 barrels of water. A heavy cement cover in the form of an arch was placed over the top. It takes two men to lift it so that no one will look in from curiosity and leave the cover displaced. The cement was reinforced with heavy woven wire fence to make it strong. The walls and cover are so thick and the shade of the oaks, elms and maples surrounding it is so dense that the water does not freeze in winter and is kept cool in summer. A waste pipe was laid in the cement six inches from the top of the reservoir to allow the surplus water to flow off if the reservoir should become overfull. It is in the nature of a water trap as the opening is beneath the surface of the water and both ends are covered with fine screen to prevent anything from entering the pipe.

The pipe that brings the water down to the buildings is in the lower side of the reservoir about a foot from the bottom. It was laid in the cement when the wall was built so that it is firmly embedded. The end which projects into the water was fitted with a drive well point, screened to keep out foreign substances and prevent sand and gravel from washing into the pipe. The pipe is laid 2 feet under ground all the way to the buildings and grass grows thickly over it for the whole distance. Because of this the water does not become heated while passing thru in warm weather and there is no danger of its freezing and bursting the pipe in winter. The screen in the drive well point is brass and the pipes are heavily galvanized inside and out. There is, therefore, no taste of iron or rust added to the water. We have moved the spring so that it flows into a corner of the kitchen as pure as at its source.

- - - - - -

We have multiplied our spring as well as moved it. We revel in water! There is a hydrant in the hen house, one in the barn, one in the calf lot, one in the garden and one at the back of the house, besides the faucets in the house. The supply of water is ample, for we tried it thoroly during a dry season. By attaching a hose to a hydrant, we can throw water over the top of the house or barn in a steady stream with the full force of a 60-foot fall and 30 barrels of water behind, so we feel we have protection in case of fire.

- - - - - -

A man came out from town one day and after seeing the water works and drinking some of the water he exclaimed, "Why, this is better than living in town!"

We have saved more than time enough to dig a well but now we do not need to dig it so we find that time seems to run in doubles this way as well as the other.

- - - - - -

We are told that "There is no great loss without some small gain." Even so I think that there is no great gain without a little loss. We do not carry water from the spring any more which is a very great gain, but it was sometimes pleasant to loiter by the way and that we miss a little.

Folks Are "Just Folks"

Why Shouldn't Town and Country Women Work and Play Together?

May 5, 1916

"The Athenians," is a woman's club just lately organized, in Hartville, for purposes of study and self-improvement. Hartville was already well supplied with social organizations. There was an embroidery club also a whist club and the usual church aid societies and secret orders which count for so much in country towns. Still there were a few busy women who felt something lacking. They could not be satisfied altogether with social affairs. They wanted to cultivate their minds and increase their knowledge, so they organized the little study club and have laid out a year's course of study.

- - - - - -

The membership of the club is limited to twenty. If one of the twenty drops out then some one may be elected to take the vacant place. Two negative ballots exclude anyone from membership. There are no dues. "The Athenians" is, I think, a little unique for a town club, as the membership is open to town and country women alike and there are several country members. Well, why not? "The Colonel's lady and Judy O'Grady are sisters under the skin." (Mind I have not said whether Judy O'Grady is a town or country woman. She is just as likely, if not a little more likely, to be found in one place as the other.)

- - - - - -

Surely the most vital subjects in which women are interested are the same in town and country, while the treasures of literature and the accumulated knowledge of the world are for all alike. Then why not study them together and learn to know each other better? Getting acquainted with folks makes things pleasanter all around. How can we like people if we do not know them? It does us good to be with people whose occupation and surroundings are different from ours. If their opinions differ from ours, it will broaden our minds to get their point of view and we will likely find that they are right in part at least, while it may be that a mutual understanding will lead to a modification of both opinions.

- - - - - -

While busily at work one afternoon I heard the purr of a motor and going to the door to investigate, I was met by the smiling faces of Mr. and Mrs. Frink and Mr. and Mrs. Curtis of Hartville. Mrs. Curtis and Mrs. Frink have taken an active part in organizing "The Athenians" and they had come over to tell me of my election to membership in that club. What should be done when there is unexpected company and one is totally unprepared and besides must be at once hostess, cook, and maid? The situation is always so easily handled in a story. The lovely hostess can perform all kinds of conjuring tricks with a cold bone and a bit of leftover vegetable, producing a delicious repast with no trouble whatever and never a smut on her beautiful gown. In real life it sometimes is different, and during the first of that pleasant afternoon my thoughts would stray to the cook's duties. When the time came, however, it was very simple. While I made some biscuit, Mrs. Frink fried some home cured ham and fresh eggs, Mrs. Curtis set the table. The Man Of The Place opened a jar of preserves and we all had a jolly, country supper together before the Hartville people started on the drive home. It is such a pleasure to have many friends and to have them dropping in at unexpected times that I have decided when it lies between friendships and feasting and something must be crowded out the feasting may go every time.

- - - - - -

At a recent meeting of the "The Athenians" some very interesting papers, prepared by the members were read. Quoting from the paper written by Mrs. George Hunter: "The first societies of women were religious and charitable. These were followed by patriotic societies and organizations of other kinds. At present there exists in the United States a great number of clubs for women which may be considered as falling under the general heads—educational, social and practical. The clubs which may be classified as practical include charitable organizations, societies for civic improvement or for the furthering of schools, libraries, and such organizations as have for their object the securing, by legislation, of improved conditions for working women and children. In 1890 the General Federation of Women's Clubs was formed. There were in the United States at the last enumeration more than 200,000 women belonging to clubs." Get the number? Two hundred thousand! Quite a little army this.

- - - - - -

A very interesting paper and one that causes serious thought was that prepared by Mrs. Howe Steel on "The Vocation of Woman." "Woman," says Mrs. Steel, "has found out that, with education and freedom, pursuits of all kinds are open to her and by following these pursuits she can preserve her personal liberty, avoid the grave responsibilities, the almost inevitable sorrows and anxieties which belong to family life. She can choose her friends and change them. She can travel and gratify her tastes and satisfy her personal ambitions. The result is that she frequently is failing to discharge satisfactorily some of the most imperative demands the nation makes upon her. I think it was Longfellow who said: 'Homekeeping hearts are happiest.' Dr. Gilbert said, 'Thru women alone can our faintest dreams become a reality. Woman is the creator of the future souls unborn. Tho she may be cramped, enslaved and hindered, tho she may never be able to speak her ideal, or touch the work she longs to accomplish, yet in the prayer of her soul is the prophecy of her destiny.'

Here's to woman the source of all our bliss.
There's a foretaste of Heaven in her kiss.
From the queen upon her throne to the maiden in the dairy,
They are all alike in this."

- - - - - -

In "Soldiers of the Soil," a story of country life in California by Rose Wilder Lane, a real country woman says: "It is my opinion there are lots more happy homes in the country than there are in the city. If everybody lived in the country you wouldn't hear all this talk about divorce." I wonder how true that is and if true, or if not true, what are the reasons for it? I suppose there are statistics on the subject. There are on most things, but you know "there are three kinds of lies—lies, d— lies and statistics," so why bother about them? The reasons given by the women quoted were that while the woman in the country worked, to help out the family income, her work was at home, while if the woman in the city worked she must leave home to do so; that, working together, man and wife were drawn together, while working apart they drifted apart.

- - - - - -

There may be fewer divorces in the country without it necessarily following that there are more happy homes. It seems to me that the deadly monotony of working with, and playing with, the same person in the same place for days and weeks and months and years would be more apt to drive a person to divorce or suicide than if they were separated during the working day and could meet when it was over with different experiences to talk about and to add variety to their companionship. To be sure, in the city a woman can live in one apartment as well as another so long as her pay envelop comes to hand regularly, while in the country when a woman leaves her home she leaves her job too. Perhaps this has more effect in lessening divorce in the country than the happy home idea. We carry our own environment with us to a certain extent and are quite likely to stand or fall by the same principles wherever we may live.

When Is a Settler an Old Settler?

June 5, 1916

"Why you are an old settler," said a new comer to us recently. "Yess," I replied proudly, "we consider ourselves natives," yet when we drove into the Ozarks 20 years ago,[4] with a covered hack and a pony team, we found the "old settler" already here. In conversation with us he made the remark: "My father was an old settler here. He came up from Tennessee before the war."[5] Since then, in working the fields, we have found now and then a stone arrow or spear head made by a settler older still.

When we came to the Ozarks a team of fairly good horses would trade for 40 acres of land. The fences were all rail fences and a great many of the houses were built of logs. The country was a queer mixture of an old and a new country. A great many of the fields had been cropped continually since the war and were so worn out that as one of the neighbors said, "You can't hardly raise an umbrella over it." Aside from these old fields the land was covered with timber and used for range. The "old settlers" told us that the thick growth of timber was comparatively a new thing; that before the country was so thickly settled there were only a few scattering large trees. The fires were allowed to run and they kept down the young growth of timber. Wild grass grew rankly over all the hills and cattle pastured free.

It has always been a great pleasure to hear the tales of earlier days. A neighbor, Mrs. Cleaver, told us stories of her experience in war times and the days, equally as bad which immediately followed. Her husband did not go to the war but one night a band of men came and took him away. She never knew what became of him. Then came hard days for her and her young step-son. They raised a little crop and a hog or two for their living but whenever they had stored a little corn or meat some of the lawless bands of raiders that infested the Ozark hills, would come and take it from them. When the war ended, some of the leaders of these lawless bands continued their depredations, only in a little different fashion. Thru the machinations of one of

4. This trip in 1894 is written about in her diary, published as Laura Ingalls Wilder and Rose Wilder Lane, *On the Way Home* (New York: Harper Collins, 1962).
5. The Civil War.

them, Mrs. Cleaver's step-son was taken from her, by due process of law, and bound out to him until the boy should be of age, to work without wages, of course. When Mrs. Cleaver protested, I suppose in rather a frantic way, she was driven from the court house, with a horse whip, by the sheriff.

- - - - - -

Not all the old time stories were so serious. There is the story of the green country boy who never had seen a carpeted floor. A new family moved in from the North somewhere and this boy went to the house one day. As he started to enter the door he saw the carpet on the floor. Standing in the door he swung his long arms and jumped clear across the small room landing on the hearth before the fireplace. Turning to the astonished woman of the house he exclaimed: "Who Mam! I mighty nigh stepped on your kiverled!"[6] Our friend in telling this story always ended with: "I never could make out whether that boy was as big a fool as he pretended to be or not. He made a mighty smart business man when he was older and made the business men of Kansas City and St. Louis hustle to keep up with him," which is a way the hill boys have.

- - - - - -

One old lady, who has lived here since the war, says that when she came the "old settlers" told her of the time when a band of Spanish adventurers came up the Mississippi River and wandered thru the Ozarks. Somewhere among the hills they hid their treasure in a cave and it never has been discovered to this day.

- - - - - -

But how old must a settler be to be an "old settler"? or if you prefer the famous question, "How old is Ann?"[7]

Facts Versus Theories

June 20, 1916

Facts will not always bear out theories! It was a Missouri judge, at a little inland county seat, who adjourned court without a proper regard for the in-

6. Coverlet or bedspread.
7. Slang for "Who knows?"

terests of the case that was being tried before him, and who, when remonstrated with and told that he "could not do that," replied, "Well, I have." And now a Missouri farmers' club has also set at naught the opinions of experts.

- - - - - -

In an article, on women's clubs, in a late magazine, I find this opinion by Eugene J. Grant a prominent New York man whose wife is a leader in club work in the state: "I do not believe that clubs for men and clubs for women should ever be combined. I say keep them separate. They won't mix well. Men and women may work toward the same ends, but they work differently, and there's no use in trying to combine the clubs." To this the Bryant Farmers' club of Bryant, Mo., may reply, "Well, I have."

- - - - - -

Article 2, section 1 of the constitution of The Bryant Farmers' club says, "Any one in good standing may become a member of this club by paying the annual fee of 25 cents." This is well clinched in section 2 of the same article. "When the head of a family joins the club, all members of his or her family under 21 years old, may become active members without paying additional fees." Not only the women but the children are taken into this Farmers' club and made active workers, all as a matter of course.

- - - - - -

The Bryant Farmers' club was started about 17 months ago and was planned to help pass the winter evenings and in order that neighbors might become better acquainted. The meetings are held at homes of the different members. At each meeting the place for the next meeting is decided upon and three members are selected to make a talk or write a paper upon some farm topic. After the business of the meeting is disposed of, the members talk over their successes and failures and compare notes. The talks and discussions are followed by a short literary program. The homes of the members are scattered and the long distances to go makes it difficult at times for them all to be present at the meetings but there usually is a good attendance. At times as many as 68 have answered at roll call. Advising with and helping one another in this way the club members, of course, raised some fine crops. Making a collection among themselves, they exhibited it at the fairs at Mansfield and Ava last fall. The exhibit received a great deal of favorable comment and won, for the Bryant Farmers' club, 85 blue and red ribbons. During the busy summers, when the evenings are short and the days, tho long, are still too short to accomplish the work waiting to be done, the meetings of the club are discontinued unless something especial comes up, when a meeting is called by 'phone.

- - - - - -

The club is growing and branching out in several directions. The members are planning to build a hall, in some central location, in which to hold their meetings and social entertainments and also as a place in which to keep a permanent exhibition of their best grains, grasses and other farm products. As a start toward this hall they have already given one entertainment which netted them $25 for the building fund. They also are co-operating in the purchase and management of livestock and in the sale of livestock, farm and garden products.

- - - - - -

The officers who have led the members in making this farmers' club so successful surely deserve honorable mention. They are as follows—M. L. Andrews, president; Miss Hattie Williams, secretary-treasurer; C. A. Williams, D. B. McMillan and J. E. Williams members of executive board. The president and secretary-treasurer also are members of the executive board by reason of their office.

Haying While the Sun Shines

July 20, 1916

One of the neighbors needed some help in the hay harvest. Being too busy to go himself, he called a town friend by telephone and asked him, if possible, to send out some one to work thru haying. Mansfield has made a beautiful shady park of the public square in the center of the town and it is the gathering place for those who have idle time on their hands. Everyone enjoys it, the busy man with just a few idle minutes as well as the town loafers who, perhaps, have a few busy minutes now and then. It seemed like a very good place to look for a man to help in the hay field, so here the obliging friend went.

"Any of you fellows want a job?" he asked of a group resting in the shade. "Yes" said one man. "I do." "Work on a farm?" asked the friend. "Yes, for I need a job," was the reply. "Can you go out in the morning?" was the next question. "How far out is it?" asked the man who needed a job. "Two miles and a half," he was told. "Can't do it!" he exclaimed, dropping back into the restful position from which he had been disturbed. "I wouldn't go that far from town to work for anybody."

- - - - - -

The Man Of The Place, inquiring in town for help, was told that it was not much use to look for it. "Jack was in the other day and begged with tears in his eyes for some one to come help him get in his hay and he couldn't get anyone." Jack's place is only half a mile from town so surely it could not be too far out, but to be sure the sun was shining rather warm in the hay field and the shade in the park was pleasanter. All of which reminds one of the tramp of whom Rose Wilder Lane tells in her Soldiers Of The Soil. She met him, one of many, while on her walking tour thru the state of California. After listening to his tale of woe, she asked him why he did not look for work on a farm. She was sure there must be a chance to find a job there, for the farmers were very short of help. To her suggestion the tramp replied, "Who wants to work like a farmer anyway!"

- - - - - -

No one seems to want to "work like a farmer," except the farmer's wife. Well! Perhaps she does not exactly want to, but from the way she goes about it no one would suspect that she did not. In our neighborhood we are taking over more of the chores to give the men longer days in the field. We are milking the cows, turning the separator, feeding the calves and the pigs and doing whatever else is possible, even going into the fields at times. Farmers are being urged to raise more food for the world consumption, to till more acres and also produce more to the acre. Their hands are quite full now and it seems that about the only way they could procure more help would be to marry more wives.

- - - - - -

A few days ago, I ran away from a thousand things waiting to be done and stole a little visit with a friend. And so I learned another way to cut across a corner and save work. Here it is, the way Mrs. Craig makes plum jelly. Cook the plums and strain out the juice: then to 3 cups of the boiling juice add 4 cups of sugar and stir until dissolved. Fill jelly glasses at once and set to one side. If the juice is fresh it will be jelled in the morning but if the juice is from canned plums it takes longer and may have to set over until the next day but it jells beautifully in the end.

Kin-folks or Relations?

August 5, 1916

"I do like to have you say kin-folks. It seems to mean so much more than relations or relatives," writes my sister from the North. They do not say kin-folks in the North. It is a Southern expression.

This remark was enough to start me on a line of thought that led me far a-field. Kin-folks! They are such homey sounding words and strong, too, and sweet. Folks who are akin—why they need not even be relatives or "blood kin!" What a vista that opens up! They are scattered all over the world, these kin-folks of ours and we will find them wherever we go, folks who are akin to us in thought and belief, in aspirations and ideas, tho our relatives may be far away. Not but what those of our own family may be akin to us also, tho sometimes they are not.

Old Mr. Weeks died last winter. His will left the fine farm to his youngest son, subject to providing a home for his mother so long as she lived. A comparatively small sum of money was left each of the seven other children who were scattered in other states. And now a strange thing happened! We always expect to hear of trouble and quarreling among the heirs, over a will and an estate and in this case we were not disappointed. There was trouble, serious trouble and disagreement. The surprising thing was in the form it took. The youngest son refused flatly to abide by his father's will. He would not take that whole farm for himself! "It was not fair to the others!"

His brothers and sisters refused absolutely to take any share of the farm. "It would not be right," they said, when their brother had made the farm what it was by staying at home and working on it, while they had gone away on their own affairs. Lawyers were even called into the case, not to fight for a larger share for their clients, but to persuade the other party to take more of the property than he wished to take. There is nothing new under the sun we are told, but if anything like this ever happened before it has not been my good fortune to hear of it. The members of this family were surely kin-folks as well as relatives.

Two sisters, Mabel and Kate were left orphans when 18 and 20 years old. There was very little for their support, so as they would be obliged to add to their income in some way they went into a little business of ladies' furnishing goods. All the responsibility was left with Mabel altho they were equal partners and she also did most of the work. Kate seemed to have no sense of honor in business nor of the difference between right and wrong in her dealings with her sister. At last Mabel had a nervous breakdown under the strain and the shock of the sudden death of her fiance. While Mabel was thus out of the way, Kate sold the business, married and left town, and when Mabel was recovered she found that the business and her sister were gone, that the account at the bank was overdrawn and a note was about due which had been given by the firm and to which her own name had been forged. Because of the confidence which her honor and honesty had inspired, Mabel was able to get credit and make a fresh start. She has paid the debts and is becoming prosperous once more.

Were Mabel and Kate kin-folks? Oh no, merely relatives!

Showing Dad the Way

Mansfield Has a Boys' Good Road Club That Works and Plays

August 5, 1916

The science of road making was brought to such perfection in the days of ancient Rome, that some of the old Roman roadways are in existence today. But it remained for the Ozark Mountain town of Mansfield, in the year 1915, to show the world something new in the way of road building.

Mansfield is situated on one of the highest points of the Ozarks, so exactly at the crest of the slopes to the north and south that the rainfall from the caves, on the north side of the railway station, runs north to the Gasconade river, which drains the northern slopes of the Ozarks, while the rain that falls on the south side of the station roof, finds its way south to Bryant River which is the waterway for the southern slope.

Steep hillsides and swift flowing mountain streams make beautiful scenery but also they make it very hard to keep the roads in fit condition to be traveled and last summer a new element entered into the problem—the urge of competition.

One of the proposed routes, for the state automobile road, runs thru Mansfield and consequently the citizens of the town and surrounding country had quite a severe attack of roadmaking fever.

Other places were affected also and there was a strong, tho friendly rivalry, among the nearby town and different road districts, as to which should make the best showing in working the roads.

Then the mayor of Mansfield, Dr. F. H. Riley, had an idea. He has an idea every once in a while, but this has proved to be one of the happiest,—"Why not make use of the energy and activity of the boys of the road district, which were going to waste?

"Growing boys must have some excitement. They must have an outlet for their exuberant spirits and some way to work off their superfluous energy. Without proper guidance these things run riot and make trouble for themselves and all concerned. I have it! We will guide this energy and it shall help to turn the wheels of industry even as do the swift streams of the Ozarks, when properly controlled."

Mansfield is a town with only 900 inhabitants but they are very much alive and quite capable of following an idea to see where it will lead, so the "Mansfield Boys Good Roads Club" was organized with 50 members and started out to help work the road.

It is astonishing how much work 50 good lively boys can do in a day when their hearts are in it. They raked the loose rocks out of the road; cleaned out ditches and culverts; picked up rocks from adjoining fields to be used on the road; cut brush from the roadway; and thoroly enjoyed it all.

Especially did they enjoy themselves when noontime came, for, with the dinner hour, arrived their mothers and their sisters and their aunts, with well filled baskets. And you all know what happens when a small boy meets a picnic.

The boys were not all so small at that—though it made no difference with what happened to the picnic—for the business and professional men of Mansfield, learning what was afoot, had begged to be taken on as associate members of the boys' club. They were present with their picks and shovels and acquired a good appetite for the noontime lunch.

Some of the business men of the town, who were unable to take an active part, opened their purses and contributed to help along the work.

Farmers, who knew of the plans, not to be outdone by the townspeople, came with their teams and gave their time and strength to the cause.

All worked with great enthusiasm and the spirit of the old time country "workings" and the roads leading into Mansfield presented the appearance of an elongated beehive.

The club spent two days on the road last summer and, besides other work accomplished, the boys themselves picked up and hauled more than 200 loads of rock, which were used in bad places in the road bed and in building a culvert.

The Mansfield Boys Good Roads Club has been a great success, not only in the amount of work accomplished, but because of the example it has set. Which example will be followed, when spring comes, by the organization of several other boys' clubs, for work on the roads of the Ozarks.

As the Mansfield club was the first organized, its members intend to stay in the lead and Dr. Riley and the boys expect to do very much better next summer than they did last. There will be at least one "working" a month, during the summer season, Dr. Riley thinks, and the picnic lunch, at noon, will be a special feature of each occasion.

Being the originator of the plan and one of the three road commissioners for the district, Dr. Riley is in a position to greatly influence the boys of the club and he intends to lead them in beautifying the roads as well as improving their driving condition. He says there is no need for anything to be ugly in order to be useful, and nut and fruit trees, by the roadside, give a pleasant shade on warm days; and make of a road a beautiful driveway. Planting and caring for these trees would be an education in itself for the boys.

Some of the effects of organizing the boys for this work are shown in the increased interest their elders take in the subject of good roads. The Mansfield road district, last fall, voted a bond issue of $20,000 for road work and it is hoped that it will result in putting in good shape the 35 miles of road in the district.

But it is expected that the effects of this work on the boys themselves will be very far reaching. It keeps them occupied during some of their idle time and thus out of mischief; gives them a good, healthy, live interest and makes them feel themselves responsible members of the community.

It teaches them the necessity for good roads; and a proper respect for public property. What boy, after realizing the work it takes to make a good road; and feeling that he owns an interest in it, because of his labors in making it good, but would feel indignant to see the road carelessly or wantonly damaged?

This feeling of a proprietary interest in public property, if wisely handled, will surely extend to other things and help to make, of these boys, public spirited, intelligent citizens.

A Dog's a Dog for A' That

Intelligent Pets Sometimes Seem Almost Like Real Folks

August 20, 1916

A redbird swinging in the grape arbor saw himself in the glass of my kitchen window not long ago. He tried to fly thru the glass to reach the strange bird he saw there and when his little mate came flitting by he tried to fight his reflection. Apparently he was jealous. During all one day he fretted and struggled to drive the stranger away. He must have told his little wife about it that night, I think, for in the morning they came to the arbor together and she alighted before the window while he stayed in the background. She gave Mr. Redbird one look, after glancing in the glass, then turned and flew fiercely at her reflection, twittering angrily. One could imagine her saying: "So that's it! This strange lady Redbird is the reason for your hanging around here instead of getting busy building the nest. I thought something was wrong, but I'll soon drive her away!" She tried to fight the strange lady bird until her husband objected to her paying so much attention to his rival and then they took turns, he declaring there was a gentleman there, she vowing there was a lady and doing her best to drive her away. At last between them they seemed to understand and now they both come occasionally to swing on the grape vine before the window and admire themselves in the glass.

There are many interesting things in the out-of-doors life that comes so close to us in the country, and if we show a little kindness to the wild creatures they quickly make friends with us and permit us a delightful intimacy with them and their homes. A bird in a cage is not a pretty sight, to me, but it is a pleasure to have the wild birds and the squirrels nesting around the house and so tame that they do not mind our watching them. Persons who shoot or allow shooting on their farms drive away a great deal of amusement and pleasure with the game, as well as do themselves pecuniary damage, while a small boy with a stone handy can do even more mischief than a man with a gun.

It is surprising how like human beings animals seem when they are treated with consideration. Did you ever notice the sense of humor animals have? Ever see a dog apologize—not a cringing fawning for favor, but a frank apology as one gentleman to another?

Shep was trying to learn to sit up and shake hands, but try as he would he could not seem to get the knack of keeping his balance in the upright position. He was an old dog, and you know it has been said that, "It is hard to teach an old dog new tricks." No sympathy has ever been wasted on the dog but I can assure you that it also is hard for the old dog. After a particularly disheartening session one day, we saw him out on the back porch alone and not knowing that he was observed. He was practicing his lesson without a teacher. We watched while he tried and failed several times, then finally got the trick of it and sat up with his paw extended. The next time we said, "How do you do, Shep," he had his lesson perfectly. After that it was easy to teach him to fold his paws and be a "Teddy Bear" and to tell us what he said to tramps. We never asked him to lie down and roll over. He was not that kind of character. Shep never would do his tricks for any one but us, tho he would shake hands with others when we told him to do so. His eyesight became poor as he grew older and he did not always recognize his friends. Once he made a mistake and barked savagely at an old friend whom he really regarded as one of the family tho he had not seen him for some time. Later as we all sat in the door yard, Shep seemed uneasy. Evidently there was something on his mind. At last he walked deliberately to the visitor, sat up and held out his paw. It was so plainly an apology that our friend said: "That's all right Shep old fellow! Shake and forget it!" Shep shook hands and walked away perfectly satisfied.

- - - - - -

My little French Poodle, Incubus, is blind. He used to be very active and run about the farm, but his chief duty, as he saw it, was to protect me. Altho he cannot see, he still performs that duty, guarding me at night and flying at any stranger who comes too near me during the day. Of what he is thinking, when he sits for long periods in the yard, with his face to the sun, I am too stupid to understand perfectly, but I feel that in his little doggy heart, he is asking the eternal, "Why?" as we all do at times. After awhile he seemingly decides to make the best of it and takes a walk around the familiar places, or comes in the house and does his little tricks for candy with a cheery good will. If patience and cheerfulness and courage, if being faithful to our trust and doing our duty under difficulties count for so much in man that he expects to be rewarded for them, both here and hereafter, how are they any less in the life of my little blind dog? Surely such virtues in animals are worth counting in the sum total of good in the universe.

Do Not Waste Your Strength

September 5, 1916

"Clothes are much more sanitary if not ironed after washing," said a physician in an article, on fresh air and sunshine which I read the other day. Isn't that delightful news and especially so in hot weather? I have not ironed knit underwear, stockings, sheets or towels for years but, altho I knew there was a very good reason for not doing so, I have always felt rather apologetic about it. Science is surely helping the housewife! Now instead of fearing that the neighbors will say I am lazy or a poor housekeeper, when they find out that I slight my ironing, I can say: "Oh no, I never do much ironing, except the outside clothes. We must not iron out the fresh air and sunshine, you know. It is much more healthful not, the doctors say." Seriously, there is something very refreshing about sheets and pillow slips just fresh from the line, after being washed and dried in the sun and air. Just try them that way and see if your sleep is not sweeter.

Our inability to see things that are right before our eyes, until they are pointed out to us, would be amusing if it were not at times so serious. We are coming, I think, to depend too much on being told and shown and taught, instead of using our own eyes and brains and inventive faculties, which are likely to be just as good as any other person's.

I should like to know who designed our furniture as we use it today? It must have been a man. No woman, I am sure, at least no woman who has the care of a house, would ever have made it as it is. Perhaps, if some physician or some domestic science teacher would point out to us the unnecessary dirt and the extra work caused by the height of our furniture, we would insist on having it different. Otherwise it is quite likely we shall keep on in the same old way, breaking our backs and overworking tired muscles, or we shall become careless and let the dirt accumulate.

Most furniture, and especially that in the bedroom, where of all places cleanliness should be most observed, is just high enough from the floor to permit dust and dirt to gather underneath but not high enough to be cleaned easily. It is more than likely, also, not to fit back smoothly against the wall but to set out just far enough to make another hiding place for dust. The only way to clean under and behind such articles is to move them bodily from their place, clean the wall and floor, and then move them back. This should be done every few days. However, dragging heavy dressers and wardrobes from their places and then putting them back again is hard work and it is a great deal worse than time wasted to do it.

Built-in furniture does away with a great deal of heavy work. A little built-in cupboard and a light dressing table may take the place of the heavy dresser. One does not have to clean under, behind, or on top of closets and wardrobes that reach smoothly from floor to ceiling, nor do sideboards and china closets built into the walls need to be moved when cleaning the dining room.

All the World Is Queer

September 20, 1916

"All the world is queer, except for thee and me," said the old Quaker to his wife, "and sometimes I think thee is a little queer."

The Man of the Place once bought me a patent churn. "Now," said he, "throw away that old dash churn. This churn will bring the butter in 3 minutes." It was very kind of him. He had bought the churn to please me and to lighten my work, but I looked upon it with a little suspicion. There was only one handle to turn and opposite it was a place to attach the power from a small engine. We had no engine so the churning must needs to be done with one hand, while the other steadied the churn and held it down. It was hard to do, but the butter did come quickly and I would have used it anyway because the Man of the Place had been so kind.

The tin paddles which worked the cream were sharp on the edges and they were attached to the shaft by a screw which was supposed to be loosened to remove the paddles for washing, but I could never loosen it and usually cut my hands on the sharp tin. However, I used the new churn, one hand holding it down to the floor with grim resolution, while the other turned the handle with the strength of despair when the cream thickened. Finally, it seemed that I could use it no longer. "I wish you would bring in my old dash churn," I said to the Man of the Place. "I believe it is easier to use than this after all."

"Oh!" said he; "you can churn in 3 minutes with this and the old one takes half a day. Put one end of a board on the churn and the other on a chair and sit on the board, then you can hold the churn down easily!" And so when I churned I sat on a board in the correct mode for horseback riding and tho the churn bucked some I managed to hold my seat. "I wish," said I to the Man of the Place, "you would bring in my old dash churn." (It was where I could not get it.) "I cut my hands on these paddles every time I wash them."

"Oh, pshaw!" said he, "you can churn with this churn in 3 minutes—"

One day when the churn had been particularly annoying and had cut my hand badly, I took the mechanism of the churn, handle, shaft, wheels and paddles all attached, to the side door which is quite high from the ground and threw it as far as I could. It struck on the handle, rebounded, landed on the paddles, crumpled and lay still and I went out and kicked it before I picked it up. The handle was broken off, the shaft was bent and the paddles were a wreck.

"I wish," I remarked casually to the Man of the Place, "that you would bring in my old dash churn. I want to churn this morning."

"Oh, use the churn you have," said he. "You can churn in 3 minutes with it. What's the use to spend half a day—"

"I can't," I interrupted. "It's broken."

"Why, how did that happen?" he asked.

"I dropped it—just as far as I could," I answered in a small voice and he replied regretfully, "I wish I had known that you did not want to use it. I would like to have the wheels and shaft, but they're ruined now."

This is not intended as a condemnation of patent churns—there are good ones—but as a reminder that being new and patented is no proof that a thing is better, even tho some smooth tongued agent has persuaded us that it will save time.

Also, as the old Quaker remarked to his wife, "Sometimes I think thee is a little queer."

Just a Question of Tact

Every Person Has Said Things They Didn't Mean

October 5, 1916

"You have so much tact and can get along with people so well," said a friend to me once. Then after a thoughtful pause she added, "But I never could see any difference between tact and trickery." Upon my assuring her that there was no difference, she pursued the subject further.

"Now I have no tact whatever, but speak plainly," she said pridefully. "The Scotch people are, I think, the most tactful and the Scotch, you know, are the trickiest nation in the world."

As I am of Scotch descent, I could restrain my merriment no longer and when I recovered enough to say, "You are right, I am Scotch," she smiled ruefully and said, "I told you I had no tact."

- - - - - -

Tact does for life just what lubricating oil does for machinery. It makes the wheels run smoothly and without it there is a great deal of friction and the possibility of a breakdown. Many a car on the way of life fails to make the trip as expected for lack of this lubricant. Tact is a quality that may be acquired. It is only the other way of seeing and presenting a subject. There are always two sides to a thing, you know, and if one side is disagreeable, the reverse is quite apt to be very pleasant. The tactful person may see both sides but uses the pleasant one.

"Your teeth are so pretty when you keep them white," said Ida to Stella; which, of course was equal to saying that Stella's teeth were ugly when she did not keep them clean, as frequently happened, but Stella left her friend with the feeling that she had been complimented and also with the shamed resolve that she would keep those pretty teeth white.

Tom's shoulders were becoming inclined to droop a little. To be sure he was a little older than he used to be and sometimes very tired; but the droop was really caused more by carelessness than by anything else. When Jane came home from a visit to a friend whose husband was very round shouldered indeed, she noticed more plainly than usual the beginning of the habit in Tom.

Choosing a moment when he straightened to his full height and squared his shoulders, she said: "Oh, Tom! I'm so glad you are tall and straight, not round shouldered like Dick. He is growing worse every day until it is becoming a positive deformity with him." And Tom was glad she had not observed the tendency in his shoulders and thereafter their straightness was noticeable.

Jane might have chosen a moment when Tom's shoulders were drooping and with perfect truthfulness have said: "Tom! You are getting to be round shouldered and ugly like Dick. In a little while you will look like a hunchback."

Tom would have felt hurt and resentful and probably would have retorted, "Well you're getting older and uglier too," or something like that, and his hurt pride and vanity would have been a hindrance instead of a help to improvement.

The children, of course, get their bad tempers from their fathers, but I think we get our vanity from Adam, for we all have it, men and women alike, and like most things it is good when rightly used.

- - - - - -

Tact may be trickery but after all I think I prefer the dictionary definition—"nice discernment." To be tactful one has only to discern or distinguish, or in other words to see nicely and speak and act accordingly.

- - - - - -

My sympathy just now, however, is very much with the persons who seem to be unable to say the right thing at the proper time. In spite of oneself there are times when one's mental fingers seem to be all thumbs. At a little gathering, not long ago, I differed with the hostess on a question which arose and disagreed with just a shade more warmth than I intended. I resolved to make it up by being a little extra sweet to her before I left. The refreshments served were so dainty and delicious that I thought I would find some pleasant way to tell her so. But alas! As it was a very hot day, ice water was served after the little luncheon and I found myself looking sweetly into my hostess's face and heard myself say, "Oh, wasn't that water good." What could one do after that, but murmur the conventional, "Such a pleasant afternoon," at leaving and depart feeling like a little girl who had blundered at her first party.

An Autumn Day

October 20, 1916

King Winter has sent warning of his coming! There was a delightful freshness in the air the other morning, and all over the low places lay the first frost of the season.

What a beautiful world this is! Have you noticed the wonderful coloring of the sky at sunrise? For me there is no time like the early morning, when the spirit of light broods over the earth at its awakening. What glorious colors in the woods these days! Did you ever think that great painters have spent their lives trying to reproduce on canvas what we may see every day? Thousands of dollars are paid for their pictures which are not so beautiful as those nature gives us freely. The colors in the sky at sunset, the delicate tints of the early spring foliage, the brilliant autumn leaves, the softly colored grasses and lovely flowers—what painter ever equalled their beauties with paint and brush? I have in my living room three large windows uncovered by curtains which I call my pictures. Everchanging with the seasons, with wild birds and gay squirrels passing on and off the scene, I never have seen a landscape painting to compare with them.

As we go about our daily tasks the work will seem lighter if we enjoy these beautiful things that are just outside our doors and windows. It pays to go the top of the hill, now and then, to see the view and to stroll thru the wood lot or pasture forgetting that we are in a hurry or that there is such a thing as a clock in the world. You are "so busy"! Oh yes I know it! We are all busy, but what are we living for anyway and why is the world so beautiful if not for us? The habits we form last us thru this life and I firmly believe into the next. Let's not make such a habit of hurry and work that when we leave this world we will feel impelled to hurry thru the spaces of the universe using our wings for feather dusters to clean away the star dust.

The true way to live is to enjoy every moment as it passes and surely it is in the everyday things around us that the beauty of life lies.

I strolled today down a woodland path—
A crow cawed loudly and flew away.
The sky was blue and the clouds were gold
And drifted before me fold on fold;
The leaves were yellow and red and brown
And patter, patter the nuts fell down,
On this beautiful, golden autumn day.

A squirrel was storing his winter hoard,
The world was pleasant: I lingered long,
The brown quails rose with a sudden whirr
And a little bundle, of eyes and fur,
Took shape of a rabbit and leaped away.
A little chipmunk came out to play
And the autumn breeze sang a wonder song.

Our Fair and Other Things

November 5, 1916

The annual fair at Mansfield was a success in spite of the summer's drouth. Farmers surely are the most optimistic people in the world! Altho badly punished, in the conflict with the forces of nature this season, they were by no means defeated, as was proved by the agricultural exhibits and everywhere could be overheard planning for next year's campaign.

Discouraged? Not a bit of it! "It's been a bad season but we'll come out all right," said one man. "The old cows will take us thru." One could understand his confidence after looking at the stock exhibited. Purebred Jerseys, Holsteins and Polled Durhams were there, each so good in its way that one could not be partial to any. In the hog pens were fine Duroc Jerseys and Poland Chinas, one weighing 800 pounds. It looked as tho the day of the "hazel splitter" was past in the Ozarks.

The women as usual did their part toward the fair in a very satisfactory manner in every department. Mrs. C. A. Durnell of Hillside Poultry Farm made a good superintendent of poultry and M. L. Andrews, poultry judge, is conceded to be one of the best in the state. Mr. Andrews is very helpful to anyone interested in poultry. As he examined bird after bird, he displayed their fine points and explained where they failed to come up to standard, to a small interested audience which followed him from coop to coop. Altogether we farmers and people of Mansfield feel very proud of our fair.

- - - - - -

One amusement feature provided as a free show on the street was, to me, shocking. I knew of course that the thing is often done, but I never have watched while knives were thrown around a human target. The target as usual was a woman and a man threw the knives. Effacing myself behind a convenient corner, which hid the spectacle, I watched the faces of the crowd. They reminded me strongly of the faces of the crowd watching a Mexican bull fight that I saw in a moving picture. There happened to be no bloodshed in the knife throwing but judging by the expression of some of the faces there was a tense expectancy and unconsciously almost a hope that there might be. In the crowd were women and children as well as men and boys, all eager, alert and watching—for what? A failure of nerve, perhaps, in one of the performers; an instant's dimming of vision or slight miscalculation on the part of the man. There is something thrilling and ennobling in seeing a person brave death in a good cause or for an ideal, but to watch anyone risk being butchered merely to make holiday sport savors too much of other things. We condemn the bull fight and the spectators you know. Is it perhaps a case of the pot calling the kettle black?

- - - - - -

It is not alone "one touch of nature" which "makes the whole world kin," but every emotion which writes itself on the human countenance creates a family likeness, with others of its kind, even between people of different races. I saw this plainly when present at a Chinese Salvation Army meeting, on a street corner in San Francisco's Chinatown. The crowd was large and all Chinese except myself and escort. Altho Chinese was the only language spoken and I could not understand a word, I could follow the exhorter's meaning and by the expressions on the faces about me could tell the state of mind of his audience. It was one of my many curious experiences in the city and when the leader started singing "Onward Christian Soldiers," in Chinese and the crowd joined in, I felt as tho my ears must be bewitched. It was quite as startling as it was to see the words "Methodist Episcopal Church" over the door of a beautiful building, built in Chinese style, on another street corner in Chinatown. The words seemed no more to belong with the fanciful Chinese architecture than the Chinese words belonged with the good old American hymn tune sung by Oriental folks.

Thanksgiving Time

November 20, 1916

As Thanksgiving day draws near again, I am reminded of an occurrence of my childhood. To tell the truth, it is a yearly habit of mine to think of it about this time and to smile at it once more.

We were living on the frontier in South Dakota then. There's no more frontier within the boundaries of the United States, more's the pity, but then we were ahead of the railroad in a new unsettled country. Our nearest and only neighbor was 12 miles away and the store was 40 miles distant.

Father had laid in a supply of provisions for the winter and among them were salt meats, but for fresh meat we depended on father's gun and the antelope which fed, in herds, across the prairie. So we were quite excited, one day near Thanksgiving, when father hurried into the house for his gun and then away again to try for a shot at a belated flock of wild geese hurrying south.

We would have roast goose for Thanksgiving dinner! "Roast goose and dressing seasoned with sage," said sister Mary. "No not sage! I don't like sage and we won't have it in the dressing," I exclaimed. Then we quarreled, sister Mary and I, she insisting that there should be sage in the dressing and I declaring there should not be sage in the dressing, until father returned,—without the goose! I remember saying in a meek voice to sister Mary, "I wish I had let you have the sage," and to this day when I think of it I feel again just as I felt then and realize how thankful I would have been for roast goose and dressing with sage seasoning—with or without any seasoning—I could even have gotten along without the dressing. Just plain goose roasted would have been plenty good enough.[8]

This little happening has helped me to be properly thankful even tho at times the seasoning of my blessings has not been just such as I would have chosen.

- - - - - -

8. This story appears in Laura Ingalls Wilder, *By the Shores of Silver Lake* (New York: Harper and Row, 1971), chapter 26.

"I suppose I should be thankful for what we have, but I can't feel very thankful when I have to pay $2.60 for a little flour and the price still going up," writes a friend, and in the same letter she says, "we are in our usual health." The family are so used to good health that it is not even taken into consideration as a cause of thanksgiving. We are so inclined to take for granted the blessings we possess and to look for something peculiar, some special good luck for which to be thankful.

I read a Thanksgiving story, the other day, in which a woman sent her little boy out to walk around the block and look for something for which to be thankful.

One would think that the fact of his being able to walk around the block and that he had a mother to send him would have been sufficient cause for thankfulness. We are nearly all afflicted with mental farsightedness and so easily overlook the thing which is obvious and near. There are our hands and feet,—who ever thinks of giving thanks for them, until indeed they, or the use of them, are lost. We usually accept them as a matter of course, without a thought, but a year of being crippled has taught me the value of my feet and two perfectly good feet are now among my dearest possessions. Why! There is greater occasion for thankfulness just in the unimpaired possession of one of the five senses than there would be if some one left us a fortune. Indeed how could the value of one be reckoned? When we have all five in good working condition we surely need not make a search for anything else in order to feel that we should give thanks to Whom thanks are due.

- - - - - -

I once remarked upon how happy and cheerful a new acquaintance seemed always to be and the young man to whom I spoke replied, "Oh he's just glad that he is alive." Upon inquiry, I learned that several years before this man had been seriously ill, that there had been no hope of his living, but to everyone's surprise he had made a complete recovery and since then he had always been remarkably happy and cheerful.

So if for nothing else, let's "just be glad that we are alive" and be doubly thankful if like the Scotch poet, we have a good appetite and the means to gratify it.

> Some hae meat that canna eat
> And some want meat that lack it,
> But I hae meat and I can eat,
> And sae the Lord be thanket.

Learning to Work Together

December 5, 1916

The Bryant Farmers' Club held their first annual auction and stock sale November 2. This plan of an auction sale for a neighborhood is something new, I think, in the work of farmers' clubs. The idea originated in the mind of the president, M. L. Andrews and was eagerly adopted by the club members.

Every member listed what he had for sale and it was surprising how a little from every one mounted up in the total. There were 40 head of stock listed and a wagon load of household goods.

The day of the auction was pleasant and the old mill yard and the one street of the little town of Bryant were filled with wagons, buggies, horses and motor cars, while a lively crowd of about 400 men, women and children surrounded the auctioneer as he cried the sale, or gathered at the lunch counter for refreshment.

The sale was a success, considering the fact that it was the first of the kind and rather an experiment, it went off very well indeed. The members and officers of the club are learning from experience, however, and already plans are being made to insure that next year's sale shall be more satisfactory still. Some farmers are saying that, if they can list their stock together to sell at auction, there is nothing to hinder their shipping together in carload lots to market. And so the idea of co-operation keeps growing, when once it has taken root.

- - - - - -

I know a little band of friends that calls itself a woman's club. The avowed purpose of this club is study, but there is an undercurrent of deeper, truer things than even culture and self improvement. There is no obligation and there are no promises, but in forming the club and in selecting new members, only those are chosen who are kind hearted and dependable as well as the possessors of a certain degree of intelligence and a small amount of that genius which is the capacity for careful work. In short, those who are taken into membership are those who will make good friends and so they are a little band who are each for all and all for each.

If one needs the helping hand of comradeship, not one but all are eager and willing to help, with financial aid if needed, but more often with a good word or a small act of kindness. They are getting so in the habit of speaking good words that I expect to see them all develop into Golden Gossips.

Ever hear of golden gossip? I read of it some years ago. A woman who was always talking about her friends and neighbors, made it her business to talk of them in fact, never said anything but good of them. She was a gossip but it was "golden gossip." This woman's club seems to be working in the same way and associations of friendship and mutual helpfulness are being built up which will last for life. It is a beautiful thing, and more than ever one is impressed with the idea that it is a pity there are—

So many gods, so many creeds,
So many paths that wind and wind
When just the art of being kind
Is all the sad world needs.[9]

- - - - - -

"Money is the root of all evil" says the proverb, but I think that proverb maker only dug down part way around the plant of evil. If he had really gotten to the root of the matter, I am sure he would have found that root to be selfishness—just selfishness pure and simple. Why all the mad scramble for money? Why are we all "money-mad Americans?" It is just for our selfish gratification with things that money can buy, from world dominion to a stick of striped candy—selfishness, just selfishness.

Not long ago I was visiting in a family where there were several children. The father lost his memorandum book and was inquiring for it. No one had seen it. "I wish," he said, "that you children would find it for me before I come back at noon." There was silence for a minute and then one of the children said: "Why don't you put up a quarter? That'll find it!"

"Well, I will," his father answered and at once the children were all eagerness to search. It seemed to me such a pity to appeal to a selfish interest in the home where there should be loving service freely given.

- - - - - -

In the blacksmith shop, one hot day last summer, the blacksmith was sweating over his hot irons when two idle boys sauntered in and over to the water bucket. It was empty. "Ain't yuh got no water?" asked one of the boys.

"Not if the bucket is empty," answered the blacksmith.

Then the man, for whom the blacksmith was working, spoke up. "Why don't you go get a bucket of water?" he asked.

"I will for a nickel," said the boy.

9. From the poem "The World's Need" by Ella Wheeler Wilcox.

"Yes, we'll go for a nickel," agreed the other boy.

"Were you going to pay for your drink?" asked the man innocently and the boys looked at him surprised and then slunk away, without filling the bucket. Just an example of selfishness made more contemptible by being so plainly unfair.

Co-operation, helpfulness, and fair dealing are so badly needed in the world and if they are not learned as children at home it is difficult for grownups to have a working knowledge of them.

So much depends on starting the children right!

Before Santa Claus Came

December 20, 1916

Hundreds of years ago when our pagan ancestors lived in the great forests of Europe and worshiped the sun, they celebrated Christmas in a somewhat different fashion than we do today.

The sun, they thought, was the giver of all good. He warmed and lighted the earth. He caused the grass to grow for their flocks and herds to eat and the fruits and grains for their own food, but every year after harvest time he became angry with them and started to go away, withdrawing his warmth and light farther and still farther from them. The days when he showed them his face became shorter and shorter and the periods of darkness ever longer. The farther away he went the colder it grew. The waters turned to ice and snow fell in place of the gentle summer showers.

If their god indeed left them as he seemed to be doing, if he would not become reconciled to them, they must all perish, for nothing would grow upon which they could live and if they did not freeze they would die of hunger. Their priests' prayers availed nothing and something must be done to make the sun god smile upon them once more. The priests demanded a human sacrifice, the sacrifice of a child!

What is now our Christmas eve was the night chosen for the ceremony. On that night the door of every hut in the village must be left unfastened that the priests might enter and take the child. No one knew which house would be entered nor what child taken to be sacrificed on the altar of the Sun God.

Perhaps the priests knew that the shortest day of the year had arrived and that the sun would start on its return journey at this time. They may have taken advantage of this knowledge to gain greater control over the people, but it may be that the selection of the right day at first was purely accidental and they believed, with the people, that the Sun God was pleased by the sacrifice. It was, to them, proof of this that he immediately started to return and smiled upon them for another season.

Do you suppose the children knew and listened in terror for footsteps on Christmas eve? The fathers and mothers must have harkened for the slightest noise and waited in agony, not knowing whether their house would be passed by or whether the priests would enter stealthily and bear away one of their children or perhaps their only child. How happy they must have been when the teachers of Christianity came and told them it was all unnecessary. It is no wonder they celebrated the birth of Christ on the date of that awful night of sacrifice, which was now robbed of its terror, nor that they made it a children's festival.

Instead of the stealthy steps of cruel men, there came now, on Christmas eve, a jolly saint with reindeer and bells, bringing gifts. This new spirit of love and peace and safety that was abroad in the land did not require that the doors be left unbarred. He could come thru locked doors or down the chimney and be everywhere at once on Christmas night, for a spirit can do such things. No wonder the people laughed and danced and rang the joy bells on Christmas day and the celebration with its joy and thankfulness has come on down the years to us. Without all that Christmas means, we might still be dreading the day in the old terrible way instead of listening for the sleigh bells of Santa Claus.

What's in a Word?

January 5, 1917

A group of friends was gathered around a glowing fire the other evening. The cold outside and the warmth and cheer and soft lights within had opened their hearts and they were talking freely together as good friends should.

"I propose that we eliminate the word can't from our vocabularies for the coming year," said Mrs. Betty. "There ain't no such animile anyhow."

"But sometimes we just c—" began sister Sue, then stopped abruptly at the sound of an amused chuckle.

"Oh, well—if you feel that way about it!" rejoined Mrs. Betty, "but I still insist that if you see such an animal it is only a creature of the imagination. When I went to school they tried to teach me that it was noble to say, 'I'll try' when confronted with a difficult thing to be done, but it always sounded weak to me. Why! the very expression presupposes failure," she went on with growing earnestness. "Why not say I will, and then make good? One can, you know, for if there is not one way to do a thing there are usually two."

"That word 'can't' with its suggestion of failure!" exclaimed George. "Do you know a man came up to me on the street the other day and said, 'You can't lend me a dollar, can you?' He expected to fail in his request—and he most certainly did," he added grimly.

"After all," said brother James slowly, "people do a good deal as they are expected to do, even to saying the things they are expected to say. The power of suggestion is very strong. Did you ever notice how everyone will agree with you on the weather? I have tried it out many a time just for fun. Before the days of motor cars, when we could speak as we passed driving along the road, I have said to the first man I met, 'This is a fine day,' and regardless of what the weather might be, he never would fail to answer, 'Sure, it's a fine day,' or something to that effect and pass on smiling. To the next man I met I would say, 'Cold weather we're having,' and his reply would always be, 'Coldest I ever knew at this season,' or 'Mighty cold this morning,' and he would go on his way shivering. No matter if it's raining, a man usually will agree with you that it's awfully dry weather, if you suggest it to him right."

"Speaking of friends," said Philip, which no one had been doing tho all could trace the connecting thought, "Speaking of friends,—I heard a man say not long ago that he could count all the friends he had on the fingers of one hand. I wonder"—and his voice trailed off into silence as his thought carried him away. A chorus of protest arose.

"Oh, how awful!" exclaimed Pansy, with the tender eyes. "Anyone has more friends than that. Why, if everybody is sick or in trouble everybody is his friend."

"It all depends on one's definition of friend," said Mrs. Betty in a considering tone. "What do we mean when we say 'friend?' What is the test for a friend?" A silence fell upon the little group around the glowing fire.

"But I want to know," insisted Mrs. Betty. "What is the test for a friend? Just what do you mean Philip, when you say, 'He is my friend?'"

"Well," Philip replied, "when a man is my friend I expect he will stand by me in trouble, that he will do whatever he can to help me if I am needing help and do it at once even at cost of inconvenience to himself."

"Now, Pansy! How do you know your friends?" still insisted Mrs. Betty.

"My friends," said Pansy, with the tender eyes, "will like me anyway, no matter what my faults are. They will let me do as I please and not try to change me but will be my friends whatever I do."

"Next," began Mrs. Betty, but there were exclamations from every side. "No! No! It's your turn now! We want to know what your test of friendship is!"

"Why! I was just asking for information," answered Mrs. Betty with a brilliant smile, the warmth of which included the whole circle. "I wanted to know—"

"Tell us! Tell us!" they all insisted.

"Well, then," earnestly, "my friends will stand by me in trouble. They will love me even tho I make mistakes and in spite of my faults, but if they see me in danger of taking the wrong course they will warn me. If necessary, they will even tell me of a fault which perhaps is growing on me unaware. One should dare anything for a friend, you know."

"Yes, but to tell friends of a fault is dangerous," said gentle Rosemary. "It is so likely to make them angry."

"To be sure," Mrs. Betty answered. "But if we are a friend we will take it thankfully for the sake of the spirit in which it is given as we do a Christmas present which otherwise we would not care for."

> "Remember well and bear in mind
> A constant friend is hard to find
> And when you find one good and true
> Change not the old one for the new."[1]

quoted Philip as the group began to break up.

"No, don't change 'em," said George, in the bustle of the putting on of wraps. "Don't change 'em! Just take 'em all in!"

Giving and Taking Advice

January 20, 1917

I have just learned something new! Isn't it a wonderful thing that we are "never too old to learn" and also sometimes isn't it strange that no matter how many years we have numbered we still learn best from that old, old teacher Experience? For instance, there was the time when I read, (not in a farm paper) that the addition of a little vinegar to the lard in which doughnuts were fried would keep them from soaking fat. I was preparing a company dinner not long afterward, and wishing to have my doughnuts especially good, was about to pour the vinegar into the lard when the Man of the Place came into the kitchen. From long association with the cook, he knew that she was doing something different and demanded to know why. When I had explained, he advised me not to try any experiments at that particular time. "Oh, it will be all right," I answered easily, "or it would not have been in that paper." I added the vinegar and learned it was perfectly true that the doughnuts would not soak the grease. They would hardly soak anything they were so tough.

Experience had taught me one more lesson!

It is so easy to give advice. It is one thing with which the most of us are well supplied and are perfectly willing to part. Sometimes I think we are too

1. From a folk song, writer anonymous.

quick to do this, too free in handing out unasked an inferior article. There is no way of estimating the mischief done by the well meant but ill-considered advice of friends and acquaintances. Knowing only one side of a question, seeing imperfectly a part of a situation, we say: "Well I wouldn't stand for that a minute," or "You'll be foolish if you do," or "I would" do this or that and go light heartedly on our way never thinking that by a careless word or two we may have altered the whole course of human lives, for some persons will take advice and use it.

- - - - - -

There were once two men who had different ways of treating their horses when they went around them in the barn. One always spoke to his horses as he passed so that they might know he was there and not kick. The other never spoke to them. He said it was their business to look before they kicked. This last man often spoke of his way as being much the best. One day he advised the other to change his way of doing because someday he would forget to speak and get kicked. Not long after, this actually happened and the man was seriously injured. His wife said to me, "If he had spoken to the horse when he went into the barn as he used to do he would not have been hurt, but lately he had stopped doing that and the horse kicked before it saw him." I always have thought that the accident happened because of his friend's advice and I have seen so often where what was best for me might not be just the thing for the other fellow that I have decided to keep my advice until asked for and then administer it in small doses.

- - - - - -

There are ways of profiting by the experience of others, besides taking advice carelessly given. We might watch, you know, while some one else tried the vinegar on the doughnuts. And that brings me back to where I started to tell of the new thing I had learned. It is a great help with the work of sewing to cover the tread of the sewing machine with a piece of soft, thick carpet. The carpet will act as a cushion and one's feet will not become so tired as they otherwise would when using the machine a great deal. There is another advantage in the use of the carpet in cold weather as it is much warmer for the feet to rest on than the cold iron of the machine.

According to Experts

February 5, 1917

In the late issue of a St. Louis paper, I find the following: "Experts in the office of home economics of the United States Department of Agriculture have found it is possible to grind whole wheat in an ordinary coffee mill fine enough for use as a breakfast cereal and even fine enough for use in bread making."

If the experts of the Department of Agriculture had asked anyone of the 200 people who spent the winter of 1880–81 in De Smet, S. Dak., they might have saved themselves the trouble of experimenting. I think, myself, that it is rather a joke on our experts at Washington to be 36 years behind the times.

That winter, known still among the old residents as "the hard winter," we demonstrated that wheat could be ground in an ordinary coffee mill and used for bread making. Prepared in that way it was the staff of life for the whole community. The grinding at home was not done to reduce the cost of living, but simply to make living possible.

De Smet was built as the railroad went thru, out in the midst of the great Dakota prairies far ahead of the farming settlements, and this first winter of its existence it was isolated from the rest of the world from December 1 until May 10 by the fearful blizzards that piled the snow 40 feet deep on the railroad tracks. The trains could not get thru. It was at the risk of life that anyone went even a mile from shelter, for the storms came up so quickly and were so fierce it was literally impossible to see the hand before the face and men have frozen to death within a few feet of shelter because they did not know they were near safety.

The small supply of provisions in town soon gave out. The last sack of flour sold for $50 and the last of the sugar at $1 a pound. There was some wheat on hand, brought in the fall before for seed in the spring, and two young men dared to drive 15 miles to where a solitary settler had also laid in his supply of seed wheat. They brought it in on sleds. There were no mills in town or country so this wheat was all ground in the homes in coffee mills. Everybody ground wheat, even the children taking their turns, and the resultant whole wheat flour made good bread. It was also a healthful food and there was not a case of sickness in town that winter.

It may be that the generous supply of fresh air had something to do with the general good health. Air is certainly fresh when the thermometer registers all the way from 15 to 40 degrees below zero with the wind moving at blizzard speed. In the main street of the town, snow drifts in one night were piled as high as the second stories of the houses and packed hard enough to drive over and the next night the wind might sweep the spot bare. As the houses were new and unfinished so that the snow would blow in and drift across us as we slept, fresh air was not a luxury. The houses were not overheated in daytime either, for the fuel gave out early in the winter and all there was left with which to cook and keep warm was the long prairie hay. A handful of hay was twisted into a rope, then doubled and allowed to twist back on itself and the two ends tied together in a knot, making what we called "a stick of hay."

It was a busy job to keep a supply of these "sticks" ahead of a hungry stove when the storm winds were blowing, but everyone took his turn good naturedly. There is something in living close to the great elemental forces of nature that causes people to rise above small annoyances and discomforts.

A train got thru May 10 and stopped at the station. All the men in town were down at the tracks to meet it, eager for supplies, for even the wheat had come to short rations. They found that what had been sent into the hungry town was a trainload of machinery. Luckily, there were also two emigrant cars well supplied with provisions, which were taken out and divided among the people. Our days of grinding wheat in coffee mills were over, but we had learned without expert aid that it can be done and that the flour so ground will make good bread and mush. Perhaps I would better say that we had all become experts and demonstrated the fact. After all necessity is the mother of invention and experience is a good old teacher.

Are You Going Ahead?

February 20, 1917

"I cannot stand still in my work. If I do not keep studying and going ahead, I slip back," said a friend the other day.

"Well, neither can I in my work," I thought. My mind kept dwelling on the idea. Was there a work that one could learn to do with a certain degree of excellence, and then keep that perfection without a ceaseless effort to advance?

How easy and delightful life might be if we could do this, if when we had attained the position we wished we might rest on our oars and watch the ripples on the stream of life.

Turning my mind resolutely from the picture of what would happen to the person who rested on his oars, expecting to hold his position where the tide was rippling, I began looking around for that place in life where one could stand still, without troubling to advance and without losing what already had been gained.

My friend who plays the piano so beautifully was a fair performer years ago, but has improved greatly as time went by. She spends several hours every day at the instrument practicing. "I have to practice," she says, "or I shall lose my power of execution," and because she does practice to keep what she already has, she goes on improving from day to day and from year to year.

In contrast to this, is the other friend who used to sing so much and who had such a lovely voice. She hardly ever sings now and told me the other day that she thought she was losing her voice. She also said that she was so busy she had no time to practice.

There is also the woman who "completed her education" some years ago. She thought there was no need for further effort along that line and that she had her education for all time, so she settled down to the house work and the poultry. She has read very little of anything that would help her to keep abreast of the times and does not now give the impression of being an educated, cultured person but quite the reverse. No doubt she has forgotten more than I ever knew, but the point is that she has lost it. Refusing to go ahead, she has dropped back.

Even a housekeeper who is a good housekeeper and stays such becomes a better and more capable one from the practice and exercise of her art and profession. If she does not, you may be sure she is slipping back and instead of being proficient will soon be careless, a woman who will say, "I used to be a good housekeeper, but—"

The same rule applies to character. Our friends and neighbors are either better friends and neighbors today than they were several years ago or they are not so good. We are either broader minded, more tolerant and sympathetic now than we used to be or the reverse is true. The person who is selfish, or mean or miserly—does he not grow more so as the years pass, unless he makes a special effort to go in the other direction?

Our graces are either growing or shrinking. It seems to be a law of nature that everything and every person must move along. There is no standing still. The moment that growth stops, decay sets in.

One of the greatest safeguards against becoming old is to keep growing mentally, you know.

If we do not strive to gain we lose what we already have, for just so surely as "practice makes perfect," the want of practice or the lack of exercise of talents and knowledge makes for the opposite condition.

We must advance or we slip back and few of us are bright enough to turn a slip to good account as did the school boy of long ago. This particular boy was late at school one icy winter morning and the teacher reproved him and asked the reason for his tardiness.

"I started early enough," answered Tom, "but it was so slippery that every time I took one step ahead I slipped back two steps."

There was a hush of astonishment and then the teacher asked, "But if that is true, how did you ever get here?"

"Oh, that's easy," replied Tom. "I was afraid I was going to be late and so I just turned around and came backwards."

Getting the Worst of It

March 5, 1917

Whenever two or three women were gathered together during the winter, sooner or later someone would ask, "Are your hens laying?"

In one such small crowd where town and country women mingled, I was very much interested and also amused by a conversation which took place between a country woman and a woman who lives in town. Of course the inevitable question was asked and the country woman answered that her hens were doing their duty. Then a town woman inquired, "What are you getting for eggs?"

"Thirty cents," replied the country woman.

"They make us pay 33 cents when we get them at the store," said the town woman. "Why can't you bring me my eggs?"

"I can," said the country woman. "How many would you want?"

"Oh! Bring me three dozen. Might as well save 9 cents," replied the town woman.

Perhaps I imagined it, but I certainly thought that the country woman's left eyelid dropped for an instant as she looked up at me, but her glance was so quick I could not be sure. Her reply was quick too.

"Why! I thought you were offering me the 3 cents a dozen more," she said. The town woman disclaimed this in a tone of surprise and the country woman asked, "How about dividing it?"

"Oh! I wouldn't bother with it for that," said the other in a tone of disgust.

"It is less bother for me to deliver our eggs all in one place. We sell them by the case, you know," said the country woman and again I thought her eyelid dropped as she glanced once more in my direction. I wish I could be sure about that wink. It would make such a difference in the conclusions one might draw.

There I said to myself, is the producer and consumer question in a nutshell, with the real reason why that terrible bogey, "the middleman" gets such a chance at us. Too much bother, unwillingness to co-operate and compromise, or in other words just plain selfishness is the cause at the bottom of all the trouble. The consumer wants something done about the high cost of living, but he wants all the benefit to accrue to himself. The producer wants something done to lessen the difference between the price at which he sells and what the consumer pays but he also desires what is thus saved to come his way, while the speculator standing between smiles to himself, secure in his position because of this weakness of human nature. For the rest of us, the punishment fits the crime and I am inclined to think that we get no more than we deserve.

After all, it is thru some fault or weakness of our own that the most of the evils of life come to us. It is as if our strength of character and virtues formed a guard around us, but a fault or weakness of character makes an opening thru which our punishment comes.

There was once a small boy with a quarrelsome disposition and a great unwillingness to obey the rules his mother made. At school he would seek a quarrel and get the thrashing he deserved; then he would come home, disobey his mother and be punished; then he would sit down and wail. "O-o-h! I always get the worst of it. I don't know why, but at school and everywhere I always get the worst of it!"

It was tragic for the child, but to me there was always something irresistibly comic about it also, because it reminded me so strongly of grown-ups I knew. We have all seen such persons. There are those who persistently disobey the laws of health, which being nature's laws are also God's laws, and then when ill health comes, wonder why they should be compelled to suffer.

Others by their bad temper and exacting dispositions estrange their relatives and repel friendly advances. Then they bewail the fact that their friends are so few.

From these, clear on down to the man who carelessly picked up the lid lifter from the hot part of the stove and then turned impatiently upon his wife exclaiming, "Why didn't you tell me that was hot!" we are all alike eager to lay upon some one else the blame for the troubles that come from our own faults and all remind me of the boy who wailed, “I always get the worst of it! I don’t know why but—I always get the worst of it!”

Buy Goods Worth the Price

April 5, 1917

We were speaking of a woman in the community who was ignoring the conventions, thereby bringing joy to the gossips’ hearts and a shock to those persons who always think first of what people will say.

“Well of course,” said my friend; “it is all perfectly harmless and she has the satisfaction of doing as she pleases, but I’m wondering whether it’s worth the price.”

There are very few things in this world that we may not have if we are willing to pay their price. You know it has been said that “Every man has his price,” which may or may not be true, but without doubt nearly every other thing has its market value and we may make our choice and buy. We must pay, in one way or another, a greater or less amount for everything we have and sometimes we show very poor judgment in our purchases.

Many a woman and girl has paid her good eyesight for a few pieces of hand embroidery or her peace of mind for a new gown, while many a man’s good health or good standing in the community, goes to pay for his indulgence in a bad habit.

Is there something in life that you want very much? Then pay the price and take it, but never expect to have a charge account and avoid paying the bills. Life is a good collector and sooner or later the account must be paid in full. I know a woman who is paying a debt of this kind on the installment plan. She wanted to be a musician and so she turned her children into the streets and neglected her husband that she might have more time for practice. She already has paid too high a price for her musical education and the worst of it is that she will keep on paying the installments for the rest of her life.

There are persons who act as if the things life has to offer were on sale at an auction and if some one else is likely to secure an article, they will raise their bid without regard to the value of the goods on sale. Indeed the most of us are like people at an auction sale in this respect, that during the excitement and rivalry we buy many things we do not need, nor want, nor know just what to do with, and we pay for them much more than they are worth.

Is it your ambition to outshine your neighbors and friends? Then you are the foolish bidder at the auction sale, raising your bid just because someone else is bidding. I knew a man like this. He owned a motor car of the same size and make as those his friends had but decided he would buy a larger, more powerful, and much more expensive one. His old car was good enough for all his needs, he said, but he was going to have a car that would be "better than the other fellow's." I suppose he figured the cost of the car in dollars and cents, but the real price he paid was his integrity and business honor, and for a bonus, an old and valued friendship. He had very poor judgment as a buyer in my opinion.

Do you desire an education? No matter who pays the money for this, you cannot have it unless you also pay with long hours of study and application.

Do you wish to be popular? Then there is a chance to buy the real lasting thing which means to be well thought of and beloved by people worth while, or the shoddy imitation, a cheap popularity of the "hail fellow well met" sort depending mostly on one's ability to tell a good story and the amount one is able to spend on so called pleasure. As always, the best is the cheapest, for poor goods are dear at any price. The square dealing, the kindness and consideration for others, the helpfulness and love which we must spend if we wish lasting esteem enrich us in the paying besides bringing us what we so much desired. On the other hand, in buying a cheap popularity, people sometimes bankrupt themselves in things, the value of which cannot be estimated. If popular favor must be paid for by the surrender of principles or loss in character, then indeed the price is too high.

Does "Haste Make Waste"?

April 20, 1917

A few days ago, with several others, I attended the meeting of a woman's club in a neighboring town. We went in a motor car, taking less than an hour for the trip on which we used to spend 3 hours, before the days of motor cars, but we did not arrive at the time appointed nor were we the latest comers by any means. Nearly everyone was late and all seemed in a hurry. We hurried to the meeting and were late. We hurried thru the proceedings; we hurried in our friendly exchanges of conversation; we hurried away and we hurried all the way home where we arrived late as usual.

What became of the time the motor car saved us? Why was everyone late and in a hurry? I used to drive leisurely over to this town with a team, spend a pleasant afternoon and reach home not much later than I did this time and all with a sense of there being time enough, instead of a feeling of rush and hurry. We have so many machines and so many helps, in one way and another, to save time and yet I wonder what we do with the time we save. Nobody seems to have any!

Neighbors and friends go less often to spend the day. Instead they say, "We have been planning for so long to come and see you, but we haven't had time," and the answer will be: "Everyone makes the same complaint. People don't go visiting like they used to. There seems to be no time for anything." I have heard this conversation, with only slight variations, so many times that I should feel perfectly safe to wager that I should hear it any time the subject might be started. We must have all the time there is the same as always. We should have more, considering the time saving, modern conveniences. What becomes of the time we save?

The reason oftenest given for not joining the Ruralist Poultry Club, by the girls I tried to interest was that they hadn't the time. Their school duties, their music and the like kept them so busy that there was no time for a new interest. There was one pleasing exception. Lulu was hesitating about sending in her application for membership and when I inquired if she lacked time for it I found that she was already giving all the time necessary to the care of the poultry and that she had an incubator of her very own already at work hatching eggs for a purebred flock.

Then I inquired if the record keeping was what made her hesitate and learned that she already kept most minute records of expense and income and of every egg laid. Not only this, but she keeps her father's farm accounts and in good condition, too. Here was a girl with time and ability enough to have a business of her own and to keep track of it and of her father's also. I think it was really shyness that made Lulu hesitate about joining the poultry club. She did send in her application at last and it was too late, but if the girls in the club do not hustle I feel sure this outsider will beat them, except for the prizes.

If there were any way possible of adding a few hours to the day they could be used handily right now, for this is surely the farm woman's busy time. The gardens, the spring sewing, the housecleaning, more or less, caused by the change from cold to warm weather and all the young things on the place to be cared for call for agility, to say the least, if a day's work is to be done in a day.

Some people complain that farm life is monotonous. They surely never had experience of the infinite variety of tasks that come to a farm woman in the merry springtime! Why! the ingenuity, the quickness of brain and the sleight of hand required to prevent a young calf from spilling its bucket of milk at feeding time and the patience necessary to teach it to drink is a liberal education in itself, while the vagaries of a foolish sitting hen will relieve the monotony for the entire day.

So much of the work of the farm that we take as a matter of course is strange and interesting to a person who is not used to it. A man who has been in business in town for over 20 years is moving his family to the farm this spring and expects to be a farmer. The old order, you see, is reversed. Instead of retiring from a farm to town he is retiring from town to a farm. I was really surprised, in talking with him, to find how many things there are for a beginner to learn.

Each in His Place

May 5, 1917

I know a farm woman who is wearing overalls this spring at her outdoor work. "They wear overalls in the munition factories," she says. "Isn't the raising of food to preserve life as important as the making of shells to take it? Why should I be hampered in my work and tormented by skirts flapping around my ankles when I am out in the field?"

Why, indeed! When every bit of one's time and strength can be put to such good use in work that is so very necessary to the world, it seems foolish to spend any of it uselessly. The simpler and more suitably we can dress the better. This year of our Lord 1917 is no time for giving much attention to frills, and when we remember the tight skirts of recent date, we surely cannot accuse overalls of being immodest. As the Man of the Place said to me, "Just hunt up a couple of your old tight skirts and sew them together, then you'll have a pair of overalls."

We all feel that we would like to do something to help our country in these perilous times, however much we may regret the necessity. We may do this; may do our share of the work and bear our share of the burden of the world without leaving our homes or exposing ourselves to new and fearful dangers. Not that country women would hesitate to take these risks if it were necessary, but it is natural to be glad that we may help as much or more in our own accustomed ways. Women in the towns and cities can be spared to work in the factories, to make munitions, to join the navy or to go as nurses with the Red Cross, but what would happen to the world if the farm women should desert their present posts?

Our work is not spectacular and in doing it faithfully we shall win no war medals or decorations, but it is absolutely indispensable. We may feed the field hands, care for the poultry and work in the garden with the full assurance that we are doing as much for our country as any other person. Here in the Hills we have helped plant the potatoes and corn, we help with the milking and feed the calves and hogs and we will be found on the line just behind the trenches, "fighting for Uncle Sam," as I heard one woman say, and every extra dozen eggs, pound of meat or bushel of vegetables we raise will help beat back the enemy, hunger.

Some women were talking over an entertainment that had been planned for the crowd. They seemed to be taking only a half-hearted interest in the subject and finally one of them exclaimed: "I can't feel right about doing this! It does not seem to me that this is a time to be feasting and frolicking. I do not think we ought to eat an unnecessary mouthful and sometimes I feel like choking on the food I do eat when I think of the people in the world who are hungry and starving."

I fully agreed with her. When there seems not to be enough food to go around, we ought to be as careful and economical with it as possible. If it is true, as we are told, that most of us have the bad habit of overeating, now is a good time to break that habit.

I am sure that we farm women will not be found second to those of any other occupation in willingness to bear our part in effort or in self denial, and if, as experts say, "armies travel on their stomachs," we are doing our best to enable the soldiers of the United States to go as far as those of any other nation.

Just Neighbors

May 20, 1917

There are two vacant places in our neighborhood. Two neighbors have gone ahead on "the great adventure."

We become so accustomed to our neighbors and friends that we take their presence as a matter of course forgetting that the time in which we may enjoy their companionship is limited, and when they are no longer in their places there is always a little shock of surprise mingled with our grief.

When we came to the Ozarks more than 20 years ago, Neighbor Deaver was one of the first to welcome us to our new home and now he has moved on ahead to that far country from which no traveler returns. Speaking of Mrs. Case's illness and death, a young woman said, "I could not do much to help them but I did what I could, for Mrs. Case was mighty good to me when

I was sick." That tells the story. The neighborhood will miss them both for they were good neighbors. What remains to be said? What greater praise could be given?

I wonder if you all know the story of the man who was moving from one place to another because he had such bad neighbors. Just before making the change, he met a man from the neighborhood to which he was going and told him in detail how mean his old neighbors were, so bad in fact that he would not live among them any longer. Then he asked the other man what the neighbors were like in the place to which he was moving. The other man replied, "You will find just the same kind of neighbors where you are going as those you leave behind you."

It is true that we find ourselves reflected in our friends and neighbors to a surprising extent and if we are in the habit of having bad neighbors we are not likely to find better by changing our location. We might as well make good neighbors in our own neighborhood, beginning, as they tell us charity should, at home. If we make good neighbors of ourselves, we likely shall not need to seek new friends in strange places. This would be a tiresome world if everyone were shaped to a pattern of our own cutting and I think we enjoy our neighbors more if we accept them just as they are.

Sometimes it is rather hard to do, for certainly it takes all kind of neighbors to make a community. We once had a neighbor who borrowed nearly everything on the place. Mr. Skelton was a good borrower but a very poor hand to return anything. As he lived just across a narrow road from us, it was very convenient—for him. He borrowed the hand tools and the farm machinery, the grindstone and the whetstone and the harness and saddles, also groceries and kitchen tools. One day he came over and borrowed my wash boiler in which to heat water for butchering. In a few minutes he returned and making a separate trip for each article, he borrowed both my dishpans, my two butcher knives, the knife sharpener, a couple of buckets, the boards on which to lay the hog, some matches to light his fire and as an after thought, while the water was heating he came for some salt. There was a fat hog in our pen and I half expected him to come back once more and borrow the hog, but luckily he had a hog of his own. A few days later when I asked to borrow a paper I was told that they never lent their papers. And yet this family were kind neighbors later when we really needed their help.

The Smiths moved in from another state. Their first caller was informed that they did not want the neighbors "to come about them at all," didn't want to be bothered with them. No one knew the reason but all respected their wishes and left them alone. As he was new to the country, Mr. Smith did not make a success of his farming but he was not bothered with friendly advice.

Doing Our Best

June 5, 1917

I am proud of Marian because she is not a quitter; because she can take disappointment without a whimper and go bravely ahead with her undertakings even tho things do not always work out as she would like. I am sure, as the years pass, Marian will answer perfectly that good, old description of a lady, "Still mistress of herself tho china fall."

Marian failed to send her application in time to become a member of the Ruralist Poultry Club, but she is a hustler nevertheless and should not be classed as being too slow to win in the race for membership. It was not really her fault, for the Missouri Ruralist does not come to her home, so she had not read about the club and as she is a little girl, only 10 years old, I did not tell her of the club until I had spent some time telling older girls about it. You see she did not have a fair start.

When she received word that the club membership was complete and her application was too late, the least that might have been expected was a crying spell, but not this little girl! She sat still a moment and then said quietly: "Well I'm going ahead just the same. Maybe some of the other girls will drop out and then there will be a place for me, anyway I'll be learning how." She is keeping her record carefully and trying to reform a farm flock of egg-eating hens while she is waiting for her purebred Buff Orpingtons to grow up and take their place.

Many a grown person might learn a lesson from the way she took her disappointment. I am certainly proud of Marian.

- - - - - -

"In the spring a young man's fancy lightly turns to thoughts of love," sings the poet, but in the spring the fancy of a hawk surely turns to spring chicken. Day after day he dines on the plumpest and fairest of the flock. I may spend half the day watching and never catch a glimpse of him then the moment my back is turned—swoop!—and he is gone with a chicken.

I should like to sentence that ex-governor who vetoed the state bounty on hawks to make his living raising chickens in the hills and not permit him to have a gun on the place, just by way of fitting the punishment to the crime. I know it is said that hawks are a benefit to the farmers because they catch field mice and other pests, but I am sure they would not look for a mouse if there were a flock of chickens near by. Even if they do catch mice, that is small comfort to the farmer's wife who loses half, or perhaps all her hatch of chicks, especially when she knows that the expense of feeding the poultry is doubled because they dare not range the fields freely.

If there were enough of a bounty on hawks to make it an object to hunt them, farm women would surprise the food controller by the amount of poultry products they would put on the market. I believe the present output would be doubled if the hawks could be exterminated, for many a chicken dinner and dozens of eggs fly away on the wings of the hawks. At the price of eggs and dinners this is rather expensive and it is certainly discouraging to lose chicks that way after one has overcome all the other difficulties of their raising. I suppose tho that we will be as game as Marian and do the best we can under the circumstances. Doing the best we can is all that could be expected of us in any case, but did you ever notice how hard it is to do our best if we allow ourselves to become discouraged? If we are disheartened we usually lag in our efforts more or less. It is so easy to slump a little when we can give the blame to circumstances. I think Marian has found the way to overcome this by being so busy with mind and muscle at the work in hand that there is no time for thoughts of failure or for bemoaning our hard luck.

Chasing Thistledown

June 20, 1917

Did you ever chase thistledown? Oh, of course, when you were a child, but I mean since you have been grown! Some of us should be chasing thistledown a good share of the time.

There is an old story, for the truth of which I cannot vouch, which is so good that I am going to take the risk of telling it and if any of you have heard it before it will do no harm to recall it to your minds. A woman once confessed to the priest that she had been gossiping. To her surprise, the priest instructed her to go gather a ripe head of the thistle and scatter the seed on the wind, then to return to him. This she did wondering why she had been told to do so strange a thing, but her penance was only begun, for when she returned to the priest, instead of forgiving her fault, he said: "The thistledown is scattered as were your idle words. My daughter, go and gather up the thistledown!"

It is so easy to be careless and one is so prone to be thoughtless in talking. I told only half of a story the other day heedlessly overlooking the fact that by telling only a part, I left the listeners with a wrong impression of some very kindly persons. Fortunately I saw in time what I had done and I pounced on that thistledown before the wind caught it or else I should have had a chase.

A newcomer in the neighborhood says, "I do like Mrs. Smith! She seems such a fine woman."

"Well y-e-s," we reply, "I've known her a long time," and we leave the new acquaintance wondering what it is we know against Mrs. Smith. We have said nothing against her but we have "damned with faint praise" and a thistle seed is sown on the wind.

The noun "Gossip" is not of the feminine gender. No absolutely not! A man once complained to me of some things that had been said about his wife. "Damn these gossiping women!" he exclaimed. "They do nothing but talk about their neighbors who are better than they. Mrs. Cook spends her time running around gossiping when she should be taking care of her children. Poor things, they never have enough to eat, by their looks. Her housework is never done and as for her character everybody knows about—" and he launched into a detailed account of an occurrence which certainly sounded very compromising as he told it. I repeated to myself his first remark with the word men in place of the word "women" just to see how it would sound.

And so we say harmful things carelessly; we say unkind things in a spirit of retaliation or in a measure of self-defense to prove that we are no worse than others and the breeze of idle chatter, from many tongues, picks them up, blows them here and there and scatters them to the four corners of the earth. What a crop of thistles they raise! If we were obliged to go gather up the seed before it had time to grow as the woman in the story was told to do, I am afraid we would be even busier than we are.

- - - - - -

The busy hands of farm women are growing browner and browner as the season advances. Two country women were in a gathering of town women the other day and the first one there exclaimed to the other as she came in, "Oh! I'm so glad you came! I was thinking of putting my gloves on to cover up my hands, they're so brown."

"Why I'm proud of the tan on my hands," answered the other. "I've enlisted, you know, and my hands show that I'm doing my part."

There is no time for gloves and primping for the enemy is storming the position. There are hawks over the poultry range and insect pests in the garden while the weeds make raids in the night. It is hand to hand fighting on the farms now and sometimes the enemy gains, but the farmers, both men and women, are people of courage. They planted the crops and cold and frosts made a great deal of replanting necessary. They replanted and the floods came so that much of the planting must be done once more, but there is no thought of anything but keeping up the fight.

Without Representation

July 5, 1917

In answer to the call sent out by the State College of Agriculture, the park in Mansfield was filled with a crowd of farm folks and town folks to listen to the address of the man from the college who was organizing farmers' clubs thru the county. As I looked around at the people, I thought what a representative gathering it was. Judging from the appearance of the crowd, the women were as much interested in the subject of food production as a means of national defense as the men were, for fully as many women as men were present and they were seemingly as eager to learn from the speaker anything that farmers could do to increase the food supply. A farmers' club was formed after the address but the women took no part in the organization nor were they included in any way. As arrangements were being made for a meeting of the club, some one near the speaker said, "The women must come, too," but it was only after a broad and audible hint from a woman that this remark was made and it was so plainly because of the hint, instead of from a desire for the women's presence and co-operation, that it made no impression.

At the first meeting of the club, the following week, there were only two women present. Quite likely it was the women's own fault and if they had taken part as a matter of course it would have been accepted as such, but it seems rather hard to do this unless we are shown the courtesy of being mentioned. We will get over this feeling in time no doubt and take the place we should, for a farmer may be either a man or a woman and farmers' clubs are intended for both.

Everyone knows that women raise the poultry and Missouri receipts from poultry products are more than from cattle, horses and mules combined. If farm women refused to help in the work of the farm how much difference do you suppose it would make in the output of dairy products?

What would happen to the "increase of production" if the women did not cook for the harvest hands, to say nothing of taking care of the hired help the remainder of the year?

A man in authority at Washington urges farm women to increase their power of production and all along down the line, agricultural colleges, farmers' club organizers, domestic science lecturers and farm papers join in the urge.

"Raise more garden truck; increase the egg production; caponize the cockerels and keep them until they will yield more meat to the fowl when killed; feed the calves and let them grow up instead of selling them for veal." (Who feeds the calves?) "Can; pickle; preserve and dry fruits and vegetables; let nothing go to waste from the garden or orchard."

As one farm paper says, "The women and children can do it!" "Eliminate all waste from the kitchen! It is conceded that it will take more time and work to do all this but it is a patriotic duty and will increase the farm profits." Why shouldn't farm women's work be recognized by state authorities and others in other ways than urging her to more and yet more work when her working day is already somewhere from 14 to 16 hours long?

There is a woman's commission of the Council of National Defense and under this commission committees are being organized in every state for the purpose of co-operating with the National Woman's Trade Union league of America. The league is fighting to protect the women and children who are working in factories and in the cities. It asks that the American people demand the 8-hour day, the living wage and one day of rest in seven.

But mark this! These things are for women and children working in the cities. They are not intended to extend to the women and children on farms. There is not yet, so far as I know, any committee to co-operate with the farm women in obtaining for them either an 8-hour day or a living profit and if they are denied an active part in the farmers' clubs they are the only class of workers who are absolutely without representation.

Did the farmers' club organized in your neighborhood recognize the women and if so in what way? We would all be interested to know. Write to me and tell me about it!

And a Woman Did It

The Wilson Stock Farm Is One of Missouri's Best

July 20, 1917

Down in the Ozarks, in Wright county, Missouri, is a 1000-acre farm where the purebred Shorthorn cattle and registered Poland China hogs roam over blue grass and clover pastures in the sunny days of summer time and in winter feast on bright alfalfa hay and succulent silage. These upper class animals come of aristocratic lineage and are cared for royally and this stock farm is managed by a woman and has been brought up from a rundown "hog and hominy" farm to its present state of efficiency by her knowledge, hard work and good business judgment.

A part of the present Wilson farm owned by Dr. and Mrs. Wilson, late of St. Louis, was bought by them 13 years ago. While on a visit to relatives in Wright county, Dr. Wilson became so enamored of the Ozarks as a place to make a home that he tried to buy a small farm near the one he now owns, but failed to obtain it and went back to St. Louis disappointed. Some time later a brother-in-law wrote him that a small place, adjoining the one he had wished to purchase, could be bought at a reasonable figure and that he would take charge and manage it for them.

So the farm was bought and stocked and the brother-in-law took charge but that was as far as he kept his agreement. He did not stay to manage. Becoming possessed of the idea that he could do better for himself farther west, he left the Wilson farm at a moment's notice.

The farm was well stocked with common stock and a good deal of money had been spent for them and for the farming tools as well as the farm itself. Dr. Wilson could not leave his practice in the city without too great a sacrifice, neither could he take it with him, so it became necessary that Mrs. Wilson should save the investment and come to the rescue of the home that was to be. Both of these things she has done and more. Not only has she saved what was then put into the place but she has more than trebled the original investment. Other tracts of land have been added to the first small piece until there is now, to be exact, 997 acres in the Wilson farm. This land was purchased for $10 and $12 an acre and is now easily worth from $30 to $50 an acre.

"All I know about farming," said Mrs. Wilson, "I have learned since we bought Fern Cliff. This is the real name of the farm. The neighbors began calling it Wilson Farm and it has gone by that name, but I always call it Fern Cliff to myself." The name was chosen because of a very beautiful spot on the farm where the face of a sheer cliff is nearly covered with lovely drooping ferns.

"I was born on the farm," continued Mrs. Wilson, "and from the age of 9 until I was 14 I lived with my grandparents on their place in the country, but I always hated it and thought the worst calamity that could befall me would be to marry a farmer and live on a farm. This thought was a real nightmare to me and I always said it was one thing I never would do, but the old saying has proved true that 'what you say you will not do, that you have to do.'"

Mrs. Wilson has learned the business of farming and stock breeding from books and farm papers, attending farmers' meetings, talking with other farmers and breeders and from practical experience. The Wilson farm was the first in this part of the Ozarks to have a field of alfalfa. Having read about alfalfa, it was decided to try it and 4 acres were sown. It made a good catch and so 20 acres more were seeded. This also was a success. Mrs. Wilson has been generous and the soil from this field has gone to many other farms to inoculate the soil for growing alfalfa. The spirit of the farming operations on the Wilson farm is shown in Mrs. Wilson's answer to a question. "No," she said, "I did not send any soil away to be analyzed. I read about alfalfa and I just tried it."

There are 400 acres in cultivation on the Wilson farm. The rest is pasture and woodland. Corn, wheat, oats and hay are raised on the place, in addition to the alfalfa.

"After taking charge," said Mrs. Wilson, "I soon learned to love the stock, especially the cattle which at that time were grades. I decided that it took no longer to raise and care for purebreds than it did grades and so we looked around for something better. I had no knowledge of stock except horses. Grandfather was from Kentucky and knew and kept good horses and he always said that I could point my finger at the best one every time, but I have learned about cattle since I began farming."

Mrs. Wilson became quite enthusiastic when asked why they chose the Shorthorn Durham cattle. After enumerating their many good qualities she summed it up thus: "The Shorthorns have all other breeds beaten when it comes to making money for their owners. Besides they are aristocrats and we think them the most beautiful of any." Trust a woman to think of that last reason.

The animals of the Wilson farm are certainly aristocrats. The first Shorthorn owned on the place was a son of Lavender Viscount many times champion and grand champion at the American Royal Stock show of Kansas City and the International of Chicago. Next came Champion Monarch from Purdy Brothers' herd, Harris, Missouri, and now the head of the herd is Violet Chief out of the herd of N. H. Gentry, of Sedalia, Missouri. Good females have been bought from time to time and there is now on the Wilson farm a herd of 100 head of purebred Shorthorns as fine as one would care to see.

Nothing seems to have been overlooked, that makes for success on this farm owned and operated by these city people who have gone "back to the land." Beside the registered Shorthorn cattle and Poland China hogs there is on the place a flock of purebred Bronze turkeys. From the flock of 34 raised four years ago, the number has increased to 100 and during these four years they have brought in, in cash, $781.92.

"I farmed at first because it was necessary," says Mrs. Wilson. "Now I farm because I like it. Dr. Wilson, from the first, has been more in love with the farm than I have been. He knows nothing about the stock or farming because he has been tied to his practice in the city, but now he has given it up and come home to the farm he can learn as I did." Dr. Wilson fully intends to do so, but already his professional services are being called for and he may not be allowed time.

This building of a farm business literally "from the ground up" has been no light task. Mrs. Wilson says that most of the time she is "too busy to think twice in the same place." She is very modest about what she has accomplished but the beautiful Wilson farm with its rich bottom fields and rolling pasture lands, with its silos and barns and stacks of alfalfa and above all the fine stock at home on the place speak for her.

A Bouquet of Wild Flowers

July 20, 1917

The Man of the Place brought me a bouquet of wild flowers this morning. It has been a habit of his for years. He never brings me cultivated flowers but always the wild blossoms of field and woodland and I think them much more beautiful.

In my bouquet this morning was a purple flag. Do you remember gathering them down on the flats and in the creek bottoms when you were a barefoot child? There was one marshy corner of the pasture down by the creek, where the grass grew lush and green; where the cows loved to feed and could always be found when it was time to drive them up at night. All thru the tall grass were scattered purple and white flag blossoms and I have stood in that peaceful grassland corner, with the red cow and the spotted cow and the roan taking their goodnight mouthfuls of the sweet grass, and watched the sun setting behind the hilltop and loved the purple flags and the rippling brook and wondered at the beauty of the world, while I wriggled my bare toes down into the soft grass.

The wild Sweet Williams in my bouquet brought a far different picture to my mind. A window had been broken in the schoolhouse at the country crossroads and the pieces of glass lay scattered where they had fallen. Several little girls going to school for their first term had picked handfuls of Sweet Williams and were gathered near the window. Someone discovered that the blossoms could be pulled from the stem and, by wetting their faces, could be stuck to the pieces of glass in whatever fashion they were arranged. They dried on the glass and would stay that way for hours and, looked at thru the glass, were very pretty. I was one of those little girls and tho I have forgotten what it was that I tried to learn out of a book that summer, I never have forgotten the beautiful wreaths and stars and other figures we made on the glass with the Sweet Williams. The delicate fragrance of their blossoms this morning made me feel like a little girl again.

The little white daisies with their hearts of gold grew thickly along the path where we walked to Sunday school. Father and sister and I used to walk the 2½ miles every Sunday morning. The horses had worked hard all the week and must rest this one day and Mother would rather stay at home with baby brother[2] so with Father and Sister Mary I walked to the church thru the beauties of the sunny spring Sundays. I have forgotten what I was taught on those days also. I was only a little girl, you know. But I can still plainly see the grass and the trees and the path winding ahead, flecked with sunshine and shadow and the beautiful golden-hearted daisies scattered all along the way.

Ah well! That was years ago and there have been so many changes since then that it would seem such simple things should be forgotten, but at the long last, I am beginning to learn that it is the sweet, simple things of life which are the real ones after all.

We heap up around us things that we do not need as the crow makes piles of glittering pebbles. We gabble words like parrots until we lose the sense of their meaning; we chase after this new idea and that; we take an old thought and dress it out in so many words that the thought itself is lost in its clothing like a slim woman in a barrel skirt and then we exclaim, "Lo, the wonderful new thought I have found!"

"There is nothing new under the sun," says the proverb. I think the meaning is that there are just so many truths or laws of life and no matter how far we may think we have advanced we cannot get beyond those laws. However complex a structure we build of living we must come back to those truths and so we find we have traveled in a circle.

The Russian revolution has only taken the Russian people back to the democratic form of government they had at the beginning of history in medieval times and so a republic is nothing new. I believe we would be happier to have a personal revolution in our individual lives and go back to simpler living and more direct thinking. It is the simple things of life that make living worth while, the sweet fundamental things such as love and duty, work and rest and living close to nature. There are no hothouse blossoms that can compare in beauty and fragrance with my bouquet of wild flowers.

2. Charles Frederick Ingalls, born November 1, 1875, died August 27, 1876.

Put Yourself in His Place

August 5, 1917

Once upon a time, a crowd of men were working in the woods where they had to do their own cooking. They took turns at being cook and they made a rule that when any one of them found fault with the food provided, that man must take the cook's place, until he in turn was released from the distasteful job by someone's finding fault with his cooking.

This worked very well, with frequent changes in the occupancy of the cook shanty, until the men had learned better than to criticize the food. No one wanted to take the cook's place so they became very careful about what they said and the poor unfortunate who was cooking for the hungry crew saw no chance of escape. He was careless as to how his work was done but no one found fault; he burned the biscuit, then he made the coffee too weak but still no one objected.

At last he cooked a mess of beans and made them as salt as brine. One of the men at supper that night took a huge mouthful of the beans and as he nearly strangled, he exclaimed, "These beans are sure salty!" Then as the eye of the cook, alight with hope, glanced in his direction, he added, "But my, how good they are!"

It is so much easier to find fault with what others do than to do the thing right one's self. Besides, how much pleasanter to let some one else do it. Of course a mere woman is not expected to understand politics in Missouri, but there is no objection to her understanding human nature and it is certainly amusing to watch the effects of the working of human nature on men's political opinions. I know of some men who were all for war during President Wilson's first term. "The United States soldiers ought to go down there and take Mexico! A couple of months would do it! The United States should fight if our shipping is interfered with. It would be easily settled." There was much more to the same effect, but now that the fight is on and there is a chance for them to show what they can do, their fighting spirit seems to have evaporated. It was easy to find fault, but rather than do the work themselves, almost anything is good enough. It is the quiet ones who hoped we might be able to keep out of war who are volunteering.

One after another our young men are enlisting. Eight in a body volunteered a few days ago. The war, the terrible, has been something far off, but now it is coming closer home and soon we shall have a more understanding sympathy with those who have been experiencing its horrors for so long. There is nothing quite like experience to give one understanding and nothing more sure than that if we could be in the other fellow's place for a while we would be less free with our criticisms.

In the days of long ago when armored knights went journeying on prancing steeds, two knights, coming from opposite directions, saw between them a shield standing upright on the ground. As the story goes, these fighting men disagreed about the color of the shield and each was so positive, the one that it was black, and the other that it was white, that from disputing about it they came to blows and charged each other right valiantly. The fury with which they rode their steeds carried each one past the shield to where the other had stood before, and as they turned to face each other again, each saw the side of the shield which the other had first seen and the man who had said the shield was white found the side he was now looking at to be black, while the one who had declared the shield was black found himself facing the white side, so each got the other's point of view and felt very foolish that they had fought over so simple a thing. It makes a difference when you're in the other fellow's place.

Let Us Be Just

September 5, 1917

Two little girls had disagreed, as was to be expected because they were so temperamentally different. They wanted to play in different ways and as they had to play together all operations were stopped while they argued the question. The elder of the two had a sharp tongue and great facility in using it. The other was slow to speak but quick to act and they both did their best according to their abilities.

Said the first little girl: "You've got a snub nose and your hair is just a common brown color. I heard Aunt Lottie say so! Ah! Don't you wish your hair was a be-a-utiful golden like mine and your nose a fine shape? Cousin Louisa said that about me. I heard her!"[3]

The second little girl could not deny these things. Her dark skin, brown hair and snub nose as compared with her sister's lighter coloring and regular features, were a tragedy in her little life. She could think of nothing cutting to reply for she was not given to seeing unkind things nor was her

3. This story appears in Laura Ingalls Wilder, *Little House in the Big Woods* (New York: Harper and Row, 1971), chapter 10.

tongue nimble enough to say them, so she stood digging her bare toes into the ground, hurt, helpless and tongue-tied.

The first little girl, seeing the effect of her words, talked on. "Besides you're two years younger than I am and I know more than you so you have to mind me and do as I say!"

This was too much! Sister was prettier, no answer could be made to that. She was older, it could not be denied, but that gave her no right to command. At last here was a chance to act!

"And you have to mind me," repeated the first little girl. "I will not!" said the second little girl and then, to show her utter contempt for such authority, this little brown girl slapped her elder, golden-haired sister.

I hate to write the end of the story. No, not the end! No story is ever ended! It goes on and on and the effects of this one followed this little girl all her life, showing in her hatred of injustice. I should say that I dislike to tell what came next, for the golden-haired sister ran crying and told what had happened, except her own part in the quarrel, and the little brown girl was severely punished. To be plain, she was soundly spanked and set in a corner. She did not cry but sat glowering at the parent who punished her and thinking in her rebellious little mind that when she was large enough she would return the spanking with interest.

It was not the pain of the punishment that hurt so much as the sense of injustice, the knowledge that she had not been treated fairly by one from whom she had the right to expect fair treatment, and that there had been a failure to understand where she had thought a mistake impossible. She had been beaten and bruised by sister's unkind words and had been unable to reply. She had defended herself in the only way possible for her and felt that she had a perfect right to do so, or if not, then both should have been punished.

Children have a fine sense of justice that sometimes is far truer than that of older persons, and in almost every case, if appealed to, will prove the best help in governing them. When children are ruled thru their sense of justice there are no angry thoughts left to rankle in their minds. Then a punishment is not an injury inflicted upon them by someone who is larger and stronger but the inevitable consequences of their own acts and a child's mind will understand this much sooner than one would think. What a help all their lives, in self control and self government this kind of a training would be!

We are prone to put so much emphasis on the desirability of mercy that we overlook the beauties of the principle of justice. The quality of mercy is a gracious, beautiful thing, but with more justice in the world there would be less need for mercy and exact justice is most merciful in the end. The difficulty is that we are so likely to make mistakes we cannot trust our judgment and so must be merciful to offset our own shortcomings, but I feel sure when we are able to comprehend the workings of the principle of justice, we shall find that, instead of being opposed to each other, infallible justice and mercy are one and the same thing.

To Buy or Not to Buy

September 20, 1917

I have been very much impressed by a sentence I read in an advertisement of farm machinery and here it is for you to think about. "The minute we need a thing, we begin paying for it whether we buy it or not."

That is true of farm machinery on the face of it. If a farm tool is actually needed it will, without question, have to be bought in time and the farmer begins paying for it at once in loss of time or waste or damage resulting from not having it. He might even, if buying was put off long enough, pay the whole price of the machine and still not have it.

A dentist once said to me, "I don't care whether people come to me when they should, or put off coming as long as they possibly can. I know they'll come in time and the longer they put it off the bigger my bill will be when they do come." We begin to pay the dentist when our teeth first need attention whether they have that attention or not.

"I can't afford to build a machine shed this year," said Farmer Jones and so his machinery stood out in the weather to rot and rust. The next year he had to spend so much for repairs and new machines that he was less able than before to build the shed. He is paying for that protection for his machinery but he may never have it.

We think we cannot afford to give the children the proper schooling, "besides, their help is needed on the farm," we say. We shall pay for that education which we do not give them. Oh! We shall pay for it! When we see our children inefficient and handicapped, perhaps thru life, for the lack of the knowledge they should have gained in their youth, we shall pay in our hurt pride and our regret that we did not give them a fair chance, if in no other way, tho quite likely we shall pay in money too. The children, more's the pity, must pay also.

Mr. Colton's work kept him outdoors in all kinds of weather and one autumn he did not buy the warm clothing he needed. He said he could not afford to do so and would make the old overcoat last thru. The old coat outlasted him for he took a chill from exposure and died of pneumonia. So he paid with his life for the coat he never had and his widow paid the bills which amounted to a great deal more than the cost of an overcoat.

Instances multiply as one looks for them. We certainly do begin paying for a thing when we actually need it whether we buy it or not, but this is no plea for careless buying as it is just as great a mistake to buy what we do not need as it is not to buy what we should. In the one case we pay before and in the other we usually keep paying after the real purchase. One thing always leads to another or even to two or three and it requires good business judgment to buy the right thing at the right time.

Are We Too Busy?

October 5, 1917

The sunlight and shadows in the woods were beautiful that morning, the sunlight a little pale and the air with that quality of hushed expectancy that the coming of autumn brings. Birds were calling to one another and telling of the wonderful Southland and the journey they must take before long. The whole, wide outdoors called me and tired muscles and nerves rasped from the summer's rush pleaded for rest, but there was pickle to make, drying apples to attend to, vegetables and fruits that must be gathered and stored, the Saturday baking and the thousand things of the everyday routine to be done.

"Oh, for a little time to enjoy the beauties around me," I thought. "Just a little while to be free of the tyranny of things that must be done!" A feeling of bitterness crept into my soul. "You'll have plenty of leisure someday when you are past enjoying it," I thought. "You know, in time, you always get what you have longed for and when you are old and feeble and past active use then you'll have all the leisure you ever have wanted. But my word! You'll not enjoy it!"

I was horrified at these thoughts, which almost seemed spoken to me. We do seem at times to have more than one personality, for as I gave a dismayed gasp at the prospect, I seemed to hear a reply in a calm, quiet voice.

"You need not lose your power of enjoyment nor your sense of the beautiful if you desire to keep them," it said. "Keep the doors of your mind and heart open to them and your appreciation of such things will grow and you will be able to enjoy your well earned leisure when it comes even tho you should be older and not so strong. It is all in your own hands and may be as you wish."

We are all beginning to show the strain of the busy summer. Mrs. Menton has put up a full two years' supply of canned and dried fruits and vegetables. She says that, even tho no part of it should be needed to save anyone from starving, she will feel well repaid in the smallness of their grocery bills the coming year. She also confessed she was glad the lull in work was in sight for there wasn't "a whole pair of socks on the place."

Several women were comparing notes the other day. Said one, "My man says he doesn't mind a decent patch but he does hate to go around with a hole in his khakis." Everyone smiled understandingly and another took up the tale.

"Joe said this morning that he wished I'd make a working and call the neighbors in to fix up his clothes," she said, "but I told him you were all too busy to come."

There has been no time this summer to do the regular work properly. Mrs. Clearly says that if the rush of work does not stop soon she will have to stop anyway. She is a recent comer to the Ozarks and thru the dry seasons she has hoped for a good crop year. Now she does not know whether she will pray for rain next year or not. A good crop year does bring work with it and tho the worst may be over, there are still busy days ahead. There are the late fruits and garden truck to be put up, potato harvest and corn harvest, the second crop of timothy and clover and more cutting of alfalfa. There is the sorghum to make and the silos to fill and everything to be made snug for winter. Some of us will help in the actual work and others will be cooking for extra help. Whatever may be expected of us later, women have certainly done their utmost during this summer so nearly gone.

The Man of the Place and I have realized with something of the shock of a surprise that we do not need to buy anything during the coming year. There are some things we need and much that we would like to get but if it were necessary we could go very comfortably thru the year without a thing more than we now have on the place. There is wheat for our bread and potatoes, both Irish and sweet, there are beans and corn and peas. Our meat, milk, cream, butter and eggs are provided. A year's supply of fruit and sweetening are at hand and a plentiful supply of fuel in the wood lot. All this, to say nothing of the surplus.

During the summer when I have read of the high wages paid in factories and shops there has been a little feeling of envy in the back of my mind, but I suppose if those working people had a year's supply of fuel and provisions and no rent to pay they would think it wonderful good fortune. After all, as the Irishman said, "Everything is evened up in this world. The rich buy their ice in the summer but the poor get theirs in the winter."

The Man of the Place and I had known before that farmers are independent but we never had realized it and there is a difference between knowing and realizing. Have you realized it personally or do you just know in a general way? Thanksgiving will soon be here and it is time to be getting our blessings in order. But why wait for Thanksgiving? Why not just be thankful now?

Get the Habit of Being Ready

October 20, 1917

Did the first frost catch you unready? It would be quite unusual if it didn't because I never knew anyone to be ready for cold weather, in the fall, or for the first warm spell in the spring. It is like choosing the right time to be ill or an out-of-the-way place for a boil—it simply isn't done!

I know a man who had a little patch of corn. He was not quite ready to cut it and besides he said, "it is just a little green." He let it wait until the frost struck it and now he says it is too dry and not worth cutting. The frost saved him a lot of hard work.

This man's disposition reminds me of that of a renter we once had who was unable to plow the corn in all summer. Before it rained the ground was so hard he could not keep the plow in, and besides if it did not rain there would be no corn anyway and he believed it was going to be a dry season. When it did rain it was too wet to plow and never was he ready and able to catch that cornfield when the ground was right for plowing.

And that reminds me of the other renter who was always ready to take advantage of his opportunities. His horses would break into the cornfield at night, or were turned in (we never knew which), and in the fall, when The Man Of the Place wanted a share of what corn was left, he was told that the horses had eaten all his share.

These anecdotes are not intended as any reflection on renters. I could tell some in which the joke is on the other side if I had the space.

The tragedy of being unready is easy to find for, more often than not, success or failure turn upon just that one thing. There was a time, perhaps long ago, when you were not ready for examinations and failed to pass, then there was the time you were not ready to make that good investment because you had been spending carelessly. We can all remember many times when we were not ready. While being ready for and equal to whatever comes may be in some sense a natural qualification, it is a characteristic that may be cultivated, especially if we learn easily by experience.

It was interesting to see the way different persons showed their character after the first frost. One man considered that the frost had done his work for him and so relieved him of further effort. Others went along at their usual gait and saved their fodder in a damaged condition. They had done the best they could, let providence take the responsibility. Still others worked thru the moonlight nights and saved their feed in good condition in spite of the frost. They figured that it "was up to them" and no little thing like the first frost should spoil their calculations.

It does not so much matter what happens. It is what one does when it happens that really counts.

"Thoughts Are Things"

November 5, 1917

As someone has said, "Thoughts are things," and the atmosphere of every home depends on the kind of thoughts each member of that home is thinking.

I spent an afternoon a short time ago with a friend in her new home. The house was beautiful and well furnished with new furniture but it seemed bare and empty to me. I wondered why this was until I remembered my experience with my new house. I could not make the living room seem homelike. I would move the chairs here and there and change the pictures on the wall, but something was lacking. Nothing seemed to change the feeling of coldness and vacancy that displeased me whenever I entered the room.

Then, as I stood in the middle of the room one day wondering what I could possibly do to improve it, it came to me that all that was needed was someone to live in it and furnish it with the everyday, pleasant thoughts of friendship and cheerfulness and hospitality.

We all know there is a spirit in every home, a sort of composite spirit composed of the thoughts and feelings of the members of the family as a composite photograph is formed of the features of different individuals. This spirit meets us at the door as we enter the home. Sometimes it is a friendly, hospitable spirit and sometimes it is cold and forbidding.

If the members of a home are ill-tempered and quarrelsome, how quickly you feel it when you enter the house. You may not know just what is wrong but you wish to make your visit short. If they are kindly, generous, good-tempered people you will have a feeling of warmth and welcome that will make you wish to stay. Sometimes you feel that you must be very prim and dignified and at another place you feel a rollicking good humor and a readiness to laugh and be merry. Poverty or riches, old style housekeeping or modern conveniences do not affect your feelings. It is the characters and personalities of the persons who live there.

Each individual has a share in making this atmosphere of the home what it is, but the mother can mold it more to her wish. I read a piece of poetry several years ago supposed to be a man speaking of his wife and this was the refrain of the little story:

> "I love my wife because she laughs,
> Because she laughs and doesn't care."

I'm sure that would have been a delightful home to visit, for a good laugh overcomes more difficulties and dissipates more dark clouds than any other one thing. And this woman was the embodied spirit of cheerfulness and good temper.

Let's be cheerful! We have no more right to steal the brightness out of the day for our own family than we have to steal the purse of a stranger. Let us be as careful that our homes are furnished with pleasant and happy thoughts as we are that the rugs are the right color and texture and the furniture comfortable and beautiful!

Everyone Can Do Something

November 20, 1917

How many women have said, "If I were a man I would go and fight for my country?" And how many men who are exempt from the draft for any reason have said, "If I were young"—or "If I could pass the physical examinations, I would be glad to go and help?"

If you ever have said these things, you now have a chance to show your good faith and prove that you meant what you said.

If you are a woman, you can fight for your country at home in your own kitchen. If you are a man who cannot pass the physical tests, you can help, even without bodily strength, at home in your own dining room.

"Your country needs you," say the posters at the recruiting stations. Our country needs us all and the issue of the war depends a good deal upon those who stay at home.

We must fight our appetites, overcome our inclinations and conquer our selfishness. The self-government of our republic, of which we are so proud, is nothing after all but the governing of self and the whole cannot be greater than the sum of the parts. The work for those who cannot go and fight is to so govern themselves that they may not cast discredit upon a free country.

Did you know that the United States will not be able to send France the amount of sugar that country has asked for?

A certain amount of sugar is needed, especially by growing children, to keep the body in proper condition. A child's craving for sweets is a call of nature. It is necessary to the proper development of their bodies. The sugar beets and refineries of France and Belgium have been destroyed by the enemy and the people are starving for sugar while we have eaten so much that we cannot send them what they need. We could all do with a little less and a little saved from each home would amount to a great deal.

We would not revel in plenty while the family of a neighbor was starving. Let's divide with our neighbors overseas!

Our harvests have been so bountiful this year that we have more than we can possibly use for ourselves. We have done our duty by working almost day and night to save it, but if we do not understand and rightly use what we have saved, we will not have helped so much as we should after all.

There are some things that can be used at home that are too perishable to ship to Europe. Surely we can use those things and save from our abundance, the wheat and meat and sugar to feed our soldiers and the dear ones of those who are standing shoulder to shoulder with them in the fight—the hungry women and children of Belgium and France.

If We Only Understood

December 5, 1917

Mrs. Brown was queer. The neighbors all thought so and, what was worse, they all said so.

Mrs. Fuller happened in several times, quite early in the morning and, altho the work was not done up, Mrs. Brown was sitting leisurely in her room or else she would be writing at her desk. Then Mrs. Powers went thru the house one afternoon and the dishes were stacked back unwashed, the beds still airing, and everything "at sixes and sevens," except the room where Mrs. Brown seemed to be idling away her time. Mrs. Powers said Mrs. Brown was "just plain lazy" and she didn't care who heard her say it.

Ida Brown added interesting information when she told her schoolmates, after school, that she must hurry home and do up the work. It was a shame the neighbors said, that Mrs. Brown should idle away her time all day and leave the work for Ida to do after school.

It was learned later that Mrs. Brown had been writing for the papers to earn money to buy Ida's new winter outfit. Ida had been glad to help by doing the work after school so that her mother might have the day for study and writing, but they had not thought it necessary to explain to the neighbors.

I read a little verse a few years ago entitled, "If We Only Understood," and the refrain was:

> "We would love each other better,
> If we only understood."

I have forgotten the author and lost the verse, but the refrain has remained in my memory and comes to my mind every now and then when I hear unkind remarks made about people.

The things that people do would look so differently to us if we only understood the reasons for their actions, nor would we blame them so much for their faults if we knew all the circumstances of their lives. Even their sins might not look so hideous if we could feel what pressure and perhaps suffering had caused them. The safest course is to be as understanding as possible and where our understanding fails call charity to its aid. Learn to distinguish between persons and the things they do, and while we may not always approve of their actions, have a sympathy and feeling of kindness for the persons themselves.

It may even be that what we consider faults and weaknesses in others are only prejudices on our own part. Some of us would like to see everybody fitted to our own pattern and what a tiresome world this would be if that were done. We should be willing to allow others the freedom we demand for ourselves. Everyone has the right to self expression.

If we keep this genial attitude toward the world and the people in it, we will keep our own minds and feelings healthy and clean. Even the vigilance necessary to guard our thoughts in this way will bring us rewards in better disciplined minds and happier dispositions.

Make a New Beginning

January 5, 1918

We should bring ourselves to an accounting at the beginning of the New Year and ask these questions: What have I accomplished? Where have I fallen short of what I desired and planned to do and be?

I never have been in favor of making good resolutions on New Year's Day just because it was the first day of the year. Any day may begin a new year for us in that way, but it does help some to have a set time to go over the year's efforts and see whether we are advancing or falling back.

If we find that we are quicker of temper and sharper of tongue than we were a year ago, we are on the wrong road. If we have less sympathy and understanding for others and are more selfish than we used to be, it is time to take a new path.

I helped a farmer figure out the value of his crops raised during the last season, recently, and he was a very astonished person. Then when we added to that figure the amount he had received for livestock during the same period, he said: "It doesn't seem as if a man who had taken in that much off his farm would need a loan."

This farmer friend had not kept any accounts and so was surprised at the money he had taken in and that it should all be spent. Besides the help in a business way, there are a great many interesting things that can be gotten out of farm accounts, if they are rightly kept.

The Man of the Place and I usually find out something new and unexpected when we figure up the business at the end of the year. We discovered this year that the two of us, without any outside help, had produced enough in the last year to feed 30 persons for a year—all the bread, butter, meat, eggs, sweetening and vegetables necessary—and this does not include the beef cattle sold off the place.

I do not know whether Mr. Hoover would think we have done as much as we should, but I do think it is not so bad. I had been rather discouraged with myself because I have not had so much time to spend with Red Cross work as some of my friends in town, but after I found out just what we have done, I felt better about it.

The knitting and making of garments for the Red Cross is very necessary and important but the work of making the hens lay and filling the cream can is just as commendable. Without the food which the farm women are helping to produce, the other work would be of no value.

If you have not already done so, just figure up for yourselves and you will be surprised at how much you have accomplished.

Santa Claus at the Front

January 20, 1918

A Santa Claus went from San Francisco to the battle front in France carrying with him more than $600 worth of presents for the French soldiers. This Santa Claus was Alphonse Gabriel Nicole. When the war began he was a waiter in one of San Francisco's restaurants. He went at once to Europe and has fought in the French army ever since. He has been wounded twice and wears a cross given him by the French government for bravery in battle.

Alphonse was in the battle of the Marne, the battle of the Somme and at Verdun. Once he was buried beneath the ground for 40 minutes and at another time he was hurled into the air and fell to the ground unconscious where he remained for some time apparently dead.

After three years of fighting he was given a 30 days furlough and permission to spend the time with his friends in San Francisco. During his stay in San Francisco, Alphonse was persuaded to tell in public of the life of the soldiers and of his experiences in the war. He made several speeches to large audiences and, because of the sympathy he aroused for the French soldiers and his habit of wishing they might enjoy the good things that were making his visit so pleasant, his friends decided they would supply him with some gifts to take back with him for the soldiers over there.

The idea was given a little publicity in the papers with the result that besides many donated gifts, $600 was raised for the purchase of other gifts.

Alphonse went back to the battle front loaded with presents for his poorly paid, ill-fed comrades; happy because he can, in this way, share with them his visit home.

Alphonse says it is a different world over there, a world of kindness and friendship where people do things as a matter of course for each other, which would be thought very remarkable in any but a war world. He says, "My friend saves my life today and I save his life tomorrow and nothing is thought of it and always we share with each other." Friendship is not just a name over there. It means braving danger for, suffering for, and sharing with one's friends. Alphonse could not have been happy with the good things showered upon him during his visit unless he had known he could share them with his soldier friends.

And so amid the awfulness of war, we find the spirit of loving and giving which three terrible years of fighting at the front has not killed but greatly strengthened. It certainly gives us cause to believe in the ultimate triumph of that spirit, if only we who stay at home can stand the test as well.

How will we be affected by the stress and strain, the anxiety and perhaps the grief which we must go thru together? Will struggle brighten and strengthen our good qualities as it has those of Alphonse and his soldier friends of France? Will our feeling of comradeship grow until we cannot be happy unless others share the good things which we enjoy and until we will do the helpful thing for friend and neighbor as a matter of course?

If when anyone is in difficulty we would all help instead of taking advantage of the situation; if when trouble comes to those we know, we would do our utmost to make it lighter instead of gossiping unkindly about it; and if we would not be satisfied until we had passed a share of our happiness on to other people, what a world we could make!

When our soldiers come home from that "war world" of which Alphonse has told, what a delightful surprise it would be for them if they should find themselves at home in a world of that kind—where the loving and sharing and good comradeship reached all the year around.

Make Your Dreams Come True

February 5, 1918

Now is the time to make garden! Anyone can be a successful gardener at this time of year and I know of no pleasanter occupation these cold, snowy days, than to sit warm and snug by the fire making garden with a pencil, in a seed catalog. What perfect vegetables we do raise in that way and so many of them! Our radishes are crisp and sweet, our lettuce tender and our tomatoes smooth and beautifully colored. Best of all, there is not a bug or worm in the whole garden and the work is so easily done.

In imagination we see the plants in our spring garden, all in straight, thrifty rows with the fruits of each plant and vine numerous and beautiful as the pictures before us. How near the real garden of next summer approaches the ideal garden of our winter fancies depends upon how practically we dream and how we work.

It is so much easier to plan than it is to accomplish. When I started my small flock of Leghorns a few years ago, a friend inquired as to the profits of the flock and, taking my accounts as a basis, he figured I would be a millionaire within five years. The five years are past, but alas, I am still obliged to be economical. There was nothing wrong with my friend's figuring, except that he left out the word "if" and that made all the difference between profits figured out on paper and those worked out by actual experience.

My Leghorns would have made me a millionaire—if the hens had performed according to schedule; if the hawks had loved field mice better than spring chickens; if I had been so constituted that I never became weary; if prices—but why enumerate? Because allowance for that word "if" was not made in the figuring, the whole result was wrong.

It is necessary that we dream now and then. No one ever achieved anything, from the smallest object to the greatest, unless the dream was dreamed first, yet those who stop at dreaming never accomplish anything. We must first see the vision in order to realize it; we must have the ideal or we cannot approach it; but when once the dream is dreamed it is time to wake up and "get busy." We must "do great deeds; not dream them all day long."

The dream is only the beginning. We'd starve to death if we went no further with that garden than making it by the fire in the seed catalog. It takes judgment to plant the seeds at the right time, in the right place, and hard digging to make them grow, whether in the vegetable garden or in the garden of our lives. The old proverb says, "God helps the man who helps himself," and I know that success in our undertakings can be made into a habit.

We can work our dreams out into realities if we try, but we must be willing to make the effort. Things that seem easy of accomplishment in dreams require a lot of good common sense to put on a working basis and a great deal of energy to put thru to a successful end. When we make our dream gardens we must take into account the hot sun and the blisters on our hand; we must make allowance for and guard against the "ifs" so that when the time to work has come they will not be of so much importance.

We may dream those dreams of a farm of our own; of a comfortable home; of that education we are going to have and those still more excellent dreams of the brotherhood of man and liberty and justice for all; then let us work to make this "the land where dreams come true."

Victory May Depend on You

February 20, 1918

"It is a war in each man's heart. Each man is fighting as the spirit moves him," said Hira Singh, speaking of the war, in the absorbing story of Talbot Mundy.[1]

Every day is showing more plainly that Hira Singh was right and that his statement is true in more ways than the author meant. It is a fact that not only is it a "war in each man's heart," but that the issues of this war are being fought over in the hearts of all the people—men, women and children.

The keynote of the statement of the nation's war aims, made by President Wilson recently, was unselfishness, an unselfish championing of the rights of nations too small to defend themselves and of people who have been oppressed so long they are helpless.

As a nation we stand for unselfishness, courage and self-sacrifices in defence of the right. Our soldiers are fighting on the battlefields that these principles shall be recognized as governing the nations of the world. And our hearts are the battlefields where these same qualities strive to become rulers of our actions.

It is indeed a "war in each man's heart," and as the battles go in these hearts of ours so will be the victory or defeat of the armies of the field, for a nation can be no greater than the sum of the greatness of its people. There never before has been a war where the action of each individual had such a direct bearing on the whole world.

One of the liveliest skirmishes of which I know takes place when our spirit of patriotism and duty comes in conflict with our instinct of hospitality, for here a seeming generosity to those near at hand blinds us to the fact that in these days when we feed those who are not hungry we are stealing from those who are starving, even tho the food is our own.

We are all in the habit of feeding our friends when we entertain them and we feel we have failed as hosts if we do not offer our guests the usual feast

1. Talbot Mundy was an author of adventure stories.

of good things. Now is our opportunity to substitute for this the "feast of reason and the flow of soul" which is the only thing that makes the meeting of friends worth while. Now is our chance to see that the food and the companionship are placed in their proper relation to each other, with the food, of course, secondary.

The refreshments at an evening gathering during the holidays were brown bread sandwiches and coffee. The entertainment is an annual affair and altho elaborate refreshments always were served in previous years, the evening was a bigger success this year than ever before.

Keep Journeying On

March 5, 1918

> "Youth longs and manhood strives, but age remembers,
> Sits by the raked-up ashes of the past
> And spreads its thin hands above the glowing embers.
> That warm its shivering life-blood till the last."[2]

Those lines troubled me a great deal when I first read them. I was very young then and I thought that everything I read in print was the truth. I didn't like it a little bit that the chief end of my life and the sole amusement of my old age should be remembering. Already there were some things in my memory that were not particularly pleasant to think about. I have since learned that few persons have such happy and successful lives that they would wish to spend years in just remembering.

One thing is certain, this melancholy old age will not come upon those who refuse to spend their time indulging in such dreams of the past. Men and women may keep their life blood warm by healthy exercise as long as they keep journeying on instead of sitting by the way trying to warm themselves over the ashes of remembrance.

Neither is it a good plan for people to keep telling themselves they are growing old. There is such a thing as a law of mental suggestion that makes the continual affirmation of a thing work toward its becoming an accomplished fact. Why keep suggesting old age until we take on its characteristics as a matter of course? There are things much more interesting to do than keeping tally of the years and watching for infirmities.

2. From the poem "The Iron Gate" by Oliver Wendell Holmes.

I know a woman who when she saw her first gray hair began to bewail the fact that she was growing old, and to change her ways to suit her ideas of old age. She couldn't "wear bright colors any more" she was "too old." She must be more quiet now, "it was not becoming in an old person to be so merry." She had not "been feeling well lately" but she supposed she was "as well as could be expected of a person growing old," and so on and on. I never lost the feeling that the years were passing swiftly and that old age was lying in wait for the youngest of us when in her company.

Of course, no one can really welcome the first gray hair or look upon the first wrinkles as beautiful, but even those things need not affect our happiness. There is no reason why we should not be merry as we grow older. If we learn to look on the bright side while we are young, those little wrinkles at the corners of the eyes will be "laughing wrinkles" instead of "crows feet."

There is nothing in the passing of the years by itself to cause one to become melancholy. If they have been good years, then the more of them the better. If they have been bad years, be glad they are passed and expect the coming ones to be more to your liking.

Old age is not counted by years, anyway. No one thinks of President Wilson as an old man. He is far too busy a person to be thought old, tho some men of his years consider their life work done. Then there is the white-haired, "Grandmother of the Revolution" in Russia still in the forefront of events in that country, helping to hold steady a semblance of government and a force to be considered in spite of, or perhaps because of, the many years she has lived. These two are finding plenty to do to keep warmth in their hearts and need no memories for that purpose.

Perhaps after all the poet whose verse I have quoted meant it as a warning that if we did not wish to come to that unlovely old age we must keep on striving for ourselves and for others. There was no age limit set by that other great poet when he wrote:

> "Build thee more stately mansions, oh, my soul
> As the swift seasons roll!"[3]

It is certainly a pleasanter, more worthwhile occupation to keep on building than to be raking up the ashes of dead fires.

3. From another poem by Oliver Wendell Holmes, "The Chambered Nautilus."

Make Every Minute Count

March 20, 1918

Spring has come! The wild birds have been singing the glad tidings for several days, but they are such optimistic little souls that I always take their songs of spring with a grain of pessimism. The squirrels and chipmunks have been chattering to me, telling the same news, but they are such cheerful busy-bodies that I never believe quite all they say.

But now I know that spring is here for as I passed the little creek, on my way to the mail box this morning, I saw scattered papers caught on the bushes, empty cracker and sandwich cartons strewn around on the green grass and discolored pasteboard boxes soaking in the clear water of the spring. I knew then that spring was here, for the sign of the picnickers is more sure than that of singing birds and tender green grass, and there is nothing more unlovely than one of nature's beauty spots defiled in this way. It is such an unprovoked offense to nature, something like insulting one's host after enjoying his hospitality. It takes just a moment to put back into the basket the empty boxes and papers and one can depart gracefully leaving the place all clean and beautiful for the next time or the next party.

Did you ever arrive all clean and fresh, on a beautiful summer morning, at a pretty picnic place and find that someone had been before you and that the place was all littered up with dirty papers and buzzing flies? If you have and have ever left a place in the same condition, it served you right. Let's keep the open spaces clean, not fill them up with rubbish!

It is so easy to get things cluttered up, one's days, for instance, as well as picnic places—to fill them with empty, useless things and so make them unlovely and tiresome. Even tho the things with which we fill our days were once important, if they are serving no good purpose now, they have become trash like the empty boxes and papers of the picnickers. It will pay to clean this trash away and keep our days as uncluttered as possible.

There are just now so many things that must be done that we are tempted to spend ourselves recklessly, especially as it is rather difficult to decide what to eliminate, and we cannot possibly accomplish everything. We must continually be weighing and judging and discarding things that are presented to us, if we would save ourselves, and spend our time and strength only on those that are important. We may be called upon to spend our health and strength to the last bit, but we should see to it that we do not waste them.

"Oh, I am so tired that I just want to sit down and cry," a friend confided to me, "and here is the club meeting on hand and the lodge practice and the Red Cross work day and the aid society meeting and the church bazaar to get ready for, to say nothing of the pie supper at the school house and the spring sewing and garden and—Oh! I don't see how I'm ever going to get thru it all!"

Of course she was a little hysterical. It didn't all have to be done at once, but it showed how over-tired she was and it was plain that something must give way—if nothing else, herself. My friend needed a little open space in her life.

We must none of us shirk. We must do our part in every way, but let's be sure we clear away the rubbish, that we do nothing for empty form's sake nor because someone else does, unless it is the thing that should be done.

Visit "Show You" Farm

Prosperity and Happiness Is Found on a 25-Acre Plot

March 20, 1918

There is at least one Missourian who is not asking to be "shown." A. C. Barton of Show You Farm says Missouri people have said "show me," long enough and they should now say "I will show you," which he is proceeding to do.

Mr. Barton used to be a Methodist preacher. He says that no one ever accused him of being the best preacher at the St. Louis conference, but they did all acknowledge that he was the best farmer among them. He thought perhaps he had made a mistake like the man who saw, in a vision, the letters G. P. C. and thought he had a call to preach, the letters standing for "Go Preach Christ." Later he decided that the letters meant "Go Plow Corn," so Mr. Barton made up his mind to follow the profession in which he excelled. He came to Mountain Grove from Dallas county, Nebraska, 8 years ago.

While waiting for his train in Kansas City, Mr. Barton noticed a man, also waiting, surrounded by bundles and luggage. For some reason Mr. Barton thought he was from the Ozarks and approaching him asked:

"Are you from Missouri?"

"Yes sir," the man replied.

"From the Ozarks?" Mr. Barton inquired.

"Yes sir," answered the man.

"Are there any farms for sale down there where you came from?" Mr. Barton asked.

"Yes sir. They're all for sale," replied the man from the Ozarks.

While that might have been true at the time, it would not be true now, for Show You Farm is not for sale.

When Mr. Barton bought his 80-acre farm on the "post oak flats" near Mountain Grove, the people he met gave him the encouragement usually given the new comers in the Ozarks. They told him the land was good for nothing, that he could not raise anything on it.

One man remarked in his hearing, "These new comers are workers," and another replied: "They'll have to work if they make a living on that place. Nobody's ever done it yet."

So "everybody works" and "father." The proprietors of Show You Farm are A. C. Barton, Nora L. Barton and family.

They soon found that there was more work on an 80-acre farm than they could handle, for while there were eight in the family, the six children were small, so it was decided to adjust the work to the family and 40 acres of the land, on which were the improvements, were sold for $2,500. Later 15 acres more were sold for $600. As the place had cost only $40 an acre that left only $100 as the cost of the 25-acre farm that was kept.

These 25 acres of unimproved, poor land have been made into a truly remarkable little farm. During last season it produced the following crops: Ten acres of corn, 400 bushels, 2 acres of oats, 80 bushels, 1 acre of millet hay, 2 tons, 1 acre of sorghum, 115 gallons of molasses; cowpeas, 100 bushels. Besides these crops there was a 5-acre truck patch which furnished a good income thru the summer, but of which no account was kept. There has been sold off the place this last season livestock amounting to $130, poultry $15, butter $250, and grain $35. The rest of the grain was still on the place when this was written. Not bad for a 25-acre farm, is it?

As there is a young orchard of 3 acres, a pasture of 3 acres and necessarily some ground used for building sites, you may wonder where the cowpeas were raised. Mr. Barton plants cowpeas with all other crops. He says it is the surest, quickest and cheapest way to build up the soil. When garden crops are harvested cowpeas are planted in their place, they follow the oats and rye and are planted with the corn.

There never has been a pound of commercial fertilizer used on Show You Farm. When clearing his land, Mr. Barton traded wood for stable manure in the town, so that he paid, with his labor, for 300 tons of stable fertilizer. Except for this, the soil has been built up by rotation of crops and raising of cowpeas, until from a complete failure of the corn crop the first year, because of poverty of the soil, last year's bountiful crops were harvested.

By the good farming methods of the Barton family they made their land bring them an average of $30 an acre even in the last dry seasons.

Mr. Barton believes in cultivation, both with plows and by hand. He is old fashioned enough to hoe his corn. A neighbor passing and seeing him hoeing said, "If I can't raise corn without hoeing it I won't raise it," and he didn't for it was a dry season. As Mr. Barton says, "The reason there are so many POOR farmers is because there are so many poor FARMERS." For the last four years, Show You Farm has taken the blue ribbon for general farm exhibit at the Tri-county Stock Show at Mountain Grove and never less than eight blue ribbons in all.

The Barton children have no idea of leaving the farm. They are too much interested in their business for they are full partners with their parents. Mr. Barton says it is easy to interest children in the farm. All that is necessary is to talk to them about the work as it is going on and let them help to plan.

When he is planting the crops he plans with them about the results. "Let's figure it," he will say. If we plant a hill of cantaloupes every 4 feet, we ought to raise two on every hill and if we sell them for 5 cents each that will bring us $128 an acre. But we should do better than that, we ought to make them bring us $300 an acre. And by explaining to them how to do this they are interested and eager to see how much they can make. The children work better when they are interested, Mr. Barton says, and they are willing to stay on the farm.

It is not all work and money making at the Barton home, however. In strawberry time the Sunday school is invited out and treated to strawberries with cream and sugar. Last season it took 8 gallons of strawberries to supply the feast. When melons are ripe there is another gathering and sometimes as many as 100 persons enjoy the delicious treat.

In the long winter evenings work and pleasure are mixed and while one of the family reads aloud some interesting book, the others shell the cowpeas that have been gathered in the fall.

Mr. Barton has not been allowed to drop all his outside activities. He has been elected secretary of the Farmers Mutual Fire Insurance Company and is helping them to organize for their mutual benefit. Also his services are often in demand to supply a country pulpit here and there, for once a Methodist preacher a man is always more or less a Methodist preacher, and as Mr. Barton goes on his daily way, both by acts and words, he is preaching kindness, helpfulness and the brotherhood of man.

He also preaches an agricultural theology. He says that robbing the soil is a sin, the greatest agricultural sin, and that like every other sin it brings its own punishment.

That Mr. Barton has not committed that sin, one is assured when looking over the farm and what he has accomplished is certainly encouraging for the man with a bit of poor land. Mr. Barton's advice to such a man is "not to go looking for a better place but MAKE one."

The Barton farmstead is built on rather an original plan. The house is 38 by 24 feet, with a kitchen, at the back, 12×14 feet. Joining the back porch of this kitchen is a concrete store room 12×12 feet with the well in a corner, and joining this store room is a long shed 44×56 feet. This is all under one roof and is 170 feet long. It is planned to soon build a barn beyond and joining the shed. It will then be 200 feet from the front door to the back and visitors will be welcome all the way.

What Would You Do?

April 5, 1918

What would you do if you had a million dollars?

I asked the question once of a young man of my acquaintance. He was the only son of rich parents and had been reared like the lilies of the field to "toil not." Then suddenly his father decided that he must learn to work. Working for a salary was supposed to teach him the value of money and learning the business would teach him how to care for his father's property when he should inherit it. But he did not take kindly to the lessons. He had been a butterfly so long he could not settle down to being a busy bee. Office hours came too early in the morning, and why should he keep office hours, anyway, when the fishing and hunting were good?

"Bert," I said to him one day, "what would you do if you had a million dollars?"

Bert looked at me gravely a moment and then, with a twinkle in his eye, said earnestly: "If I had a million dollars I would buy a bull dog, a big brindle one. I would keep him under my office desk and if anyone came in and said 'business' to me, I would say, 'Take him, Tige'."

I read in a California paper last week of an altogether different type of man who had arrived at somewhat the same conclusion as Bert, but by exactly the opposite route. This man was an old desert prospector, "desert rat" as they are called in the West, who had spent years hunting for gold in the desert. He came out to the nearest town with his burro and packs after supplies and found that he was heir to a fortune and that there had been quite a search thru the country to find him. He did not want the money and at first refused to take it. But it was his and he must make some disposition of it, so he insisted that a trustee be appointed to take care of it for him.

The old "desert rat," with all his worldly possessions in a pack on the back of a burro, and Bert who had grown to manhood with no wish unsatisfied, that money could gratify, had both come to the same decision—the burden of riches was more than they would bear.

The real character of men and women comes to the surface under stress, and sudden riches is as strong a test as any.

Just now there is a chance of fortune coming to unexpected places in the Ozark hills thru the boom in mining operations. Several farm women were talking over the prospects.

"What will you do when they strike it rich on your place?" some one asked.

"Oh! I'll get some new spring clothes and some more Holsteins," answered Mrs. Slade.

"Clothes, of course, but who would stop there?" exclaimed Mrs. Rice. "I shall buy motor cars and diamonds."

"I'll sell out the place and leave these hills," said Mrs. Wade. "How about you, Mrs. Woods?"

"I wouldn't go away," said Mrs. Woods slowly. "I should just like to help and I can help better where I am accustomed to people and things."

Her serious face lighted and her eyes shone as she continued.

"I do so desire to help a little and there is so much one could do with a little money, not just ordinary charity, there are so many persons looking after that, but some playthings for children here and there who do not have any; the pleasure of paying a mortgage now and then, for some hard-working family who could not pay it themselves; just helping those who need it before they become discouraged. It would be so much better than taking care of them after they have given up trying to help themselves. I'm going to do some of these things if they find ore on our place."

And so they showed their different characters and dispositions and the objects of their lives—business and show and snobbishness and love for others with a sincere desire to share good fortune with those less fortunate.

What would you do if you should suddenly become rich? Think out the answer and then look at yourself impartially by the light that answer will throw upon you! It is surprising what an opinion one sometimes forms of one's self by mentally standing off and looking on as at a stranger.

We Must Not Be Small Now

April 20, 1918

We read so much in the papers of graft and price profiteering, of federal investigation of first one business and then another, of treachery and double-dealing and strikes and riots, that one is tempted to be discouraged with people in general until one remembers that crimes and criminals are news and as such are given prominence on first pages of newspapers with glaring headlines. It is seldom that good deeds and their doers have such startling news value, but there are still plenty of them in the world. People are still kind and neighborly and are quietly and unobtrusively helping each other over hard places as they always have done.

Mrs. Sells was left a widow last winter and this spring she wishes to make a start with poultry in order to be self-supporting and able to keep her home. The neighbors have contributed the eggs and one will hatch them in her incubator to give Mrs. Sells her start.

Mr. Ashton was unable, because of illness, to put in his crop of oats. His neighbors have done the work for him.

I know a busy, up-to-date farmer who in his own way is helping his neighbors and his country. He is selling, for seed, a particularly high-priced kind of bean and some especially good cowpeas at just half the price charged in the seed catalogs. His price makes him a good profit, he says, and that is enough. Poultry is a specialty on his farm but he is selling eggs for hatching at a great reduction from his usual price. He wishes his neighbors to be successful in their farming and to increase the supply of food.

Isn't it refreshing to think of such a man as a change from excess profits? There is more of this kind of thing being done than appears on the surface for it is not given publicity. The spirit of helpfulness and comradeship is moving us all more or less.

Haven't you noticed a kinder feeling, in your heart, for your friends lately—a little more thoughtfulness for their comfort and well-being; just a touch more tenderness for your dear ones, even those who are in no danger of being called by the draft? It seems to me there is a drawing closer together, a feeling of standing shoulder to shoulder with my friends and neighbors that I have never experienced before. I am sure it is not all imagination.

There had been a little misunderstanding and consequent bad feeling in an organization to which I belong. It has been causing quite a little tempest in a teapot as such things always do, even tho they should not break out where they have more room for mischief. I was surprised to hear one of the parties in the controversy say: "I wish we might all go on and forget it. That's the only thing to do—just go on and forget it!"

Another person who has been a strong partisan on the other side said to me the same day: "What's the use of chewing the rag forever? It is much better to let it all drop and work together. There is no time to keep hashing things over and stirring up trouble." How long can any quarrel last when the parties to it begin to talk in that way?

Our common danger, a common cause and the work we are doing together is making us appreciate one another more and understand the littleness of petty jealousies and disagreements. The big things of life are crowding out the little unpleasant differences.

How can I hold a grudge against my neighbor when I know that his son, "somewhere in France," is interposing his body as a shield between my home and the danger that threatens it? How is it possible for me to do an unkind thing to my acquaintance when her son is braving the dangers of submarines and enemy warships while convoying my son safely to France to do his part in the fighting or perhaps helping to protect the ship that is bringing him home from foreign shores?

Then, too, if I can help my neighbor to raise a better crop or have better success with his stock, it will be just so much more to feed all our "kin folks" at home and abroad. Under these circumstances, how can we be selfish and self-centered? The old saying that, "everybody's business is nobody's business" is certainly all wrong now and anybody's business is everybody's business instead.

We will feel differently toward one another than ever before when we have had time to realize these things and if there has been any friction or misunderstanding, we will surely "just go on and forget it."

What the War Means to Women

May 5, 1918

"This is a woman's war and the women will see to it that before the war is ended the world shall be made safe for women." This sentiment was expressed by a woman in my hearing soon after the declaration of war by the United States.

Every war is more or less a woman's war, God knows, but is this in an especial way a woman's war? Never before in the history of the world has war been deliberately made upon the womanhood of the world and motherhood, woman's crown and glory, been made her scourge and shame. The tortures by savages, tales of which used to make our blood run cold did not equal in horror and cruelty what has been inflicted upon educated, refined women and ignorant peasant women alike.

Stripped naked and driven along the roads out of their own country a sport for drunken soldiery. Thrown by hundreds into the rivers when the crowds of soldiers had tired of them—this was a part of the war in Armenia.

Death by thousands, after nameless horrors and suffering, along the roads of Poland!

Driven over the snow covered mountains of Servia; dying of hunger and exhaustion and wounds, a fate preferred to falling into the hands of the invaders—this was the fate of the women of Servia.

Tortured and defiled, mutilated and murdered in Belgium and northern France! The mind revolts and the soul sickens at even trying to contemplate the things that women have been made to suffer by Germany's invading armies.

There has been a planned, deliberate attempt, by the enemy, to destroy the other nations of the world. To destroy a nation, its women and children must be exterminated and so a part of this incredible plot has been to so mutilate and destroy the women of those nations that they will bear no more children to perpetuate their race.

All over the world women are bravely taking their part in the conflict and doing what they can to defend those things they hold most sacred, their homes, their children and their honor. In all the allied countries women are filling places of responsibility and danger, doing hard, unpleasant work to help in the struggle to "make the world safe for women."

Women are showing their fearlessness on all the battle fronts. In Russia when the soldiers refused to fight, the women formed the famous "Battalion of Death" and met the enemy on the first line. They held their section of the line, too, when on every side the soldiers retreated in disorder and tho every woman in the battalion was killed or wounded. Later, with their ranks refilled, this battalion of women took part in the fighting at Petrograd, defending their position dauntlessly, seemingly without fear of death.

The women in the Red Cross units on the western front hesitate at nothing they find to do to help the allied cause. They were the last to leave the abandoned towns, before the Germans entered and they helped the refugees to escape, picked up and removed scores of wounded, driving their own trucks and motor cars, established temporary kitchens near the front to feed the soldiers who had not eaten for hours and, when the emergency arose, took charge of the military traffic and directed the columns of guns, cavalry, supply wagons and troops and prevented a traffic jam.

The women of the American Red Cross are winning honor on the western battle front. They act as cooks or chauffeurs, traffic policemen, stretcher bearers or grave diggers as the occasion arises.

Women in sheltered America have perhaps been slow to realize what the war means to them but they are beginning to understand. Among them, as among the men, are some pessimists and whiners, also some cowards and slackers, but they are few.

When the British retreated on the west, the first of April, a man remarked, "They're licking the stuffing out of us, licking us every day," and a woman answered, "What does one retreat amount to? A man isn't whipped in a fight even if he is knocked down, if he just gets up and comes again."

I like the spirit of the man whom I heard say, "We can't be whipped! We won't be whipped! We'll fight for 60 years if we must, but we'll never give up!"

A widow whose son volunteered and is now in France, said she was so proud of him that she had no time to be sorry; that she was glad he had gone and could not understand how any young man could stay at home.

Another woman, speaking of her son who had volunteered, said she was proud of him and that he would have been ashamed to look his sister in the face if he had not gone to help protect her from the fate of the girls of Belgium and France.

The congregation at the church was remarkable on Easter Sunday for the absence of new hats and the large number of Liberty Bond pins and Red Cross buttons. One woman who has always taken great pride in her apparel said to me: "I can't get a new hat this summer. I'm paying for my Liberty Bond and helping with the Red Cross and someway new hats don't seem to matter."

The little town of Mansfield and immediate vicinity, oversubscribed its quota in the Third Liberty Loan.

How About the Home Front?

May 20, 1918

When we buy Liberty Bonds and War Savings Stamps, we are open to suspicion, in our own minds at least, of not being entirely disinterested. We may be a little influenced in our saving and buying by a hope of gain, for Liberty Bonds and Savings Stamps are good investments. They are gilt-edged securities and a paying proposition.

Even when we work hard on our farms raising food to "feed the world," we are making money for ourselves and the harder we work the more we make, so perhaps we do not deserve so very much credit for the extra effort after all. We are such complex creatures and our motives are nearly always so mixed, that it is easy to deceive ourselves. I know from experience that it is very pleasant to have duty and inclination run hand in hand and to be well paid in cash for doing right.

When we give to the Red Cross, however, it is entirely different. What we give then we do not make a profit on, at least in money. We get nothing in return except a glow of satisfaction and a knowledge that we are actually helping our soldiers at the front and the ill and destitute of the world.

By the sacrifice we make in giving we show our love for humanity; our pity for the helpless and our generosity toward those less fortunate than ourselves.

It is something of which to be very proud when one's community goes over its allotment for the Red Cross as so many have done. It is another victory over the enemy, for this war is a battle of ideas and standards of life.

Disguise it as we may in concrete terms such as "the restoration of Belgium," the "rights of small nations" and the "integrity of treaties," this world war is a world conflict of ideas. This is why the fighting cannot be confined to the battle fronts; why every country is more or less in conflict internally. We are in the midst of a battle of standards of conduct and each of us is a soldier in the ranks. What we do and how we live our everyday lives has a direct bearing on the result, just as each of us will be personally affected by it.

We may have thought that a little selfishness and over-reaching on our part, a breaking of our promised word now and then if it was more convenient; a disregard of the rights of others for our own advantage, did not so much matter and were not so very wrong. Nevertheless it is these same things when done in mass by the German government and armies, that the remainder of the world abhors.

There is a connection between our motives, the way we live our lives here at home, and those vast armies facing each other in a death grapple.

In the thick of battle; under terrific bombardments that shake the earth; in the darkness of night when the poison gas comes creeping; our soldiers are fighting that right shall be the standard of the future instead of might; that the strong shall not take unfair advantage of the weak; that a pledged word and honor shall be considered sacred and shall not be broken.

Are we fighting bravely for these same things all down the line? When "Johnny comes marching home" victorious will he find that we also have won the victory on the home front?

If we are careless of our given word; if we take unfair advantage; if we are deceitful and lustful and cruel; if we spread false reports; if we are malicious and grasping and full of hate instead of kind, open-minded, fair and just, then the Prussian ideas, as insidious as their poison gas, will have vanquished in our own country those ideals for which our armies fight.

This is our battle and must be our victory, for if the standards of life approved by the German government hold the peoples of the earth then, in a different way than was intended but in a very true sense, Germany will have conquered the world.

New Day for Women

Great Responsibilities Will Be Ours after the War

June 5, 1918

How long has it been since you have seen an old maid? Oh, of course, one sees unmarried women every day, but it has been a good many years since I have seen a real "old maid" or "maiden lady." Even the terms sound strange and lead one back and back into memories. There were old maids when I was a girl. Later some of the older girls protested against being called old maids and insisted on being called "bachelor girls." There was some controversy over the question of whether women should be given such a title, I remember, but not having any special interest in the subject, I lost sight of it and awakened later to the fact that both old maids and bachelor girls had disappeared, how or when I do not know. In their place are simply women, young women, older women, (never old women), married and unmarried women, divorced women and widows, with the descriptive adjective in the background, but nowhere in the world, I think, are there any old maids.

As one considers the subject, it becomes plain that this one fact contains the whole story and explanation of the change in the world for women, the broadening and enriching of their lives. In the days when old maids flourished, the one important fact in a woman's life was whether or not she were married and as soon as a girl child reached maturity she was placed in one of two classes and labeled accordingly. She was either Mrs.—or else an old maid.

THE WORLD IS OPEN TO US

As women became more interested in other things; as the world opened up to them its storehouse of activities and absorbing interests; when the fact that a woman was a doctor, a lawyer, a farmer or what not; when her work in and for the world became of more importance to the world than her private life, the fact of whether or not she were married did not receive the emphasis that it formerly did. To be sure, everyone knows that a woman's most important work is still her children, but other interests enter so largely into her life today that she is not classified solely on the one count. Altho still a vital part of a woman's life, marriage is not now the end and aim of her existence. There are in the world many, many other ambitions and occupations to take up her attention.

Women are successful lumber dealers, livestock breeders, caterers, curators, bacteriologists, pageant managers, cable code experts and besides have entered nearly every ordinary profession. They have learned and are learning the most advanced methods of farming and scientific dairy management while it has become no uncommon thing for a woman to manage an ordinary farm. The exigencies of the war have thrust women into many new occupations that otherwise they might not have undertaken for many years if ever. Thousands of them have become expert munitions makers and, while we all hope there will be no need for that trade when the present war is ended, still there will be use for the trained technical skill which these women workers have acquired.

Women are running trains, they are doing the work in factories, they are clerks, jurors, representatives in congress and farm help. By the time the war is over most of the economic and industrial systems of the world will be in the hands of the women. Quite likely, too, they will have, thru the ballot, the control of the political governments of the world.

If by an inconceivable turn of fate, Germany should conquer in the struggle now going on, women will be held in control by the military power and without doubt will be again restricted to the home and children, according to the rule laid down by Emperor William defining their sphere of activity, but this we will not permit to be possible.

When the democratic nations are victorious and the world is ruled by the ballot instead of the cannon, there is scarcely a doubt but what women will be included in the universal suffrage. Already the franchise has been given to 6 million women in England. A suffrage amendment to the constitution of the United States missed being brought before congress by only a few votes and there is no doubt but that the women of the United States will soon have the ballot.

In Russia when the revolution occurred, the women took the franchise with the men as a matter of course and without question. In France the old idea that women should rule thru their influence over men is still alive but growing feeble. More and more women and men are coming to stand together on terms of frankness and equality.

WOMEN SHALL RULE

Italy is far behind the other nations in the emancipation of its women, still the women of Italy have a great influence. It was the use of German propaganda among the Italian peasant women that weakened Italy and caused the late reverses there.

We all realize, with aching hearts, that there is a great slaughter of men on the battle fronts and with the sexes about equal over the world before the war, what will be the result when millions of men are killed? When at last the "Beast of Berlin" is safely caged and the soldiers of freedom return home to settle quietly down into civil life once more, the women are going to be largely in the majority over the world. With the ballot in their hands, they are going to be the rulers of a democratic world.

There is a great deal of speculation about the conditions that will prevail after the war. Nearly all writers and thinkers are looking for a new order, a sort of social and industrial revolution and they all expect it to come thru the returned soldiers. No one, so far as I have found, is giving a thought to the fact that in a free democratic world, the power will be in the hands of the women who have stayed quietly at home working, sorrowing and thinking.

Will we be wise and true and strong enough to use this power for the best, or will we be deceived thru our ignorance or driven on the wrong way by storms of emotion or enthusiasm? We have been privileged to look on and criticize the way the world has been run. "A man-made world" we have called it now and then, implying that women would have done so much better in managing its affairs. The signs indicate that we are going to have a chance to remake it nearer to the heart's desire. I wish I might be sure that we would be equal to our opportunity.

I suggested this idea of the coming power of women, to a liberal-minded man, a man who is strongly in favor of woman suffrage and he replied: "The women are no more ready for such a responsibility than the people of Russia were; they are ignorant along the lines of government and too uncontrolled in their emotions."

I wonder if he is right! The majority vote in a Democratic league of nations will be a great power to hold in inexperienced hands; a great responsibility to rest upon the women of the world.

Do the Right Thing Always

June 20, 1918

"It is always best to treat people right," remarked my lawyer friend.

"Yes, I suppose so, in the end," I replied inanely.

"Oh of course!" he returned, "but that was not what I meant. It pays every time to do the right thing! It pays now and in dollars and cents."

"For instance?" I asked.

"Well for the latest instance: a man came to me the other day to bring suit against a neighbor. He had good grounds for damages and could win the suit, but it would cost him more than he could recover. It would make his neighbor expense and increase the bad feeling between them. I needed that attorney's fee, but it would not have been doing the right thing to encourage him to bring suit, so I advised him to settle out of court. He insisted but I refused to take the case. He hired another lawyer, won his case and paid the difference between the damages he recovered and his expenses.

"A client came to me a short time afterward with a suit worth-while and a good retainer's fee, which I could take without robbing him. He was sent to me by the man whose case I had refused to take and because of that very refusal."

Is it possible that "honesty is the best policy" after all, actually and literally? I would take the advice of my lawyer friend on any other business and I have his word for it that it pays to do the right thing here and now.

To do the right thing is simply to be honest, for being honest is more than refraining from short-changing a customer or robbing a neighbor's hen roost. To be sure those items are included, but there is more to honesty than that. There is such a thing as being dishonest when no question of financial gain or loss is involved. When one person robs another of his good name, he is dishonest. When by an unnecessary, unkind act or cross word, one causes another to lose a day or an hour of happiness, is that one not a thief? Many a person robs another of the joy of life while taking pride in his own integrity.

We steal from today to give to tomorrow; we "rob Peter to pay Paul." We are not honest even with ourselves; we rob ourselves of health; we cheat ourselves with sophistries; we even "put an enemy in our mouths to steal away our brains."

If there were a cry of "stop thief!" we would all stand still. Yet nevertheless, in spite of our carelessness, we all know deep in our hearts that it pays to do the right thing, tho it is easy to deceive ourselves for a time. If we do the wrong thing, we are quite likely never to know what we have lost by it. If the lawyer had taken the first case, he might have thought he gained by so doing, for he never would have known of the larger fee which came to him by taking the other course.

Are You Helping or Hindering?

July 5, 1918

A "government of the people, for the people and by the people" can be no better nor greater than the people.

My friend had been telling me a tale of graft and injustice, in relatively high places and she concluded with, "And this is a government of the people, for the people, by the people." If we could point to no such instances among those more or less in power, it would very plainly not be a government representative of the people, for there are good, bad and indifferent persons among the people and a few who make mistakes now and then.

From town constable to the chief executive, we find good officers, bad officers and those who are negligible, for the people are the government and the government is the people. If we want the one perfect, we must reform the other for I will venture to say that if there were no dishonesty, or grafting or self-seeking among the rank and file of the people, there would be none in any department of government.

I knew of one person in the recent Red Cross drive who bought as cheaply as possible at a Red Cross auction and resold at a profit. There were only a few dollars involved but there was the soul of a profiteer in a person with small means who, tho at the bottom of the social structure financially, is just as obnoxious as the man who makes millions out of the suffering of the world.

Not far from this man lives another who served in the U. S. army all thru the Spanish war and who has never been in good health since. He is entitled to a pension but never has applied for one because, in his own words, he "could make a livin'." He told me the other day when we happened to meet, that just before the United States went into this war he had decided to ask for his pension but had not done so when war was declared. He said "Then I told my wife that the government would have lots of expenses without paying me a pension and we talked it over and decided that we would not ask for a pension until this mess was straightened out and government expenses were lighter. Then I'd be older if I was alive and I'd ask for a pension. If I was dead my wife could get one. Oh! I wish I could turn things back and be young enough, I'd go and fight!"

This man is just as much a self-sacrificing patriot as George Washington, tho just a humble wood cutter like the great Lincoln. Then between the two extremes of patriotism and slackerism are numbers of indifferently good patriots sacrificing a little, doing the greater part of their duty by their country.

I have heard people who have been inoculated with I. W. W. doctrine say "if this government don't do right, we will turn it over." If it were turned over, we would have on top what had before been the bottom and we would perhaps have in power both the man who made money from the Red Cross sale and the one who is going without his pension to help his country. Tho I'll wager the moneymaker would scheme himself into some place where the graft pickings were good.

We have no king in a republic "who can do no wrong", no kaiser whom we are bound to regard as infallible with the right to both our minds and our bodies, but from the lowest to the highest we are bound by the same standards; we are sworn to the same ideals and permeated alike with good and evil and all alike we are liable to make mistakes.

When we are tempted to be impatient and too critical of our leaders, we might think as I heard a woman say, "few of us would have their jobs." Friendly, constructive criticism is one thing and unkind, nagging fault-finding is another quite different.

Imagine a man fighting, for his life and the lives of his friends, and while he is struggling to the limit of his strength his friends stand around and cry—

"Oh that was wrong! You shouldn't have hit him on the nose; you should have landed on his jaw!" "Why did you let him hit you? If you had been quicker you could have stopped him. You're too slow!" "You ought not to have taken that drink this morning! Stop now and tell us! Will you be a teetotaler after this?" "Hey! This fellow in the crowd is stepping on my toes! Make him quit!" "You never can lick him for you weren't trained. You should have been prepared for this!"

Wouldn't that man fight better if he were encouraged by cries of, "That's a good one! Hit him again! You've got him going now; keep after him!" and so forth? If the principle is good in a game of ball, why not use it in this bigger game? Let's root for our leaders now and then!

I would like to read, for instance, that congress had called Secretary Baker into its presence and said to him, "Well done, Secretary Baker! It is a remarkable achievement to transport so many troops safely to France in so short a time and we honor you for it."[4]

Instead of so much wailing because we must eat cornbread, I would like to hear someone say, "What a wonderful man Mr. Hoover is to be able to regulate the food supply of the world; to handle the food of our country so that we may not come to hunger and perhaps famine and still are able to feed other nations!"[5]

Let's talk to each other about the ideals of life and government that President Wilson is putting before the world! If we, the people hold fast to and live by these beautiful ideals, they are bound to be enacted by our government for, in a republic the ideas of the people reach upward to the top instead of being handed down from some one at the top to the people who must accept them whether they like them or not.

Swearing Is a Foolish Habit

August 5, 1918

I heard a boy swear the other day, and it gave me a distinctly different kind of a shock than usual. I had just been reading an article in which our soldiers were called crusaders who were offering themselves, in their youth as a sacrifice in order that right might prevail against wrong and that those ideals, which are in effect the teachings of Christ, shall be accepted as the law of nations.

When I heard the boy use the name of Christ in an oath, I felt that he had belittled the mighty effort we are making, and that he had put an affront upon our brave soldiers by using lightly the name of the great Leader who first taught the principles for which they are dying. The boy had not thought of it in this way at all. He imagined that he was being very bold and witty, quite a grown man in fact.

I wonder how things came to be so reversed from the right order, that it should be thought daring and smart to swear, instead of being regarded as utterly foolish and a sign of weakness, betraying a lack of self-control. If people could only realize how ridiculous they appear when they call down the wrath of the Creator and Ruler of the Universe just because they have jammed their thumbs. I feel sure they would never be guilty of swearing

4. Newton D. Baker served as secretary of war from 1916 to 1921.
5. In 1917, President Woodrow Wilson appointed Herbert Hoover head of the Food Administration.

again. It is so out of proportion, something as foolish and wasteful as it would be to use the long-range gun which bombarded Paris, to shoot a fly. If we call upon the Mightiest for trivial things, upon whom or what shall we call in the great moments of life?

There are some things in the world which should be damned to the nethermost regions, but surely it is not some frightened animal whom our own lack of self-control has made rebellious, or an inanimate object that our own carelessness has caused to smite us. Language loses its value when it is so misapplied and in moments of real and great stress or danger we have nothing left to say.

It is almost hopeless to try to reform older persons who have the habit of swearing fastened upon them. Like any other habit, it is difficult to break and it is useless to explain to them that it is a waste of force and nervous energy, but I think we should show children the absurdity of wasting the big shells of language on small insignificant objects. Perhaps a little ridicule might prick that bubble of conceit and the boy with his mouth full of his first oaths might not feel himself such a dashing, daredevil of a fellow if he feared that he had made himself ridiculous.

Overcoming Our Difficulties

August 20, 1918

"A difficulty raiseth the spirit of a great man. He hath a mind to wrestle with it and give it a fall. A man's mind must be very low if the difficulty doth not make part of his pleasure." By the test of these words of Lord Halifax, there are a number of great persons in the world today.

After all, what is a difficulty but a direct challenge? "Here I am in your way," it says, "you cannot get around me nor overcome me! I have blocked your path!" Anyone of spirit will accept the challenge and find some way to get around or over, or thru that obstacle. Yes! And find pleasure in the difficulty for the sheer joy of surmounting it as well as because there has been an opportunity once more to prove one's strength and cunning and by the very use of these qualities cause an increase of them.

The overcoming of one difficulty makes easier the conquering of the next until finally we are almost invincible. Success actually becomes a habit thru the determined overcoming of obstacles as we meet them one by one.

If we are not being successful, if we are more or less on the road toward failure, a change in our fortunes can be brought about by making a start, however small, in the right direction and then following it up. We can form the habit of success by beginning with some project and putting it thru to a successful conclusion however long and hard we must fight to do so; by "wrestling with" one difficulty and "giving it a fall." The next time it will be easier.

For some reason, of course according to some universal law, we gather momentum as we proceed in whatever way we go, and just as by overcoming a small difficulty we are more able to conquer the next, tho greater, so if we allow ourselves to fail it is easier to fail the next time and failure becomes a habit until we are unable to look a difficulty fairly in the face; but turn and run from it.

There is no elation equal to the rise of the spirit to meet and overcome a difficulty, not with a foolish over-confidence but keeping things in their proper relations by praying, now and then, the prayer of a good fighter whom I used to know. "Lord make me sufficient to mine own occasion."

When Proverbs Get Together

September 5, 1918

It had been a busy day and I was very tired, when just as I was dropping off to sleep I remembered that bit of mending I should have done for the man of the place. Then I must have dreamed, for in my fancy, I saw that rent in the garment enlarge and stretch into startlingly large proportions.

At the same time a familiar voice sounded in my ear, "A stitch in time saves nine," it said.

I felt very discouraged indeed at the size of the task before me and very much annoyed that my neglect should have caused it to increase to nine times its original size, when on the other side of me a cheerful voice insinuated, "It is never too late to mend."

Ah! There was that dear old friend of my grandmother who used to encourage her to work until all hours of the night to keep the family clothes in order. I felt impelled to begin at once to mend that lengthened rent, but paused as a voice came to me from a dark corner saying, "A chain is no stronger than its weakest link."

"Shall a man put new wine into old bottles," chimed in another. Of course not, I thought, then why put new cloth—.

But now the voices seemed to come from all about me. They appeared to be disputing and quarreling, or at least disagreeing among themselves.

"Oh what a tangled web we weave when first we practice to deceive," said a smug, oily voice.

"But practice makes perfect," piped a younger voice, sweetly tho with an impudent expression.

"And if at first you don't succeed, try, try again," chirped a small voice with a snicker and it seemed to me that the room was filled with soft laughter.

Evidently thinking that something should be done to put the younger folks in their place, a proverb with a very stern voice spoke from a far corner. "Children should be seen and not heard," he said and a demure little voice at once answered, "Out of the mouth of babes cometh wisdom."

This was really growing interesting. I had not realized that there were so many wise proverbs and that they might fall out among themselves.

Now a couple of voices made themselves heard, evidently continuing a discussion.

"A rolling stone gathers no moss," said a rather disagreeable voice and I caught a shadowy glimpse of a hoary old proverb with a long, gray beard.

"But a setting hen never grows fat," retorted his companion in a sprightly tone.

"An honest man is the noblest work of God," came a high, nasal voice with a self righteous undertone.

"Ah, yes! Honesty is the best policy, you know," came the answer in a brisk business-like tone, just a little cutting.

"A fool and his money are soon parted," said a thin, tight-lipped voice with a puckering quality, I felt sure would draw the purse strings tight.

"Oh, well, money is the root of all evil, why not be rid of it?" answered a jolly, rollicking voice with a hint of laughter in it.

But now there seemed to be danger of a really violent altercation for I heard the words "sowing wild oats," spoken in a cold, sneering tone, while an angry voice retorted hotly, "There is no fool like an old fool," and an admonitory voice added, "It is never too late to mend." Ah! Grandmother's old friend with a different meaning in the words.

Then at my very elbow spoken for my benefit alone, I heard again the words, "It is never too late to mend." Again I had a glimpse of that neglected garment with the rent in it grown to unbelievable size. Must I? At this time of night! But a soft voice whispered in my ear, "Sufficient unto the day is the evil thereof," and with a smile at grandmother's friend, I drifted into dreamless sleep.

What Days in Which to Live!

September 20, 1918

The world is growing smaller each day. It has been shrinking for centuries, but during these later years it is diminishing in size with an ever increasing swiftness, yet so gradual is the change that we do not realize what is taking place unless we compare the present with the past.

It is only a few years ago that our neighbors were only those who lived within a few miles of us. Now we make an afternoon call on our neighbors 20 miles away with no greater effort.

The King and Queen of Belgium called on the English sovereigns not long ago. Their conveyance was an airplane and it took them only a short time to make the trip from Belgium to their destination in England.

Students of the future tell us that flying machines will come into general use after the war and perhaps we shall then drop in on our friends in England and France for afternoon tea just as casually as we used to happen in at our next door neighbor's. We shall have friends in France and England by that time and those countries will never again seem far away. Even now, it is just "over there" and with so many persons passing back and forth, with millions of our common, every-day folks becoming intimately familiar with all the countries at war, the world will be much, much smaller when peace comes again.

It seems to me such a wonderful thing that the people of all the different nations of the earth are becoming so well acquainted. When people have fought and struggled and worked, gone hungry and eaten together they can never again be indifferent and distant toward one another. These people whom we have always carelessly bunched together in our minds as foreigners will be our friends and neighbors from this time on. Already we have shared our food with them; we have gone to their aid in danger and sickness, in misfortune and misery, as is and always has been the privilege of good neighbors the world over, and in doing this we are only returning the neighborly kindness of France shown to the United States in the war of Independence and that of England in protecting us from Germany during the war with Spain.[6]

As nations we have been neighbors for many years and now we are beginning to realize it as individuals. The people of the allied nations have

6. In the Spanish American War, the Germans sought to intervene against U.S. interests.

learned that our sympathy is quick and our purse open to the needy and now they are finding out that our boys are good to fight beside.

As we who stay at home follow the operations on the various battle fronts, we have come to feel a personal interest in the heroic Belgian soldiers, holding the small corner of their country in spite of the worst the enemy could do; in the gallant French soldiers who set the bounds and said, "They shall not pass!" in the Italian soldiers who accomplished almost unbelievable feats fighting above the clouds, on snowclad mountain peaks, thousands of them having left security in the United States to take part in the terrific combat; and in the Russian soldiers, surely as brave as any, who went out against armed Germans and artillery with their bare hands when there were no arms and ammunition and yet who were so simple-souled and gentle-minded as to be overcome with fair words and false promises.[7]

Our admiration and sympathy has drawn us near to the soldiers of these different armies and to the people of their countries. We have been proud of their bravery and fortitude; we have rejoiced with them in their successes and sorrowed with them in their sufferings. This is what makes of people friends and neighbors. Never again can we be strangers.

If we can but broaden our vision to see world happenings as a whole, we cannot fail to be in accord with that young and eager person who exclaimed, "Glory! What days in which to live!"

Your Code of Honor

October 5, 1918

What is your personal code of honor? Just what do you consider dishonorable or disgraceful in personal conduct? It seems to me that we had all grown rather careless in holding ourselves to any code of honor and just a little ashamed of admitting that we had such a standard. At best our rules of life were becoming a little flexible and we had rather a contemptuous memory of the knights of King Arthur's round table who fought so often for their honor and still at times forgot it so completely, while we pitied the Pilgrim Fathers for their stern inflexibility in what they considered the right way of life.

Just now, while such mighty forces of right and wrong are contending in

7. The Russian people were probably not "deceived" by false promises: internal conditions in Russia, namely revolution, made it necessary for them to sue for peace with Germany.

the world, we are overhauling our mental processes a little and finding out some curious things about ourselves. We can all think of examples of different ideas of what is dishonorable. There are the persons who strictly fulfill their given word. To them it would be a disgrace not to do as they agree, not to keep a promise, while others give a promise easily and break their word with even greater ease.

Some persons have a high regard for truth and would feel themselves disgraced if they told a lie, while others prefer a lie even tho the truth were easier.

There are persons who have no scruples to prevent them from eavesdropping, reading letters not intended for them, or any manner of prying into other persons' private affairs, and to others the doing of such things is in a manner horrifying.

There are scandal-mongers who are so eager to find and scatter to the four winds a bit of unsavory gossip that they are actually guilty in their own souls of the slips in virtue that they imagine in others, and contrasting with these are people so pureminded that they would think themselves disgraced if they entertained in their thoughts such idle gossip.

I know a woman whose standard of honor demands only, "the greatest good to the greatest number, including myself." The difficulty with this is that a finite mind can scarcely know what is good for other persons or even one's self.

Another woman's code of honor is to be fair, to always give the "square deal" to the other person and this is very difficult to do because the judgment is so likely to be partial.

There is a peculiar thing about the people who hold all these differing ideas of what they will allow themselves to do. We seldom wish to live up to the high standard to which we hold the other fellow. The person who will not keep his word becomes very angry if a promise to him is broken. Those who have no regard for truth, in what they say, expect that others will be truthful when talking to them. People who pry into affairs which are none of their business consider the same actions disgraceful in others and gossips think that they should be exempt from the treatment they give to other people. I never knew it to fail and it is very amusing at times to listen to the condemnation of others' actions by one who is even more guilty of the same thing.

It does one good to adhere strictly to a rule of conduct, if that rule is what it should be. Just the exercise of the will in refusing to follow the desires, which do not conform to the standard set, is strengthening to the character, while the determination to do the thing demanded by that standard and the doing of it however difficult, is an exercise for the strengthening of the will power which is far better than anything recommended for that purpose by books.

If you doubt that it pays in cash and other material advantages to have a high code of honor and live up to it, just notice the present plight of the German government. At the beginning of the war they threw away their honor, broke their pledged word and proclaimed to the world that their written agreements were mere scraps of paper. Now when they ask for a conference to discuss a "peace by agreement," the allies reply, in effect, "but an agreement with you would in no sense be binding upon you. We cannot trust again to your word of honor since your signed pledge is a mere 'scrap of paper' and your verbal promises even less."

It is plain, then, that nations are judged by their standards of honor and treated accordingly, and it is the same with individuals. We judge them by their code of honor and the way they live up to it. It is impossible to hold two standards, one for ourselves and a different one for others, for what is dishonorable in them would be the same for us and that seems in the end to be the only sure test, embracing and covering all the rest, the highest code of honor yet voiced—"Whatsoever ye would that men should do to you, do ye even so to them!"[8]

Early Training Counts Most

October 20, 1918

"Don't open that door again, Tom! It lets in too much cold," said Tom's mother, with what I thought was an unnecessarily sharp note in her voice.

It was the first chilly day of early autumn and there was no fire in the house except in the kitchen stove. As I was making an afternoon visit we of course sat in the front room—and shivered. In a moment the outside door opened again and Tom and a gust of raw wind entered together.

"I told you not to open that door! If you do it again I'll spank you good!" said Tom's mother and Tom immediately turned around, opened the door and went out.

We talked on busily for another moment when, feeling more chilly than usual, I looked around and saw Tom standing in the open door, swinging it to and fro.

"Tom!" exclaimed his mother, "I told you not to open that door! Come

8. Matthew 7:12.

here to me!" As the door swung shut, Tom turned and faced his mother, took a few steps toward her, raised himself on his tiptoes, with his hands behind him and—turned around, opened the door and walked out.

His mother screamed after him, "Tom! If you open that door again, I'll skin you alive!"

"You know you wouldn't do that and Tom knows it too," I said. "Oh, of course," she replied, "but I have to tell him something."

I know Tom's mother is trying to teach her boy to be truthful, but a few days ago he got into mischief and when asked who had done the damage he replied, "Sister did it."

Tom was punished for telling a lie but I imagine it would be rather difficult to explain to him why it was all right to tell a falsehood about what would happen and all wrong to tell one about what had happened; why he should be punished and his mother not.

While I was busy with my work the other morning, a great commotion arose in the dooryard. There was shouting, the dog was barking furiously and there was the noise of running and trampling. I hurried to the door and found several boys in the yard darting here and there, shouting to each other, "Catch it! There it goes!"

As I opened the door a couple of the boys put their feet into the meshes of the woven wire fence and climbed over it as tho it had been a stairs, altho the gate was only a few steps from them. Evidently that was the way they had entered the dooryard.

"Boys what are you doing?" I asked. "Oh! Just chasing butterflies," answered one, while another added as tho that excused everything, "Our teacher is just down there," indicating a place well within the fenced field.

When we had taken stock of the damage done by the butterfly chasers, we found that the barbed wire fence had been broken down where they had entered the fields and the woven wire fence was badly stretched and sagged. Wire fencing is high these days and help impossible to get so that such raids are particularly annoying just now tho they are not, by any means, anything new.

We are engaged just now in a mighty struggle to teach a certain part of the people of the world a respect for truth and for the rights and property of other people. Are we failing to teach these things at home as we should?

We are told that the reason for the warped national conscience of the German nation is, that the people have been trained from infancy for the things which they have been doing in this war, taught in such a manner that they could be brought to do the awful things which they have done. The results show with startling vividness the effects of childhood impressions and the training of youth.

If in one generation a gentle, kind-hearted people can be changed into fiends by a system of teaching, what might be accomplished if children were as carefully trained in the opposite direction. Truly, "As the twig is bent, the tree inclines."

Opportunity

November 5, 1918

"Grasp opportunity by the forelock, for it is bald behind," says the old proverb. In other words, we must be ready to meet and take advantage of opportunities as they come, or we will lose the chance. We cannot have any hold on them once they have passed by. Nor is time and endeavor spent in preparing ourselves ever wasted, for if we are ready, opportunity is sure to come.

President Wilson is one of the finest examples of a man who was prepared for the opportunity that came to him. In studying his life one comes to feel that he must have decided, while yet a boy, to become President and carefully prepared himself for it, so exactly did his life, up to the time, fit him for the position.

Virtually all his life, Wilson was a student of government. He was nearly 30 when his academic training was ended, then a two years' study of law added a practicable equipment. But all these years of hard study were only a beginning for the still more arduous study he did in preparation for the lectures he gave and the magazine articles and books he wrote, mostly on subjects relating to history and legislation.

Before there was any idea of making him President, before he could have seen any likelihood of such a thing, he knew congress and congressional procedure thoroly, far better than did many experienced congressmen.

Wilson's experience as president of Princeton university gave him a training in the handling of men and also in fighting for democratic institutions and so in this great crisis of American history, the opportunity found the man prepared, trained and waiting to take his high place in the world, a position where he is called upon to put to use all the knowledge and skill he acquired in all those long years of study and training.

There are other great persons of whom the same is true. In fact no one can become great who is not ready to take the opportunity when it comes, nor indeed succeed in smaller matters and whatever we prepare ourselves to do or become, the opportunity will come to us to do or become that thing.

Even tho we never become one of the great persons of the world, the chance is sure to come to us to use whatever knowledge we acquire.

I knew a woman who denied herself in other things in order that she might pay for French lessons. There seemed no chance that it would ever be an advantage to her except as a means of culture, but she now has a good position at a large salary which she would have been unable to fill but for her knowledge of French.

There is unfortunately a reverse side to this picture I have drawn, of efforts crowned by success—just as achievements are made possible by a careful preparation, a lack of effort to reach forward and beyond our present position works inversely, and again examples are too numerous to mention.

A hired man on a farm who always needs a boss; who is unable mentally and by disposition to work unless his employer is present and leading; who never fits himself, by being responsible and trustworthy, for the responsibility of owning and running his own farm, will always be a hired man either on a farm or elsewhere.

The tenant farmer who is not preparing himself for being an owner by putting himself mentally in an owner's place, getting his point of view and realizing his difficulties, is the tenant farmer who is always having trouble with his landlord and almost never comes to own his own farm. Realizing the difficulties and solving the problems of the next step up seem to lead inevitably to taking that step.

If we do a little less than is required by the position we now fill, whether in our own business or working for someone else; if we do not learn something of the work of the person higher up, we are never ready to advance and then we say, "I had a good chance if I had only known how, and so forth."

If we spend on our living every cent of our present income, we are not ready to take that opportunity which requires a little capital and then we say, "That was a good chance if I could only have raised the money."

There is also a touch of humor to be found in the fact that what we prepare for comes to us, altho it is rather pitiful. Humor and pathos are very close "kin."

When the influenza came to our town, Mrs. C called a friend and tried to engage her to come and nurse her thru the illness.

"Have you the influenza?" asked the friend.

"Oh, no!" replied Mrs. C. "None of us has it yet, but I'm all ready for it. I have my bed all clean and ready to crawl into as soon as I feel ill. Everything is ready but a nurse and I want you to come and take care of me."

In a very few days Mrs. C was in bed with an attack of influenza. She had prepared for the visit and she could say with the psalmist: "The thing that I feared has come upon me."

San Marino Is Small but Mighty

December 5, 1918

"In order to get my passports for Europe, I had to swear allegiance to the allies, including the King of Siam and the republic of San Marino. Of course I love 'em all if they are fighting for us but it seemed rather queer to swear allegiance to that little four-by-nine country of San Marino," says a letter which I recently received.

Hidden away within the territory of Italy, completely surrounded by that country, is the smallest republic in the world. This little country, the republic of San Marino, is 9 miles long and contains 38 square miles.

The capital of the country is built upon a mountain top which seems almost inaccessible, rising sheer from the plains of Romagna. There is a legend that this mountain was raised by the Titans in their anger when they tried to reach Jove and drive him from the throne of Heaven.

The republic of San Marino has been free and independent for 1,600 years, while around it have rolled the strife and bloodshed of the wars of the world.

The position of the country, far enough from the coast to be secure from invasion by sea, distant from the great Roman roads, up and down which armies traveled, the peaceful character of the inhabitants and the poverty of the country, were partly responsible for its being unmolested, but the principal cause of San Marino's peaceful history, is internal and exists in its institutions and the character of its people.

During all the years while other countries have been going thru the disrupting, violent process of dethroning tyrants and vindicating the rights of the common people, there were in San Marino no factions, no tyrants and the rights of the people were safe and respected. Here the people lived simply, changing their laws slowly as the changing times required and always adopting those changes which best developed and conserved their liberties.

It was in the middle of the Fourth century, during the days when Christians were persecuted, that two stone masons of Dalmatia, named Marino and Leo, crossed the Adriatic sea and came to Rimini to aid the Christian slaves who had been condemned to build the walls of that city. The lot of those who hewed the rocks from the mountains and transported them to the mouth of the river, was much the hardest and because their need of help was the greatest, Marino and Leo ascended the river and stopped before the two abruptly rising mountains. As they were experienced stone cutters, they were soon placed in charge of large numbers of slaves, whom they were able to help in many ways spiritually as well as physically.

When the walls of the city of Rimini were finished, the two stone cutters retired each to the mountain top to live in peace and solitude. Marino hewed a bed from the rock and cultivated a little garden. The rock bed and site of the garden is still to be seen in the city. Some of the slaves escaped and followed their overseers to the mountains. A little Christian church was built on each mountain and here these simple people practiced their Christian faith undisturbed and the two colonies became an asylum for the weary and oppressed. Being poor and simple, their wants were provided for by the hewing and quarrying of stone, which is today the chief industry.

A wealthy Roman woman who had been taught the Christian faith, by Marino, gave him the mountains which she owned, as absolute and perpetual property. Marino strove to found a free society upon the foundation of liberty, justice, simplicity, charity and love of peace and when he died he called his people together around him and bequeathed them his mountain, "free from every other man." He begged his followers to be true to the faith and live in perfect accord as free men.

The territory of the country was extended a little thru purchase and because of the warring times the city was fortified. The strong walls whose ruins still encircle the city show one reason why the little republic was left in peace.

The government of the country today still holds the spirit of its founder. A council of 60 citizens is the governing body. These councilors are elected every three years and they choose, from their number every six months two captains regent who hold the executive power and preside at meetings of the council

There are several co-operative institutions in San Marino, among which are a public bake house, a bank, a canteen and a grain magazine. Fine livestock is raised by the people and every family has its own vineyard.

Actual criminals are not allowed to come and remain in the country but political refugees are given haven and many famous people have found refuge there.

Marino taught his people that war, tho, a necessity in self-defense, was otherwise an unpardonable crime and so since its foundation until the present time, the country has never gone to war, but the people could not stay quietly at home while the war for the liberty of the world was raging and the young men of San Marino went into the Italian army and the country has maintained a hospital on the Italian front, for San Marino, tho the smallest of the goodly company, is one of the allies.

The American Spirit

December 20, 1918

"The food administration now becomes a great machine of mercy destined to carry the American spirit into the homes and hearts of a great host of bewildered, confused human beings, hungry, discouraged, saddened, submerged by the wreckage resulting from the war. They have gone thru fire for us. The least we can do is to help them to their feet, to see that they are fed and clothed. Don't let your community backslide! Play the game thru! America hates a quitter!"

These ringing words were spoken by Dr. Ray Lyman Wilbur, president of Stanford University.

As a nation we have made a great reputation, it now remains to live up to it. Just what is this American spirit that our overseas force of fighters and helpers have carried into Europe? It is a spirit of helpfulness and courage, of sympathy and sacrifice, of energy and of fair play.

We have sent our fighting men to the aid of the wronged and helpless and food and clothing to the starving and destitute. Never before in history have the people of a whole nation denied themselves food that they might feed the hungry of other nations.

I am sure that a great many persons felt a sort of flatness and staleness in life when the war ended. Altho they were glad and deeply thankful, there was an unpleasantness in going back to ordinary things, a letting down from the heights to which they had attained, a silence in place of the bugle call to duty, to which their spirits had become attuned.

But here is a chance to exercise still further those qualities which, in spite of all the horrors, have made of the war a glorious thing by showing how the good still rises triumphant over the bad in the heart of humanity.

The appeal of Dr. Wilbur comes most appropriately at this time for the American spirit as it has been displayed is really the spirit of Christmas or in other words the spirit of Christianity, a practicable example of loving and serving and giving.

It is a wonderful thing for us to have accepted as our own such national ideals, but we cannot hold them as a nation unless we accept them for our own as individuals. So the responsibility rests upon each of us to keep our country true to the course it has taken and up to the high standard it has reached.

1919

A Few Minutes with a Poet

January 5, 1919

Among my books of verse, there is an old poem that I could scarcely do without. It is "The Fool's Prayer" by Edward Rowland Sill and every now and then I have been impelled, in deep humiliation of spirit, to pray the prayer made by that old-time jester of the king.

Even tho one is not in the habit of making New Year's resolutions, to be broken whenever the opportunity arises, still as the old year departs, like Lot's wife, we cannot resist a backward glance. As we see in the retrospect, the things we have done that we ought not and the things we have left undone that we should have done, we have a hope that the coming year will show a better record.

In my glance backward and hope for the future, one thing became plain to me—that I valued the love and appreciation of my friends more than ever before and that I would try to show my love for them; that I would be more careful of their feelings, more tactful and so endear myself to them.

A few days later a friend and I went together to an afternoon gathering where refreshments were served and we came back to my friend's home just as the evening meal was ready. The Man of The Place failed to meet me and so I stayed unexpectedly. My friend made apologies for the simple meal and I said that I preferred plain food to such as we had in the afternoon, which was the same as saying that her meal was plain and that the afternoon refreshments had been finer. I felt that I had said the wrong thing and in a desperate effort to make amends I praised the soup which had been served. Not being satisfied to let well enough alone, because of my embarrassment,

I continued, "It is so easy to have delicious soups, one can make them of just any little things that are left."

And all the way home as I rode quietly beside The Man of The Place I kept praying "The Fool's Prayer,"

> O Lord be merciful to me, a fool.

We can afford to laugh at a little mistake such as that, however embarrassing it may be. To laugh and forget is one of the saving graces, but only a little later I was guilty of another mistake, over which I cannot laugh.

Mrs. G and I were in a group of women at a social affair, but having a little business to talk over, we stepped into another room where we were almost immediately followed by an acquaintance. We greeted her and then went on with our conversation, from which she was excluded. I forgot her presence and when I looked her way again she was gone. We had not been kind and, to make it worse, she was comparatively a stranger among us.

In a few minutes every one was leaving, without my having had a chance to make amends in any way. I could not apologize without giving a point to the rudeness but I thought that I would be especially gracious to her when we met again so she would not feel that we made her an outsider. Now I learn that it will be months before I see her again. I know that she is very sensitive and that I must have hurt her. Again and from the bottom of my heart, I prayed "The Fool's Prayer,"

> These clumsy feet, still in the mire,
> Go crushing blossoms without end;
> These hard, well-meaning hands we thrust
> Among the heart-strings of a friend.
> O Lord, be merciful to me, a fool.

As we grow old enough to have a proper perspective, we see such things work out to their conclusion, or rather to a partial conclusion, for the effects go on and on endlessly. Very few of our misdeeds are with deliberate intent to do wrong. Our hearts are mostly in the right place but we seem to be weak in the head.

> 'Tis not by guilt the onward sweep
> Of truth and right, O Lord, we stay;
> 'Tis by our follies that so long
> We hold the earth from heaven away.

Our faults no tenderness should ask
The chastening stripes must cleanse them all;
But for our blunder—oh, in shame
Before the eyes of heaven we fall.

Without doubt each one of us is fully entitled to pray the whole of "The Fool's Prayer" and more especially the refrain,

O Lord, be merciful to me, a fool.

Let's Revive the Old Amusements

January 20, 1919

The influenza epidemic has been particularly hard on farm folks, coming as it did just at the close of the season's work when country people were beginning to relax from the strain of raising the year's crops.[1] It is at this time we usually meet one another and become acquainted again. There has been so much depending on our work, especially for the last two years, that we have attended to our business even more strictly than usual and we were really lonesome for some good times together. But, being advised by the doctors not to gather in crowds, we have stayed at home as much as possible. Let's hope it hasn't become a habit!

Sometimes I wonder if telephones and motor cars are altogether blessings for country people. When my neighbor can call me up for a short visit over the phone, she is not so likely to make the necessary effort to come and spend the afternoon, and I get hungry for the sight of her face as well as the sound of her voice. When she gets into her motor car, it is almost sure to run for 12 or 15 miles before she can stop it and that takes her away down the road past me. I have no hope that my rather prosy conversation can rival the joy of a ride in the car, and we see less and less of each other.

I am not really prejudiced against the motor car and the telephone. It is the way they are used to which I am objecting. Now when my neighbor calls me up to say she is coming over, I think very highly of the telephone as an adjunct to country life, for it gives me time to dust the mantle shelf, jump into a clean dress and shut the bedroom door. Then I can meet her serene-

1. A flu epidemic swept over war-weakened Europe and North America following World War I. Millions died in this catastrophe that may have killed more people than the war itself.

ly as tho things were always that way. But I don't like to visit over the 'phone. I'd much rather be sitting in the same room with my neighbor, so I can see how her new dress is made and if she has another gray hair.

There is one social affair, which used to belong to country life, that I would like to see come back again. That is the old-fashioned Friday night literary at the school house. You older people who used to attend them, did you ever enjoy yourselves better anywhere?

At early candle light, parents and pupils from all over the district, gathered at the schoolhouse, bringing lanterns and candles and sometimes a glass lamp to give an added touch of dignity to the teacher's desk. The lighting was good enough for eyes were stronger in the days before brilliant lights were so common. Do you remember how the school children spoke their pieces and dialogs? It gave one a touch of distinction to speak a part in a dialog.

Then came the debate. Sometimes the older pupils of the school, sometimes a few of the pupils and some of the grownups and again just the grownups took part in the debate, and the questions debated were certainly threshed out to a conclusion. I have been thinking lately what a forum for discussing the questions of the day, political and others, the old-fashioned debate would be. I think that farmers do not discuss these things enough, among themselves, these days. They are more likely to talk them over with their banker or their merchant when they go to town, and their minds on the questions of the day, take their color from town opinion.

We farmers are very slow to realize that we are a class by ourselves. The bankers are organized, even internationally, as a class; merchants, both wholesale and retail, are organized and working in a body for the interests of merchants; labor, except that of the farmer, his wife and children, is very much organized and yet many farmers are still contending, single handed, as individuals against these huge organizations. We are so slow to organize and to work together for our mutual interests. The old-fashioned debates at the country school house would be a place and time where farmers could discuss these things among themselves.

An understanding, among farmers, of themselves and how their interests are affected by the questions of the hour, is seriously needed. We cannot take our opinions from our fathers nor even keep the opinions we formed for ourselves a few years ago. Times and things move too fast. We must learn to look at things, even politics, from a farmer's standpoint. The price of hogs is more important to us than whether one political party wins an election simply as a political party. I would like to hear such timely questions discussed in an old-time debate and I really think that a training in public speaking and an understanding of public questions would be worth more to pupils of the schools than games of basketball, by exercising their brains so that they might grow into intelligent, wide-awake citizens.

Well, the debate is finished and it is time for the spelling-down match. How earnestly we used to line up for the struggle and valiantly contest for the honor of remaining longest on the floor and how we used to laugh when some small school child spelled down an outsider, who had forgotten the lessons in the old spelling book.

Mrs. Jones Takes the Rest Cure

February 5, 1919

The telephone rang sharply in Mrs. Jones's dining room, early one summer morning, and Billy answered it for his mother was busy.

"This is Uncle John," said the voice on the 'phone. "We are thinking of coming out to your place for a week; it's so awfully hot in town and the children wish to play around in the country. Tell your mother!"

"Wait a minute," said careful Billy and, hanging the receiver on the hook, he turned to his mother who was clearing the breakfast table and repeated the message.

Mrs. Jones was tired that morning. It was hot in the country, too, especially over the cook stove, and there was so much work ahead that she could not see her way thru it.

She threw up her hands with a gesture of dismay. "Oh! I'm just sick!" she exclaimed.

Billy turned slowly to the telephone, but there was a twinkle in his eye. Tho slow of movement, he was not slow mentally and he was his mother's right-hand man.

"Hullo," he said and then, "I'm afraid it won't do. Mother's ill," and hung up the receiver.

Mrs. Jones gasped. "Oh Billy!" she said, and then she thought, "Well, why not?" If John and his wife and the two boys came to be fed and waited on she would get none of the week's work done and would be exhausted when the end of the week came. If she were ill (?) the work planned for the week would not be done, either, but at the end of the week she might be rested.

"Well, Billy," she said, "mother is sick. She is sick to death of this endless work, and if you will clear away the breakfast things, I believe I'll go lie down."

This was the way Mrs. Jones came to take the rest cure for a week, lend-ing the children a helping hand only now and then when they got into serious difficulty and consoling herself for her desertion of them by planning a vacation for them later.

Everyone seems to be so overburdened these days, let's be considerate about our visiting.

I had company myself one day last summer. Mr. and Mrs. P and their three children drove up in their car at just 11 o'clock one morning. I welcomed them as prettily as I knew how, made them comfortable in the cool living room and said: "If you will please excuse me now, I shall get us all some dinner."

"Oh! We can't stay for dinner," said Mrs. P; "we shall stay only a few minutes." After that I could not leave them to get dinner for the Man of The Place and his hired help, so I sat with them, trying to be entertaining, tho wondering frantically how I could hasten the dinner when I was free to get it.

They stayed on and on. At half past 11, I again urged them to stay and tried to excuse myself from the room. They only refused again, saying they must go. But they didn't. At a quarter to 12 I felt some way that if I should ask them again they would stay to dinner and let me get it, but I had become angry and resolved that if they should stay all day I would not again ask them to eat with us. They left at a few minutes past 12, just as the men appeared in the barn door coming to dinner.

We do enjoy company, all of us, but we are all tired. We have been working unusually hard for two years and have been under a nervous strain besides.[2] We have each adjusted our burden so that we are more or less able to carry it, but a little addition to it makes it, in some cases, unbearable. It was the last feather in the camel's load that broke his back, you know.

Company we must have! Visiting should be more frequent that we may exchange ideas and learn to know and love one another, and there are ways that this may be made easy for us all instead of burdening one another by being inconsiderate.

One of the pleasantest times I remember last summer was a surprise visit from a family of five persons. In the middle of the morning a team drove up and the five were unloaded at my door.

"Daddy was coming on business," cried one of the grown daughters "and we desired to visit with you so we just came along."

"Don't be scared," said the soft-voiced mother. "We took you by surprise so we brought a picnic dinner and we won't let you even build a fire. Just bring out what you have cooked and let's all picnic together."

2. The strain of the World War.

They proposed eating out under the trees, but we decided it would be pleasanter to spread the dinner on the long table on the screened north porch. How simple and easy, with nobody overworked or tired, and we did have such a good visit.

Work Makes Life Interesting

February 20, 1919

There is good in everything, we are told, if we will only look for it, and I have at last found the good in a hard spell of illness. It is the same good the Irishman found in whipping himself.

"Why in the world are you doing that?" exclaimed the unexpected and astonished spectator.

"Because it feels so good when I stop," replied the Irishman with a grin. And this thing of being ill certainly does feel good when it stops. Why, even work looks good to a person who has been thru such an enforced idleness, at least when strength is returning. Tho I'll confess if work crowds on me too soon, I am like the friend who was recovering from influenza rather more slowly than is usually the case.

"I eat all right and sleep all right," said he. "I even feel all right, but just the sight of a piece of work makes me tremble."

"That," said I, "is a terrible affliction, but I have known persons who suffer from it who never had the influenza."

But I'm sure we will all acknowledge that there is an advantage in having been ill, if it makes us eager for work once more. Sometimes I fancy we do not always appreciate the value of work and how dry and flavorless life would be without it.

If work were taken from us, we would lose rest also, for how could we rest unless we first became tired from working? Leisure would mean nothing to us for it would not be a prize to be won by effort and so would be valueless. Even play would lose its attraction for, if we played all the time, play would become tiresome; it would be nothing but work after all. In that case we would be at work again and perhaps a piece of actual work would become play to us. How topsy-turvy! But there is no cause for alarm. None of us is liable to be denied the pleasure of working and that it is good for us no one will deny. Man realized it soon after he was sentenced to "earn his bread by the sweat of his brow," and with his usual generosity he lost no time in letting his womenkind in on a good thing.

This being the case, it is particularly pleasing to read, in the advice sent out from Washington, that it would be wise the coming season not to raise any more garden stuff than will be necessary for the family use.

Does this mean that farm women are to be let down easily from their tiptoe position of reaching out for work and still more work to keep the world rolling? It would seem a sensible thing to come about in view of the fact that according to United Press stories there is a concerted action on the part of members of the New York produce exchange to do all in their power to depress the produce and provision and grain markets regardless of the cost of production.

Still more significant is the fact stated in a recent editorial of the Kansas City Drover's Telegram that the "members of the New York produce exchange have evidently lined up the leaders of organized labor at Chicago and New York to assail the prices of farm products."

It would be the height of irony if the big companies who stand between the producer and consumer robbing both of them, should be able to line them up against each other, the laborer against the farmer; the farmer against the laborer and steal away unnoticed with their ill-gotten gains, leaving them fighting.

Friendship Must Be Wooed

March 5, 1919

Sometimes we are a great trial to our friends and put an entirely uncalled for strain upon our friendships by asking foolish questions.

The Man of the Place and I discovered, the other day, that we had for sometime been saying to our friends, "Why don't you come over?" Can you think of a more awkward question than that? Just imagine the result if that question should always be answered truthfully. Some would reply, "Because I do not care to visit you." Others might say, "Because it is too much trouble," while still others who might care to come, would be swamped in trying to enumerate the many little reasons why they had not done so. We decided that we would break ourselves of such a bad habit.

I once had a neighbor who, whenever we met, invariably asked me why I had not been to visit her. Even when I did go she met me with the query, "Why haven't you been over before?" It was not a very pleasant greeting, and naturally one shuns unpleasantness when one may.

I have another neighbor who will call me on the phone and say: "It has been a long time since we have seen you and we do want a good visit. Can't you come over tomorrow?" And immediately I wish to go. It does make such a difference how things are said.

Friendship is like love. It cannot be demanded or driven or insisted upon. It must be wooed to be won. The habit of saying disagreeable things or of being careless about how what we say affects others grows on us so easily and so surely if we indulge.

"Mrs. Brown gave me an unhappy half hour a few days ago," said Mrs. Gray to me. "She said a great many unpleasant things and was generally disagreeable, but it is all right. The poor old thing is getting childish and we must overlook her oddities."

Mrs. Gray is a comparatively new comer in the neighborhood, but I have known Mrs. Brown for years and ever since I have known her, she has prided herself on her plain speaking, showing very little regard for others' feelings. Her unkindness appears to me not a reversion to the mentality of childhood, but simply an advance in the way she was going years ago. Her tongue has only become sharper with use and her dexterity in hurting the feelings of others grown with practice.

I know another woman of the same age whom no one speaks of as being childish. It is not necessary to make such an excuse for her, because she is still, as she has been for 20 years, helpful and sweet and kind. And this helpfulness and sweetness and kindness of hers has grown with the passing years. I think no one will ever say of her, "poor old thing, she is childish," as an excuse for her being disagreeable. I know she would hope to die before that time should come.

People do grow childish in extreme old age, of course, and should be treated with tenderness because of it, but I believe that even then the character which they have built during the years before will manifest itself. There is a great difference in children, you know, and I have come to the conclusion that if we live to reach a second childhood we shall not be bad-tempered, disagreeable children unless we have indulged those traits before.

Then there are the people who are "peculiar." Ever meet any of them?

The word seems to be less used than formerly, but there was a time when it was very common and I longed to shriek every time I heard it.

"Oh! You must not do that, George will be angry. He is so peculiar!"

"Of course, she doesn't belong with the rest of the crowd, but I had to invite her. She is so peculiar, you know, and so easily offended."

"I wouldn't pay any attention to that. Of course, she did treat you abominably but it is just her way. She is so peculiar."

And so on and on. I thought seriously of cultivating a reputation for being peculiar, for like charity such a reputation seemed to cover multitudes of sins, but I decided that it would be even more unpleasant for me than for the other fellow; that it would not pay to make myself an unlovely character for the sake of any little, mean advantage to be gained by it.

Keep the Saving Habit

March 20, 1919

"We may have all the sugar we want now," said an acquaintance the other day as he picked up the sugar bowl and emptied the last of its contents of about 4 or 5 spoons of sugar into his coffee cup.

"We may have all the sugar we wish now—if we have the money to pay for it," remarked a friend to me as we sat at table together, a few days later. And he helped himself to 1 spoon of sugar for his coffee.

It is interesting to notice the difference in the way people are reacting from the strain and struggle of the war. Some evidently feel that since the war is over all restraints are removed and are going back to their old, reckless ways of spending and waste. Others have thoroly learned the lesson of carefulness and economy. "When I make over an old hat or dress and save buying new, I save something when prices are as high as they are now," I overheard one woman say to another and I thought she was entirely right.

It is surely worth one's time to be careful of clothing now and to take the time to repair and make over. If we will think of how much we accomplished by being careful with food, we cannot help but realize that it pays to eliminate waste in that direction. There has been so much loss and suffering and cost in the war that we should carefully salvage from its wreck all the good that is in any way possible to bring out of it.

What we have learned of economy and frugality; of substituting for too rich dishes those which are plainer, really more palatable and much healthier; of a more simple tho equally as beautiful way of dressing, should be of great value to us personally and nationally unless we foolishly make haste to forget these lessons of the hard years just passed.

From a careful reading of the news from all over the world, it appears to me that the economy and thrift of the people of the nations will be of as much importance during the next few years as it has been during the actual warfare and may well determine in the end who are the actual victors in the conflict.

I notice that there is a systematic effort being made to buy up the bonds of small denominations from the small bond holders and I am very sorry to learn that some are selling. I wish all might be like one farm woman of my acquaintance, who with her egg money has invested $350 in Liberty Bonds and who says she has formed the habit of buying bonds and will begin buying farm loan bonds as soon as there are no more Liberty Bonds for sale.

Never before have government bonds of small denominations been placed within easy reach of the people of the United States. It has given us all a chance to own a financial interest in our government and to pay interest to ourselves instead of to the other fellow, a way of evening things by making one hand wash the other, so to speak.

Some of us have been rather inclined, at times, to envy the government pensioners and to wish that we might be assured of a pension for our old age. Now here at last is our chance to earn our old age pension from the government by practicing economy now and remembering that government bonds, either Liberty Bonds at 4¼ per cent or farm loan bonds at 4½ per cent, are good, safe investments and worth making an effort to buy and to keep.

I am not urging that we become penurious or deny ourselves or family the things we should have for our comfort and pleasure but simply that we never again fall into the way of thinking that we must buy anything because our neighbor has it or enter into the old strife for show. The reputation of a careless spender is nothing to be desired. For myself, I would prefer a government bond in a safety deposit.

Who'll Do the Women's Work?

April 5, 1919

Flaring headlines in the papers, have announced that "women will fight to hold jobs," meaning the men's jobs which they took when the men went to war. What to do about the situation seems to be a very important question. One would think that there must have been a great number of women who were idle before the war. If not, one wonders what has become of the jobs they had. To paraphrase a more or less popular song—I wonder who's holding them now?

With men by the thousands out of work and the unemployment situation growing so acute as to cause grave fears of attempted revolution, women by hundreds are further complicating affairs by adding their numbers to the ranks of labor, employed, unemployed or striking as the case may be.

We heard nothing of numbers of women who could not find work, before the war. They were all busy, apparently and fairly well satisfied. Who is doing the work they left, to fill the places of men who went into the army, or is that work undone?

It would be interesting to know and it seems strange that while statistics are being prepared and investigations made of every subject under the sun, no one has compiled the records of "The Jobs Women Left or Woman's Work Undone."

But however curious we may be about the past, we are more vitally interested in the future. Will these women take up their old work and give the men a chance to go back to the places they will thus leave vacant? The women say not.

Other women, also, besides those who took men's jobs, have gone out of the places they filled in pre-war days, out into community and social work and government positions which were created by and because of the war. Will these women go back? And again we hear them answer, "Never! We never will go back!" All this is very well, but where are they going and with them all of us? I think this query could most truthfully be answered by a slang expression, which tho perhaps not polished is very apt—"We don't know where we're going but we're on our way."

It makes our hearts thrill and our heads rise proudly to think that women were found capable and eager to do such important work in the crisis of wartime days. I think that never again will anyone have the courage to say that women could not run world affairs if necessary. Also, it is true that when men or women have advanced they do not go back. History does not retrace its steps.

But this too is certain. We must advance logically, in order and all together if the ground gained is to be held. If what has hitherto been woman's work, in the world, is simply left undone by them, there is no one else to take it up. If in their haste to do other, perhaps more showy things, their old and special work is neglected and only half done, there will be something seriously wrong with the world, for the commonplace, home work of women is the very foundation upon which everything else rests.

So if we wish to go more into world affairs, to have the time to work at public work, we must arrange our old duties in some way so that it will be possible. We cannot leave things at loose ends, no good housemother can do that, and we have been good housekeepers so long that we have the habit of finishing our work up neatly.

Women in towns and villages have an advantage over farm women in being able to co-operate more easily. There is talk now of community kitchens for them, from which hot meals may be sent out to the homes. They have of course the laundries and the bake shops already.

We farm women, at least farm mothers, have stayed on the job, our own job, during all the excitement. We could not be spared from it as we realized, so there is no question of our going back or not going back. We are still doing business at the old place, in kitchen and garden and poultry yard and no one seems to be trying to take our job from us.

But we do not wish to be left too far behind our sisters in towns and cities. We are interested in social and world betterment; in religion and politics; we might even be glad to do some work as a side line that would give us a change from the old routine. We would like to keep up, if any one can keep up with these whirling times and we must have more leisure from the treadmill if we are to do any of these things. We must arrange our work differently in some way. Why not a laundry for a farm neighborhood and a bakery also, so situated that they will be easily accessible to a group of farms? Perhaps if we study conditions of labor and the forward movements of the world as related to the farm, we may find some way of applying the best of them to our own use.

Women's Duty at the Polls

April 20, 1919

Now that women in Missouri have been given the right to vote for President of the United States and the prospect is good that they will be granted full franchise in the state, it will be interesting to observe how they will respond to the new duty laid upon them.

That it is a duty for every self-respecting woman to discharge faithfully there can be no question; and as these women are not in the habit of failing in their duties, there is no danger that they will do so now if they understand the situation.

We must get rid of the habit of classing all women together politically and thinking of the "woman's vote" as one and indivisible. When the question of woman suffrage was last before the voters of the state, one ardent advocate of the measure who was also a strong prohibitionist made the remark, "When women have the ballot we'll do away with this whisky business."

But when women secured the ballot in California, the state rejected the prohibition amendment and just lately, with the women voting, Chicago went wet, "wringing wet" as one editor says.

This simply shows what we have all really known, that there are all kinds of women as well as of men and that woman's vote will no more bring purity into politics and can no more be counted on as a unit than can man's vote.

It is easy to forecast the effect of woman suffrage on politics if the home-loving, home-keeping women should refuse to use their voting privilege, for the rougher class of women will have no hesitancy in going to the polling places and casting their ballots. There must be votes enough from other women to offset these in order to keep the balance as it has been.

Then too, there is legislation which is needed to protect farming interests. Shall farm women fail to use the power given them by the ballot, to help secure this legislation?

And so, as I said before, instead of being a privilege to be taken advantage of or neglected according to individual fancy, voting has now become, for the better class of women, a duty to be bravely and conscientiously done, even tho it may be rather distasteful. It is "up to them" to see to it that the power of their ballot is behind their influence for good clean government; for an honest administration of public affairs; for justice for all and special privileges for none. In short, as they have stood behind their soldiers, at home and abroad who were fighting for freedom and democracy, now to stand shoulder to shoulder with them and keep up the fight.

I fear that we are not quite ready to use the ballot intelligently. Tho there has been warning enough that the responsibility was coming to rest upon us, we have been careless about informing ourselves of the conditions which the people of the United States must handle and the questions they must answer.

In this reconstruction period, the most serious time which our nation and the world has ever been called upon to face, we come into the responsibility of helping to decide the fate of the world for perhaps hundreds of years, without being prepared.

Women can no longer hide behind their husbands and fathers and brothers by saying, "I don't pay any attention to politics. That is the men's business," nor can they safely vote as their men folks do without any other reason for so doing. We women know in our hearts, tho we would not admit it, that our men are not infallible. They do sometimes make mistakes and have the wrong ideas. Frankly now, is it not true? This being the case, now that the responsibility is ours, we shall be obliged to think things out for ourselves if we are honest and fair to them and ourselves.

If we expect to be fit companions of the men who did their duty so bravely, fighting and working to save our country, we must do our part in upholding our ideals in time of peace. In plain words, as the other women will vote, we must do so in order to keep things properly balanced and tho we may be unprepared at present, there is no reason why we should not be able to vote intelligently by the time we are called upon to exercise the privilege.

The Farm Home (1)

May 5, 1919

Among all the beautiful sights and sounds of spring, there is an ugly blot on the landscape here and there, a sight that is unpleasantly out of harmony and shows as little promise for the future as a blighted fruit tree. It is the presence of children at work in the fields when they should be in school.

There is a compulsory school law but I have been informed that it does not apply to children engaged in agricultural work. It is a sufficient excuse for absence from school if the parent says the children are needed to help in the farm work.

And farm children are needed at home, because every bit of help it is possible to get is usually not quite enough. But it does seem unfair to country children that they should be discriminated against; that they should have no protection from the law such as town children have. Food is needed to feed the world but that is not a good enough reason why part of the children should be allowed to work to produce it while other children are protected in their right to an education.

Tho, in a way a concession to the independence of farming, leaving them at liberty to give their children the advantages of the schools or not as they may see fit, immunity from the compulsory school law will react to the disadvantage of all farmers by making them as a class below the level of those who follow other occupations, for farmers are like other people. There are some who put the interests of their children above other things and there are others who because Johnny can save them a good deal of time and many steps, will keep him at home that he may do so even tho it will put him at a disadvantage the remainder of his life.

All the instruction in the farm papers, the wealth of knowledge, of new ideas and methods, of mutual help and the getting together spirit that all good farm papers are working to spread, does not reach the farmers who cannot read an article in a paper and understand it.

Besides the loss of all this they are at the mercy of any unfounded report that may be circulated. As for instance, in regard to the League of Nations which is now so much discussed, there is a report circulating in the back places to the effect that if the United States enters the League we shall become subject to a foreign king. And it is believed literally by farmers who cannot read understandingly. Still they would not be classed as illiterate and there are no statistics from which we may learn how many such there are.

But below them is the ignorant mass of the rural population who have not attended school for even the two years necessary to pass the literacy test and who are classed as illiterate by the Federal Bureau of Education which has compiled the statistics from the facts gathered. These illiterate persons amount to 10 per cent of the rural population.

Of the 37 million country people, 2,700,000 cannot read a farm paper nor an agricultural bulletin and must learn the news as well as trade market conditions from some rumor, perhaps deliberately untrue, perhaps only a mistake thru much passing from one to another.

"We shall have to spend great sums of money in improving our school systems! We shall have to undertake a nation-wide propaganda for the betterment of school buildings, for the replacement of unsanitary shacks with modern structures, for the adequate compensation of competent teachers," says one editor writing on this subject. But of what use will all this be to the farmer boy who in school-time is driving old Bill and Kate with the heavy lines around his shoulders while with his hands he guides the plow, making the long furrows around and around the field which later he will help to plant to corn?

Will it mean that he must begin his work earlier in the morning and keep at it later in the evening to help his father earn the added taxes to pay for these improvements that more fortunate children may have the advantage of them?

"Pap needed me to help him," said one such boy now a grown man. "Pap needed me to help him. I know, and it's all right, but it's no use for me to take a farm paper for I can't read it so I can understand it."

The Farm Home (2)

May 20, 1919

"No article or commodity shall be shipped or delivered in international trade in the production of which children less than 16 years old have been employed or permitted to work."

How would farmers like to have that kind of a law? Why! They couldn't even drive up the cows, and what would become of the pig and poultry clubs!

When the American Federation of Labor formulated its platform of principles, and made this Article X the writers surely did not intend to prohibit child labor on the farm, for they must know that it would increase greatly the cost of produce if high priced help must be hired to do the children's chores; and the high cost of living is already one of the chief grievances.

The explanation seems to be that, as a class, farmers make so little impression that they are overlooked.

Perhaps Article X might be a good law for city children, tho I doubt it. It does seem it would be much better for children to be employed under careful regulation than to be idle on the streets when they are not in school. We know it is better for farm children to help with the work they are able to do, giving them a greater interest in the farm, teaching them to be responsible, independent and energetic. If such a law became a fact it would be an injury to farm children to obey, and we should not wish to teach them to become law breakers by disregarding it.

But the fact remains that the American Federation of Labor, which is a great power in politics and national affairs, in what it considers one of its most important principles, and which it is attempting to make a law, was either so ignorant of farm affairs that its writer knew no better or absolutely ignored the farmers of the country.

It only goes to show how seldom farmers are considered by some of the powers now planning to reconstruct the United States.

- - - - - -

Things are considerably stirred up these days as we all know, and when they settle it may be along new lines. No political party nor any industrial group is going to look after the interests and welfare of farmers.

While we are slow to consider affairs from the standpoint of farmers as a class other classes have drawn closely together, into their own groups.

Far back in history, in the days when Italy was a group of small principalities and of cities ruled as independent governments; when Great Britain had not been formed, and England was just England struggling to maintain its existence as an independent country, in those old days there were labor unions. They were called guilds then. There was the weavers' guild, the dyers' guild, the builders' guild, and many others. Then there were the traders and merchants who worked for their trade interests, and the soldiers with which the overlord controlled his little principality, collecting taxes from the guilds and the merchants and peasants.

Then, as now, the peasants or farmers stood alone. While the different guilds quarreled and even fought one another they all united to oppose unjust taxation or oppression. The merchants and traders had organizations, and worked together for their own ends but the peasantry stood or fell as individuals without any organized power which they could bring to bear on rulers or guilds or traders.

There were peasant revolts sometimes but it was simply mob action. There was no organized constructive effort to win their objects.

It remains to be proved how far farmers, as a class, have advanced since the time of those peasants. We are so busy and so careless that politicians working for self interest and industrial groups who have high salaried officers who spend their time working for the interests of their people can take advantage of our ignorance.

There is occasion for all of us to be thoughtful; and we ought to do our thinking before it is too late.

The Farm Home (3)

June 5, 1919

After reading the staggering total of the indemnity demanded by the Allies from Germany and adding to that sum the amount of the country's internal war indebtedness, it is very plain to anyone that Germany is bankrupt, that it will take many, many years to pay these debts and make the credit of the country good once more.

But there is an even worse thing which has come upon Germany—the nation is morally bankrupt, also. No one has attempted to put a money value upon this failure, knowing that the honor of a nation, as of an individual, is beyond price, but it is sure that Germany will keep paying on this debt, which it owes the world, for many years, also probably for generations.

The first installment of this debt is being collected now and that it is hard for the nation to make the payment is shown by an interview with Germany's foreign minister, Brockdorff-Rantzan, in which he says, "The peace terms are simply unbelievable, because they ask the impossible. The entente[3] demands material guarantees and will not accept moral guarantees. This shows its distrust of us. We desire an organized world in which Germany will have the same rights as other people."

Germany is finding that as a nation which has for four years deliberately broken its pledged word, that word is of no value; that it is bankrupt in moral guarantees.

The entente is in the position, with Germany, of the hill man who fought another man for telling an untruth about him. He had knocked his enemy down and was still beating him tho he was crying "enough" when a stranger came along and interfered.

3. Britain, France, and Russia as allied against Germany during World War I.

"Stop! Stop!" he exclaimed. "Don't you hear him hollering enough?"

"Oh, yes!" replied the hill man, "but he is such a liar I don't know whether he is telling the truth or not."

When I was a girl at home, my father came in from the harvest field one day at noon and with great glee told what had befallen my cousin Charley. Father and Uncle Henry were harvesting a field of wheat in the old fashioned way, cutting it by hand with cradles and Charley, who was about 10 years old, followed them around the field for play. He lagged behind until the men where ahead of him and then began to scream, jumping up and down and throwing his arms around. Father and Uncle Henry dropped their cradles and ran to him thinking a snake had bitten him or that something in the woods close by was frightening him, but when they came to Charley he stopped screaming and laughed at them.

Charley fooled them this way three times, but they grew tired and warm and had been deceived so many times that when for the fourth time he began to scream they looked back at him as he jumped up and down, then turned away and went on with their work.

But Charley kept on screaming, and there seemed to be a new note in his voice, so finally they walked back to where he was and found that he was in a yellow-jackets' nest and the more he jumped and threw and screamed the more came to sting him.

"I'd like to have the training of that young man for a little while," said father, "but I don't believe I could have thought of a better way to punish him for his meanness."

Boys or men or nations it seems to be the same, if they prove themselves liars times enough, nobody will believe them when they do tell the truth.

"Getting down to first causes, what makes one nation choose the high way and another nation choose the low way? What produces character and conscience in a nation, anyhow? What produces the other thing?" asks a writer in an article in the Saturday Evening Post. And the question is left unanswered.

In a country ruled as Germany has been there is no doubt the character of the nation received the impress of the rulers, coming from them down to the people. In a country such as ours, the national character is also like that of the rulers, but in this case the rulers are the people and it is they who impress themselves upon it. The character of each individual one of us affects our national character for good or bad.

"Getting down to first causes," what forms the character of individuals?

Training! School training; home training; mother's training! And there you are back to the first causes in the making of an honorable, truthful, upright individual, the kind who becomes a good citizen, the kind of citizens who collectively make an honorable, treaty-keeping nation, a nation that chooses the high way instead of the low.

The Farm Home (4)

June 20, 1919

On the southern coast of Alaska is the greatest natural-wonder of the world, only recently discovered and not yet fully explored: a region where icebergs float in hot water, while hot streams flow out from underneath banks of snow; where large glaciers of solid ice lie next to steaming fissures and the camper may have cold storage in a cave of ice at the back of his tent and cook his food over a steaming hot hole in the ground at the front of it; where a careless step may plunge one thru the earth's crust into molten masses beneath and where the solid rock spouts steam.

The Valley Of Ten Thousand Smokes was formed by a volcanic eruption of Katmai mountain in 1912. The whole top of the mountain was blown off in this explosion and the dust and ashes and gases thrown into the upper atmosphere, by the terrific forces loosed, affected the weather conditions of the whole world.

The Valley Of Ten Thousand Smokes acts as a safety valve for the whole volcanic region surrounding Mt. Katmai. The valley was discovered and named by an exploring party in charge of Professor Griggs, sent out by the National Geographic Society in 1916. The next year it was partly explored and it is hoped to complete this great scientific research work during the present year.

One thousand seven hundred square miles of this Alaska wonderland has just recently been set aside, by President Wilson, as the Katmai National Monument, to be a national park for all the people for all time.

When transportation to this region has been made easier it will be the great natural wonder playground of America, in time taking the place of the Yellowstone, where the geyser fields are dying, while that of the Valley Of Ten Thousand Smokes is only in process of development.

To quote from President Wilson's proclamation—"The results of this eruption are still fresh offering excellent opportunities for studying the causes of the catastrophe and its results and affording a conspicuous object lesson to visitors interested in the operation of the great forces which have made and are still making America."

Here the workings of nature in making land habitable for man may be studied at first hand to better advantage than anywhere else on the earth. Nothing like it has ever before been seen by human beings. Only the geologist finds records of such in the rocks of prehistoric ages when the world was new and in process of formation.

From the summit of Katmai Pass the Valley Of Ten Thousand Smokes lies below the observer and all the volcanoes of the world set down close together side by side would be less of a spectacle than is spread before him. One of its discoverers says they named the valley too hastily; that there are at least a million smokes.

The valley is so hot that all water is instantly evaporated and for this reason there are no hot springs or geysers. Instead, hot smoke and steam and gases rise from the millions of vents in clouds and columns. The smoke from one vent registered 432 degrees of heat and melted zinc easily. The gases are smelled 20 miles from the valley.

It is not known whether the vents are chimneys thru which escape the gases, steam and vapors from a vast molten mass which has risen from the depths of the earth and nearly burst thru the crust in a body, or whether they are caused from the evaporation of surface water by the heated products of the volcanic eruption. A watch is being kept to learn which is true.

Across the head of the valley stands Mt. Magirk, its three peaks smoking away continuously into the clouds above. There are three glaciers on its sides reaching down to the level of the valley where they stop abruptly as tho their lower edges were melted away by the heat.

Near the foot of these glaciers is a fissure from 200 to 400 feet wide with one of its perpendicular walls 35 feet higher than the other. The depth of the fissure cannot be learned for it is filled with a beautiful lake the water of which is a clear green. Along its sides are many snowdrifts which feed the lake but altho filled by the water from melting snow, the water of the lake is warm.

Another wonder of the valley is called Falling Mountain. From the sides of this mountain hundreds of tons of rock shoot off daily. During the three years that it has been under observation there has not been more than 5 minutes at a time during which its slopes were quiet. Steam is continually rising from this mountain and even spouts out of the solid rocks after they have been dropped into the valley below. The cause of these falling rocks is not known but it is hoped that it will be discovered by the expedition of this year.

Novarupta is a small volcano opposite Falling Mountain. The force of the volcano seems not to have been sufficient to have cleared the crater and the lava has cooled in the throat of it in the form of a plug 12 feet in diameter and rising 250 feet above the floor of the crater. There is molten lava beneath.

The floor of the valley is a maze of vents thru which it is difficult for the explorers to pick their way. The smoke comes roaring out of these vents around them as they work and rises in columns 2 miles high when the winds are still.

Gases incrust the mud of the valley with deposits in all colors of the rainbow. Prevailing hues are caused by the gray and green and yellow alums which are in crystal formation like mosses growing on the ground. Large spots of ground are burned to a bright red and all shades of the color, caused by varying intensity of heat, which are very beautiful. These vary from orange and brick red to bright cherry reds, purples and down to black with here and there streaks of blue. Around some of the large vents the ground is a dull pink with spots of brilliant orange and yellow. In some places the deposits are of a white chalky nature. These white vents are lightly tinted with yellow and pink, a very delicate coloring. In other spots the blue mud is covered by a rich chestnut brown crust. Crystals of pure sulfur can be gathered by the bushel.

So far, no one ever has entered this valley and viewed its wonders except the members of the exploring parties sent out by the National Geographic Society but as it is more accessible than was Yellowstone Park at the time it was reserved as a national park, the time will soon come when the Valley Of Ten Thousand Smokes will be on the tourist routes and for generations travelers will be astounded by its wonders.

The Farm Home (5)

July 5, 1919

Ships, ships, I will descry you
Amidst the main,
I will come and try you
What you are protecting,
And projecting,
What's your end and aim?
One goes abroad for merchandise and trading
Another stays to keep his country from invading,
A third is coming home with rich and wealthy lading.
Hallo! My fancie, whither wilt you go?[4]

4. From the poem "The Voyage" by Washington Irving.

There would seem to be distinction enough between fact and fancy to prevent any confusing of the two, but we often do mistake the one for the other, especially in our memories.

Scientists are convinced from a study of facts that wherever there is life there is possible memory.

When we speak carelessly of remembering we may not realize all that is comprised in the simple word.

Memory is composed of impressions made upon the senses, the movements of the muscles and structures of the body. If these muscles and body structures are alive and healthy the memory of events, objects and situations will be correct. If the individual is not perfectly healthy the memory may be inaccurate, false or exaggerated.

As few persons are absolutely healthy we can understand how unreliable our memories may be.

The elements of memory are impressiveness, retention, recollection and recall, and a very good memory depends generally upon perfect and complete health for the powers of attention and retention and the ability to recall at will.

One of the best tests therefore for one's sanity, youth and health is one's memory and understanding of the most recent and current events.

And so there has been organized, at Mansfield, Justamere Club for the study and discussion of current events. The membership is composed of both town and country women with their attached men folks as social members.

One afternoon of each month the club meets at the home of a member for reading of the papers prepared on topics assigned and a general discussion of them.

Once every two months there is an evening social meeting for both regular and social members.

Justamere Club gave the first study program a few days ago and if there is anyone who has been deceived into thinking that women are not going to take an interest and an active part in affairs he should have heard those papers and the discussion following. Such a visitor might have observed a slight awkwardness in the discussion now and then but he never would deny that serious thought and study had been given to the topics.

Here is the program which is the same for each meeting during the year, each topic being assigned to a different person each month.

Roll Call .... Current event
Secretary's report.
Business.
Paper or talk by president on any subject she may choose.

Present World Political Situation . . . . (Something on)
Present Economic World Condition . . . . (Something on)
United States Politics and Legislation. (recent)
State Politics and Legislation . . . . (recent)
Recent Invention or Discovery, (Scientific, Geographical or Mechanical)
Review of Late Book, with Short Biography of Author
A Late Poem, (recited or read) Something of Interest About Author
Review of a Late Play or Photo-play
Music, (Instrumental or Vocal or Paper on)
Fashions (in anything from Dress to Architecture)
The Coming Person (Man or Woman)
The Next Thing Needed

Each paper is followed by a discussion, the paper and discussion being limited to 10 minutes.

A unique feature is the rule in regard to refreshments. The hostess of the day is excused from the program and as her contribution to the study of current events must serve for refreshments one course consisting of her first trial of a new recipe with such accessories as belong with it. Members must eat their portions of this latest dish, regardless of how it has turned out, making all comments to the hostess.

The Farm Home (6)

July 20, 1919

Rummaging thru a closet in the attic a few days ago, I unearthed some fashion magazines of the summer of 1908 and was astonished to discover that since that short time ago women have apparently changed the form of their bodies and the shape of their faces as well as the style of their gowns and hair dressing.

Perhaps the pensive lines and die-away expression of the faces, in the old-fashioned plates, were due to the tightly drawn-in waists and the over-draw-check effect of the choker collars, or it may be that faces with such an expression just naturally called for that style of dressing.

However that may be, a comparison of those fashions with the easy, comfortable styles of this summer, which give beauty and grace of line with freedom of movement and plenty of breathing room, is enough cause for celebrating a special Thanksgiving day months ahead of the regular time.

There is still room for improvement in children's clothes. They are much too fussy to be either beautiful or becoming. Why trouble with fancy, changeable, children's styles? There will be plenty of time for them to learn all the vanities of dress later and it is better to keep them simple and sweet as long as possible. It would do away with a lot of needless bother and vexation if we copied the English in their way of dressing little girls as their mothers were dressed, in the same kind of a simple little smock frock.

Fashions in other things than clothes have been and are still being simplified, for the sake of a more economic production, thus lessening the cost of manufacturing by saving time, labor and material.

Furniture makers cut down the number of their patterns several hundred per cent during the war, cutting out just that many varieties of furniture. This was done by the advice of the War Industries Board to reduce the cost of production and save materials and labor for other work. It was found to be such a benefit that it has been decided to keep on in the same way and so we shall have fewer styles in furniture.

In the hardware trade the same plan is being used. There are something like 4450 fewer styles of pocket knives for Johnnie to buy and lose than there were before the war, but it does seem that he should be able to please himself by a choice from the 250 kinds left him.

There used to be 207 kinds of lawn mowers. Now there are only six. This number does not include the regular mowing machine which the Man Of The Place uses so effectively in the front yard nor the pet colt who mows the lawn and puts the clippings to such good use.

The idea of doing away with useless, unnecessary things is at work in architecture also, in the planning and building of houses so that we are hearing a great deal these days of the dining roomless house.

The dining room, if kept strictly as a dining room, is used for only a few minutes three times a day which is not enough return for the work and thought and expense of keeping up an extra room. The fact is that most dining rooms are used by the family as a living room as well and so in the new plans the rooms are frankly combined into one. Sometimes where the kitchen is large it is the kitchen and dining room and many steps are saved. Either of these combination rooms may be made very attractive and have been in small houses where people did not wait for it to become the fashion.

Everyone is complaining of being tired, of not having time for what they wish to do. It is no wonder when they are obliged to pick and choose from such multitudes of thoughts and things.

The world is full of so many things, so many of them useless, so many, many varieties of the same thing creating confusion and a feeling of being overwhelmed by their number. It would be a wonderful relief if, by eliminating both wisely and well, life might be simplified.

The Farm Home (7)

August 5, 1919

"We are going to be late getting the hay in from the west meadow. Can't you come and rake it for us?" said The Man of the Place.

I could and did; also I drove the team on the hay fork to fill the big barn, for such is the life of a farmer's wife during the busy season.

"The colt has sprained his ankle. Come pet him while I rub on some liniment, and while you are there I wish you'd look at the red heifer's bag and see what you think best to do for that swelling on it."

And so I halter broke the colt while The Man of the Place bathed the lame ankle and then we decided that the red heifer had been bee stung and bathed her udder with salt and water.

I have finally got the weakly calf into good growing condition and turned it out in the pasture with the others, for I am by way of being an understudy for the veterinarian.

"What would you raise next year on that land we cleared of brush down by the creek? The hay on it is too thin, and it must be broken up?" This was the question for my consideration at the breakfast table, and my answer was, "Raise the same crop on that as you do on the remainder of the land on that side of the creek. One large field is better than two small ones and time is saved in working. Put it into the regular rotation with the rest."

Not that The Man of the Place would do as I said unless he agreed with me, but getting my ideas helps him to form his own opinions and he knows that two heads are better at planning than one.

One of my neighbors is managing the farm this summer during the absence of her husband. She planted and cultivated, has attended to the harvesting and threshing and haying. She, with the children, cares for the horses and cows, the pigs and poultry. She buys and sells and hires and fires. In short, she does all the work and business that her husband would do if he were here and keeps up her own work besides.

United States Commissioner of Education, Philander P. Claxton, says that on a farm it is the "Know-All and Do-Everydumthing" that makes for success. If this is true for farmers it is much more so for their wives. A farmer's wife is expected to, and usually does, know as much about the farm as her husband and in addition she must know her own business of housekeeping and homemaking.

A farmer to be successful must understand his machinery and be a sort of blacksmith. He must be a carpenter, a road builder, enough of a civil engineer to know how to handle the creeks and washouts on his farm. He must, of course, understand all about the care of the animals on the farm in sickness and in health; he must know all about the raising of crops and handling of soils, the fighting of pests and overcoming of weather conditions and in addition must be a good business man so that he shall not lose all the fruits of his toil in the buying and selling end of the game.

Besides being a helper in all these things with brains, and muscle if necessary, the farmer's wife must know her own business, which includes the greatest variety of trades and occupations ever combined in one all-around person. Think of them! Cook, baker, seamstress, laundrywoman, nurse, chambermaid and nurse girl. She is a poultry keeper, an expert in dairy work, a specialist in canning, preserving and pickling, and besides all else she must be the mother of the family and a smiling hostess.

Dr. Claxton is advocating a change in rural schools so that they shall prepare farmers and farm women for their work, for as he says, "A man's life is his work! And a woman's life is her work!"

The Farm Home (8)

September 5, 1919

What a frightful thing it would be if we were to wake some morning and find there was no fuel of any kind in the United States with which to cook our breakfast. Yet this astounding thing may happen to our grandchildren, our children or even in our own lifetime if our days should be "long in the land."

Men have usually supplied the family fuel in a large offhand manner, but women have always seen that the wood box or coal hod was filled at night to be on hand for the morning's work.

If we do not intend that the stove shall remain cold and the family be breakfastless on that surprising morning in the future, it is time we were looking after the supply of fuel, for John has been careless and the wood pile is too small.

Too many of the forests of the United States have been made into lumber even tho there never has seemed to be lumber enough and the waste of timber has been great. The great woods of the East and the North of our country have been destroyed.

Three thousand saw mills are now busily at work in the South and the timber is fast disappearing before them. Within five years they will have cut out all the timber and disappeared from the South. Then only the forests of the Pacific coast will remain and they will not last long. In less than 70 years the supply of timber in the United States will be used up.

When that time comes, those of us who have permitted this destruction, if there are any of us left, will wish to hide our faces from the generations we have robbed, but we will be unable to "take to the tall timber" as certain politicians are said to have done in the past.

There will be no lumber to build the houses and no wood to cook that breakfast. I fear that even the dim mists of the past will be no refuge for the people who have permitted such a condition to come about and that we will be held up to scorn and reproach.

People then will not be able to use coal in place of wood for the supply of coal is fast disappearing. The end of hard coal is in sight. Soft coal therefore must be the basis of the country's industrial life as well as its fuel. There is, to be sure, a great deal of soft coal left but it is of poor quality and must be especially prepared for use to be satisfactory.

Dr. Garfield, former fuel administrator, does not favor government ownership but says there should be co-operation between the government and all basic industries to eliminate waste and all needless expense. The greater difficulties and more costly equipment in mining inferior coal and also the higher wages make prices higher.

But cost alone is not the greatest problem. There is danger of a power shortage which will stop all manufacturing unless a way is found to furnish a national power supply. Two-thirds of all our coal mined goes into the production of power. Eleven million persons are working in our manufacturing plants and more than double the power was used last year that was used in 1900.

The expense of the power is from 2 to 20 per cent of the cost of an article and when we buy $50 worth of goods we can figure that about $2 goes for the coal that supplied the power to manufacture them. Quite a tax!

Electricity is the only thing that can save the situation. One ton of coal used in generating electricity will furnish power equal to 4 tons.

Secretary Lane[5] has a plan for furnishing electric power thru a large central station. He urges a power survey of the whole United States, the locating of central stations and smaller supply stations.

5. Franklin K. Lane, at that time secretary of the interior.

It is known that in the territory between Boston and Richmond is situated one-fourth of the power-generating capacity of the country and as an illustration of the plan I quote Floyd W. Parsons in the Saturday Evening Post. "The logical development is a multiple-transmission line of high voltage extending all the way from Boston to Washington and on to Richmond. Energy could be delivered into this unified system by power stations located near the mine mouths and by hydro-electric plants located at the 20 or more water power sites tributary to this area."

Thus might be created rivers of power flowing thru the country and furnishing energy and power to our manufactories at much less than half of what it costs now.

They have one such great power line in California and another 500 miles long reaching from Tonopah, Nev., to Yuma, Ariz.

There is water power enough in the Ozark Hills to furnish power and light for that section of country and if included in the national system with the coal of Kansas and Illinois, would do its part in caring for the whole. The railroads could be electrified also and by the careful handling of our natural power and fuel, by a responsible head, that cold and dreary, breakfastless morning might never arrive. It need never arrive if we see to it that our water power and what is left of our fuel supply is handled carefully and intelligently. It is time to get busy with the wood box.

The Farm Home (9)

September 20, 1919

We all, at times, have had the longing that Robert Burns so well expressed when he said, "Oh, wad some power the giftie gie us, to see oursel's as ithers see us." And lately I have had a glimpse of how we, as a class, appear to strangers, not merely strangers so far as acquaintance goes, but strangers to our life and customs.

Friends from Switzerland, motoring thru from San Francisco to New York, broke the journey by a visit to Rocky Ridge Farm. Their account of the trip was very interesting, but a part of it has given me a picture of farm folks which is not at all pleasant to look upon.

"So many farm people from adjoining states were camping at Colorado Springs," said Mme. Marquis. "And they brought so much of their work with them that I do not see how the vacation could do them any good. They brought such quantities of luggage, everything from their washboards and tubs to their talking machines. The women did the washing on those glorious mornings, rubbing away on the wrinkle boards, and they spent the most of the time left sitting around in camp talking to one another. I heard one woman say, 'No, I haven't been up on Pike's Peak. It costs $2 to go up, and that's too much money.' And so, having come all the way to the foot of the Peak, they missed the climax of the whole trip, because it would cost a couple of dollars more.

"It seemed to me that they had worked hard all their lives, and at last they had reached the point where they were able to leave all their cares behind them, to get into their own motor cars and take a trip for pleasure and adventure. And then, at the last moment, they let their lifelong habits of pinching the pennies spoil it all. And Oh! Those farm women looked so worn and tired."

The Man of the Place and I once went on a picnic fishing trip, with a family who were friends of ours. And listening to Mme. Marquis tell of these women on their camping trip to Colorado Springs brought back to me the feeling of disillusion and utter weariness I experienced then. I had expected a relaxation and rest, but instead there was the cooking, the care of the children, washing of many dishes and making of beds, all to be done in the most difficult manner possible. If we had stayed long enough so that I had been obliged to do a washing I believe I would have wished to feed myself to the fishes. Once was enough. It was never again for me.

M. and Mme. Marquis were making the journey across the United States in a car for the sake of becoming acquainted with the people at home, and we took them with us to camp-meeting and to an all-day singing, picnics and on short trips here and there.

"What do you think of us?" I asked M. Marquis. "How do we impress you?"

"Well, if I can explain," he answered with his delightful accent. "You are a very nice people. I have studied the faces in the crowd and they are good faces, fine and beautiful, some of them. But you all seem to take your pleasures so sadly. You appear to be quite happy and contented, but very sad. There seems to be a spirit of sadness over it all. Do you not feel it?"

I was obliged to admit that I did, even within myself. Do we always carry our work and our sorrows with us, I wonder, as we did on the fishing party, and as the tired farm women did at Colorado Springs? Is it the constant, unrelieved carrying-about of our burdens that has caused our lives to be permeated with sadness, so that it is felt by a sensitive person seeing us for the first time?

Another thing was revealed to us about ourselves during the visit of these strangers. That is that we have grown careless in our manners. They had time always for an exquisite courtesy, being never too tired or hurried to show their appreciation of a favor or to do a kindness when the chance came. Their courtesy never failed, even when the machine broke down on rough roads, or in the rush of farm work, in which they eagerly took a part.

"We are all so careless about those things," said The Man of the Place to me. "I think we ought to try to do better."

"Yes," I replied. "Let's take time to be at least as nice as we know how to be. And after this, when I go on a vacation I am going to leave my 'wrinkle-board' behind."

After all, a vacation is not a matter of place or time. We can take a wonderful vacation in spirit, even tho we are obliged to stay at home, if we will only drop our burdens from our minds for awhile. But no amount of travel will give us rest and recreation if we carry our work and worries with us.

The Farm Home (10)

October 5, 1919

"Now can we depend on you in this?" asked Mr. Jones. "Certainly you can," replied Mr. Brown. "I'll do it!"

"But you failed us before, you know," continued Mr. Jones, "and it made us a lot of trouble. How would it be for you to put up a forfeit? Will you put up some money as security that you will not fail; will you bet on it?"

"No-o-o," answered Mr. Brown. "I won't bet on it but I'll give you my word of honor."

How much was Mr. Brown's word worth? I would not want to risk much on it. Would you? He evidently considered it of less value than a little cash. Now and then we hear of people whose word is as good as their bond but far too often we find that "word of honor" is used carelessly and then forgotten or ignored.

Speaking to a friend of the difficulties of putting thru a plan we had in mind, I remarked that it was very difficult to do anything with a crowd any more, for so many would promise and then fail to keep the promise.

"I know," she replied, "I do that way myself, it is so much easier to say 'yes,' and then do as I please afterward."

If my friend had realized how weak and unkind her reason was for disregarding her word, she would be more careful for she prides herself on her strength of character and is a very kind, lovable woman on the whole.

Mr. Brown and my friend had mistaken ideas of value. One's word is of infinitely more worth than money. If money is lost, more money and just as good is to be had, but if you pledge your word and do not redeem it, you have lost something that cannot be replaced. It is intangible perhaps but nevertheless valuable to you. A person who cannot be depended upon, by others, in time becomes unable to depend upon himself. It seems in some subtle way to undermine and weaken the character when we do not hold ourselves strictly responsible for what we say.

And what a tangle it makes of all our undertakings when people do not keep their promises. How much pleasanter it would be and how much more would be accomplished if we did not give our word unless we intended to keep it, so that we would all know what we could depend upon!

When we think of honor we always think of duty in connection with it. They seem to be inseparably linked together. The following incident illustrates this.

Albert Bebe, a French resident of San Francisco came home from the battle front in France. He had been in the trenches for two years and for four months in an advanced position, a "listening post" only 60 yards from the German trenches. Marie Bebe, the soldier's little daughter, was very much excited over her father's coming and objected to going to school the next morning. She thought she should be allowed to stay at home on the first day of her father's visit. But her mother said: "No! Your father went to fight for France because it was his duty to go. You must go to school because that is your duty. Your father did his duty and you must do yours!" And Marie went to school.

If everybody did his duty as well in the smaller things, there would be no failures when the greater duties presented themselves.

The Farm Home (11)

October 20, 1919

The American Forestry association has sent out a plea to make a great national road of memory of the Lincoln Highway,[6] by planting trees, in memory of our national heroes, all along its 3,000 miles.

Besides using our native trees, it is planned to bring over and plant Lom-

6. Running from Times Square in New York City to Lincoln Park in San Francisco, the Lincoln Highway was built in the early 1910s as the first transcontinental route. In 1925, with the advent of numbered routes, various stretches became (from east to west) U.S. 1, U.S. 30 (nearly two-thirds of the length), U.S. 530, U.S. 40, and U.S. 50.

bardy poplars from France, chestnut and oak from England, and cherry and plum from Japan.

This plan for making a living memorial to American heroes, has been endorsed by councils of Daughters of the Confederacy, and the Department of the Interior and the Forestry Department are aiding in the work.

For sentimental reasons alone such a memorial would be most wonderful, for while in life our heroes stood between us and danger, their memory would in this way still hover over us and give us comfort and pleasure, linked ever more closely to us by our loving thought, in the planting and care, of the living, breathing monument, which will reach across our common country from coast to coast.

As an example, such a great, national, tree bordered highway might help us to realize the unnecessary ugliness of most of our country roads and perhaps in time they also may be tree embowered and beautiful.

Motoring on the Ozark highway the other day I passed over a long stretch of the road where the large, beautiful native oak and walnut trees had been cleared away from beside it, leaving the roadway unshaded, bare and ugly. A little farther on, I came to a place where the farmers on each side had set out young walnut trees in even spaces along the road in an attempt to put back the beauty and usefulness which had been destroyed by cutting down the forest trees.

It seems such a pity that we can learn to value what we have only thru the loss of it. Truly "we never miss the water 'till the well runs dry."

People painstakingly raise shade trees on the bare prairies, but where we already had the shade and beauty of the forest we have carelessly failed to preserve it and now in many places must carefully rebuild what we have destroyed, taking years to replace what was removed in only a few days.

While a drive along a shady roadway is much more pleasant than one on a hot and dusty road, still pleasure and beauty are not all that are to be considered. There is also a utility side to the idea of trees along the way, for they help to keep the roadbed in good condition by retaining moisture and preventing washing away of the soil.

In many parts of Europe the fruit and nut trees along the roads bring enough of an income to keep up the roads so that the people pay no road tax. Rather staggering, that idea of self-supporting roads, to a people who spend so much for poor roads as we do. Another curious little fact in regard to trees in Europe is that any one in Switzerland who cuts down a forest tree must plant another to take its place.

Of course, in the clearing of our great new country we could not do that, but we have destroyed trees when it was not necessary, seemingly thru a spirit of wantonness, and so we have a double task before us, to plant trees where they did not grow and to replant in some places where they have been cut down. The work has been well started in some prairie states. Six thousand trees have been set out by the United States balloon school at Fort Omaha.

J. Sterling Morton was United States Secretary of Agriculture under President Cleveland but he will be longer remembered by the work he did on the State Board of Agriculture in Nebraska when he set aside the tenth of April as Arbor Day to be observed then and thereafter by the planting of trees. Since that first Arbor Day in 1872, 300 million trees have been set out in Nebraska.

People of wooded districts can save themselves much trouble and expense later by preserving the trees along the roadways for I am sure the Lincoln Highway will set the fashion which all our country's roads will follow in time.

The Farm Home (12)

November 5, 1919

"Isn't it awful, the prices we have to pay for things!" exclaimed my neighbor to me. "Just look at these shoes! I paid $10 for them! Something ought to be done to these profiteers; poor people can't afford to live any more."

My neighbor's shoes were new, of course, and the heels were extremely high, too high to be really good style, but she seemed very proud of them and proud also in a rather shamefaced way that she had paid $10 for them.

"You need not have paid so much," I replied, "thru all these high prices for shoes I never have paid quite $4 for a pair and my shoes always have been correct in style and have worn well."

"Oh!" said my neighbor. "It's too much trouble to hunt bargains and my foot is not easily fitted. Besides you order your shoes, do you not?"

"Sometimes," I answered, "but never when I think the home retailer is asking only a fair profit. When I think he is profiteering, I protect myself without calling on the government at Washington. I do for myself at least as much as I can."

I think most of us imagined our war troubles were over when the fighting had stopped and Germany had signed the peace terms, in the famous Hall of Mirrors, but we are sadly disappointed. The whole world is in a state of unrest and disturbance caused by the after effects of the war and chief among the disturbing causes is the high cost of everything one has to buy.

In articles on the subject and in political speeches the consumer is put in a separate and distinct class by himself as opposed to the producer. Farmers think of themselves as consumers and condemn the producers and profiteers when they have to buy the high priced farm implements and other necessities of life, while the people who make these goods or sell them say that farmers are profiteering producers. And so we go on wasting our time in recriminations, just as congress, as a body, has spent its time in investigation of things that are past and gone and in oratory about the mistakes some one made, instead of citizens and congress both bending every thought and energy to the future, to the rebuilding of what has been destroyed by war and the reforming of the abuses still existing.

There are problems that should be handled for us all collectively but as in so many other things of our national life, it is also a matter for each of us to attend to. If each one of a crowd acting independently does the same things, it produces a mass action that is powerful, and we can handle this problem of high costs for ourselves much better than we have been doing if we try.

We all did seemingly impossible things in conserving and producing during the war. We can still do them until the effects of the war have passed away so far as prices are concerned, and it is as much a patriotic duty. Experts in economics say that the reason for the high prices is that the rate of production has not kept up with the inflation of currency due to war conditions and that the remedy for the evils of high prices is increased production.

According to them, prices and production work like a see-saw—when one goes up the other goes down. When money is scarce and products plentiful, a little money buys a large amount of products, but when money is plentiful and products scarce, then it takes a great deal of money to buy a small amount of products, which is where we are today.

Just now to help arrive at that balance we must practice economy and produce as much as possible. This is where every one of us can help. For instance, if by caring for a garment we can make that garment last twice as long, we have not only saved money but helped to increase the volume of products by leaving them on the market. It acts in the same way as the schoolboy described in his essay on pins—"Pins has saved many lives by not swallering of 'em."

Another way to help ourselves thru the pinch of these unsettled times and to make it harder for the actual profiteers is to buy as carefully and economically as possible even tho it is some trouble, for it is surely worth the effort.

The Farm Home (13)

November 20, 1919

"One gains a lot by going out into the world, by traveling and living in different places," Rose said to me one day, "but one loses a great deal, too. After all I'm not sure but the loss is greater than the gain."

"Just how do you mean?" I asked.

"I mean this," said Rose. "The best anyone can get out of this world is happiness and contentment and people here in the country seem so happy and contented, so different from the restless people of the cities who are out in the rush of things."

So after all there are compensations. Tho we do not have the advantages of travel, we stay-at-homes may acquire a culture of the heart which is almost impossible in the rush and roar of cities.

I think there are always compensations. The trouble is we do not recognize them. We usually are so busily longing for things we can't have that we overlook what we have in their place that is even more worth while. Sometimes we realize our happiness only by comparison after we have lost it. It really appears to be true that,

> To appreciate Heaven well
> A man must have some 15 minutes of Hell.

Talking with another friend from the city gave me still more of an understanding of this difference between country and city.

"My friends in town always are going somewhere. They never are quiet a minute if they can help it," he said. "Always they are looking for something to pass the time away quickly as tho they were afraid to be left by themselves. The other evening one of the fellows was all broken up because there was nothing doing. 'There isn't a thing on for tonight,' he said. 'Not a thing!' He seemed to think it was something terrible that there was nothing special on hand for excitement and he couldn't bear to think of spending a quiet evening at home."

What an uncomfortable condition to be in—depending altogether on things outside of one's self for happiness and a false happiness at that, for the true must come from within.

If we are such bad company that we can't live with ourselves, something is seriously wrong and should be attended to, for sooner or later we shall have to face ourselves alone.

There seems to be a madness in the cities, a frenzy in the struggling crowds. A friend writes me of New York, "I like it and I hate it. There's something you've got to love, it's so big—a people hurrying everywhere, all trying to live and be someone or something—and then when you see the poverty and hatefulness, the uselessness of it all, you wonder why people live here at all. It does not seem possible that there are any peaceful farms on earth."

And so, more than ever, I am thankful for the peacefulness and comparative isolation of country life. This is a happiness which we ought to realize and enjoy.

We who live in the quiet places have the opportunity to become acquainted with ourselves, to think our own thoughts and live our own lives in a way that is not possible for those who are keeping up with the crowd where there is always something "on for tonight," and who have become so accustomed to crowds that they are dependent upon them for comfort.

In thine own cheerful spirit live,
Nor seek the calm that others give;
For thou, thyself, alone must stand
Not held upright by other's hand.[7]

The Farm Home (14)

December 5, 1919

"The Price of Sugar May Go to 20 Cents!" was the headline that stared me in the face from the page of the paper I had picked up. "Unless Congress continues the sugar equalization board during 1920, the price of Cuban sugar to the American consumer will increase to 15 or 20 cents a pound, Attorney General Palmer says," I read on.

If the sugar equalization board is any curb on the sugar trust, it is devoutly to be hoped that the board will be continued, especially when one remembers that five persons are said to control the sugar output of the world.

Congress was asked by the President to continue the war boards in operation until conditions had adjusted themselves to peace, but with that spirit of hostility to the executive branch of the government, Congress immediately discontinued some of the most important. Among these was the labor board, which I know from private, inside information was working desper-

7. Author unknown; possibly Laura herself.

ately to be in a position to handle the labor situation. The labor troubles from which we are all suffering may not be the direct result of dismissing the board, but it is plain that all the help that could have been had in the trouble would not have been too much.

Since the removal of the restrictions on the packers and stopping of the investigation, the price of cattle and hogs has gone down and down. The situation reminds me of a flock of crows descending upon a corn field when the man with the gun is gone.

Also, it makes me wonder if the man was right who said to me, "They may talk about the Bolsheviki and the I. W. W. and imprison and deport them, but we have the same thing, in only a little different form, in high places and we won't have peace until we settle them both."

Is one any more a lawbreaker, I wonder, for trying to take that to which he is not entitled from those above him in the social scale than is the one who takes more than he is entitled to from those below him?

Some public speakers and some editorials are saying that the farmers hold the balance of power and will have to take control and handle the situation, but farmers are only partly organized and it will be difficult for them to handle anything so few understand, besides they are all divided among political parties and stand by their particular party regardless, even tho by so doing they lower the price of hogs.

I heard some farmers talking politics not long ago and they violently disagreed, passing insults on one another's popular leaders. In this they were following the lead of their daily papers.

I wonder again—I wonder if that correspondent of the Saturday Evening Post was right when she said, "The world has simply lost its kindliness and its courtesy. It has lost its ability to gauge the fitness of things."

Some writers are expressing the hope that the women will "clean house" in politics, sweeping out from both parties those who only clutter up the place, and hinder the day's work.

I think the idea of a woman's party, a political division on sex lines, is distasteful to women, especially farm women. It seems as if the time had come to reason together instead of dividing into another antagonistic group.

If farm women would make a study of just where and how the action or refusal to act, of Congress affects their interests, talking it over in the home, and then vote accordingly, I am sure that they would find themselves and their men folks supporting the same candidates and defeating, for reelection, those who have sold them out to any interests whatever, whether the higher or the lower Bolsheviki.

If women, with their entrance into a free discussion of politics, can do away with the "hot air" and insults, with "making the Eagle scream," and "twisting the Lion's tail," and "shaking the bloody shirt," and all the rest of the smoke screen, bringing politics into the open air of sane, sensible discussion—a discussion of facts and conditions, not personal discussions of leaders, they will have rendered the country a great service.

The Farm Home (15)

December 20, 1919

Peace upon earth the angel sang,
Good will unto men the chorus rang.

But that was many, many years ago at the first Christmas time. We could scarcely hear the angels, if they were singing now, for the clamor of disputing and wrangling which is going on where peace is supposed to be.

In our own country there is a gathering into groups with mutterings and threats of violence, with some bloodshed and danger of more and there is still war and threat of war over most of the world. This would be bad enough at any time, but just now when we are thinking of all the blessed meanings of Christmas tide, it becomes much more terrible.

A great deal is said and written about natural, national boundaries and learned discussions of racial antagonisms as causes of the restlessness and ill temper of the nations and there are investigations and commissions and inquiries to discover what is the matter with the world and to find a remedy.

But the cause of all the unrest and strife is easily found. It is selfishness, nothing else, selfishness deep in the hearts of the people.

It seems rather impossible that such a small thing as individual selfishness could cause so much trouble, but my selfishness added to your selfishness and that added to the selfishness of our neighbors all over the big, round world is not a small thing.

We may have thought that our own greed and striving to take unfair advantage were not noticed and never would be known, but you and I and our neighbors make the neighborhood and neighborhoods make the states and states make the nation and the nations are the peoples of the world.

No one would deny that the thoughts and actions and spirit of every person affect his neighborhood and it is just as plain that the spirit and temper of the communities are reflected in the state and nation and influence the whole world.

The nations of Europe are selfishly trying to take advantage of one another in the settlements of boundaries and territory and so the World War is like a fire that has been stopped in its wild advance only to smoulder and break out here and there a little farther back along the sides.[8]

At home, in the troubles between labor and capital, each is willing to stop disputes and eager to cure the unrest of the people if it can be done at the expense of the other party and leave them undisturbed in their own selfish gains.

Following all the unrest and unreason on down to its real source where it lurks in the hearts of the people its roots will be found there in individual selfishness, in the desire to better one's own condition at the expense of another, by whatever means possible, and this desire of each person infects groups of people and moves nations.

Here and there one sees a criticism of Christianity because of the things that have happened and are still going on. "Christian civilization is a failure," some say. "Christianity has not prevented these things, therefore it is a failure," say others.

But this is a calling of things by the wrong names. It is rather the lack of Christianity that has brought us where we are. Not a lack of churches or religious forms, but of the real thing in our hearts.

There is no oppression of a group of people but has its root and inception in the hearts of the oppressors. There is no wild lawlessness and riot and bloodlust of a mob but has its place in the hearts of the persons who are that mob. Just so, if justice and fairness and kindness fill the minds of a crowd of persons those things will be shown in their actions.

So if we are eager to help in putting the world to rights, our first duty is to put ourselves right, to overcome our selfishness and be as eager that others shall be treated fairly as we are that no advantage shall be taken of ourselves; to deal justly and have a loving charity and mercy for others as we wish them to have for us. Then we may hear the Christmas angels singing in our own hearts, "Peace upon earth! Good will unto men."

8. Some historians judge that the Treaty of Versailles, ending World War I, so exacerbated poor economic conditions in Europe that it made World War II almost inevitable.

The Farm Home (16)

January 5, 1920

The Man of the Place and I were sitting cozily by the fire. The evening lamp was lighted and the day's papers and the late magazines were scattered over the table. But tho we each held in our hands our favorite publication; we were not reading. We were grumbling about the work we had to do and saying all the things usually said at such times.

"People used to have time to live and enjoy themselves, but there is no time any more for anything but work, work, work."

Oh, we threshed it all over as everyone does when they get that kind of a grouch and then we sat in silence. I was wishing I had lived altogether in those good old days when people had time for the things they wanted to do.

What the Man of the Place was thinking, I do not know but I was quite surprised at the point at which he had arrived, when he remarked out of the silence, in rather a meek voice, "I never realized how much work my father did. Why, one winter he sorted 500 bushels of potatoes after supper by lantern light. He sold them for $1.50 a bushel in the spring, too, but he must have got blamed tired of sorting potatoes down cellar every night until he had handled more than 500 bushels of them."

"What did your mother do while your father was sorting potatoes?" I asked.

"Oh, she sewed and knit," said the Man of The Place. "She made all our clothes, coats and pants, undergarments for father and us boys as well as everything she and the girls wore, and she knit all our socks and mittens—shag mittens for the men folks, do you remember, all fuzzy on the outside?

She didn't have time enough in the day to do all the work and so she sewed and knit at night."

I looked down at the magazine in my hand and remembered how my mother was always sewing or knitting by the evening lamp. I realized that I never had done so except now and then in cases of emergency.

But the Man Of The Place was still talking. "Mother did all her sewing by hand then," he said, "and she spun her own yarn and wove her own cloth. Father harvested his grain by hand with a sickle and cut his hay with a scythe. I do wonder how he ever got it done."

Again we were silent, each busy with our own thoughts. I was counting up the time I give to club work and lodge work and—yes, I'll admit it—politics. My mother and my mother-in-law had none of these and they do use up a good many hours. Instead of all this, they took time once in a while from their day and night working to go visit a neighbor for the day.

"Time to enjoy life!" Well, they did enjoy it but it couldn't have been because they had more time.

Why should we need extra time in which to enjoy ourselves? If we expect to enjoy our life we will have to learn to be joyful in all of it, not just at stated intervals, when we can get time, or when we have nothing else to do.

It may well be that it is not our work that is so hard for us as the dread of it and our often expressed hatred of it. Perhaps it is our spirit and attitude toward life and its conditions that are giving us trouble instead of a shortage of time. Surely the days and nights are as long as they ever were.

A feeling of pleasure in a task seems to shorten it wonderfully and it makes a great difference with the day's work if we get enjoyment from it instead of looking for all our pleasure altogether apart from it, as seems to be the habit of mind we are more and more growing into.

We find in the goods we buy, from farm implements to clothing, that the work of making them is carelessly and slightingly done. Many carpenters, blacksmiths, shoemakers, garment makers and farm hands do not care how their work is done just so quitting time and the paycheck comes. Farmers are not different except that they must give more attention to how a thing is done because it is the result only that brings them any return.

It seems that many workmen take no pride or pleasure in their work. It is perhaps partly a result of machine-made goods, but it would be much better for us all if we could be more interested in the work of our hands, if we could get back more of the attitude of our mothers toward their handmade garments and of our fathers' pride in own workmanship. There is an old maxim which I have not heard for years nor thought of in a long, long time. "To sweep a room as to God's laws, makes that, and the action fine." We need more of that spirit toward our work.

As I thought of my neighbors and myself it seemed to me that we were all slighting our work to get time for a joy ride of one kind or another.

Not that I object to joy riding! The more the merrier, but I'm hoping for a change of mind that will carry the joy into the work as well as the play.

"All work and no play makes Jack a dull boy," surely, and it makes Jill also very dull indeed, but all play and no work would make hoboes of us. So let's enjoy the work we must do to be respectable.

The Man Of The Place had evidently kept right on thinking of the work his father used to do. "Oh, well," he said as he rose and lighted the lantern preparatory to making his late round to see that everything was all right at the barns, "I guess we're not having such a hard time after all. It depends a good deal on how you look at it."

"Yes," said I, "Oh yes, indeed! It depends a good deal on how you look at it."

The Farm Home (17)

January 20, 1920

The snow was falling fast and a cold wind blowing, the other morning. I had just come in from feeding the chickens and was warming my chilled self when the telephone rang.

"Hello!" said I and a voice full of laughter came over a wire. "Good morning!" it said. "I suppose you are busy making garden today."

"Making garden?" I asked wonderingly.

"Yes," replied the voice, "you said some time ago, in the Ruralist, that you enjoyed making garden in the winter time, beside a good fire, so I thought you'd be busily at it this morning."

"Well," I replied defensively, "the vegetables one raises in the seed catalogs are so perfectly beautiful." And with a good laugh we began the day right merrily in spite of the storm outside.

So after many days my words came back to me and the thoughts that followed them were altogether different from those connected with them before.

We do grow beautiful gardens beside the fire on cold winter days as we talk over the seed catalogs and our summer gardens are much more of a success because of these gardens in our minds. We grow many other things in the same way. It is truly surprising how anything grows and grows by talking about it.

We have a slight headache and we mention the fact. As an excuse to ourselves for inflicting it upon our friends we make it as bad as possible in the telling. "Oh I have such a dreadful headache," we say and immediately we feel much worse. Our pain has grown by talking of it.

If there is a disagreement between friends and the neighbors begin talking about it, the difficulty grows like a jimson weed, and the more it is talked about the faster it grows.

When there is a disagreement between workmen and their employers the agitators immediately begin their work of talking and the trouble grows and grows until strikes and lockouts and riots are ripened and harvested and the agitators grow fat on the fruits thereof.

The same law seems to work in both human nature and the vegetable kingdom and ideas, with the changes caused by them, as well as peas and cabbages grow by cultivation, by keeping the soil stirred about them.

Now it isn't enough in any garden to cut down the weeds. The cutting out of weeds is important but cultivating the garden plants is just as necessary. If we want vegetables we must make them grow; not leave the ground barren where we have destroyed the weeds. Just so we must give much of our attention to the improvements we want, not all to the abuses we would like to correct. If we hope to improve conditions, any conditions, anywhere, we must do a great deal of talking about the better things.

If we have a headache we will forget it sooner if we talk of pleasant things. If there is misunderstanding and bad feeling between neighbors we can cultivate their friendliness by telling each of the other's kind words before the trouble began. Perhaps a crust has formed around the plant of their friendship and it only needs that the soil should be stirred in order to keep on growing.

In the matter of labor disputes which so nearly left the country to freeze this winter, I think everything possible has been said against conditions that would allow such things to happen. The time has come to give our attention to a better way of settling such disputes than by strikes and lockouts. One plan proposed is the establishing of an industrial court for the hearing of both sides of any dispute between laborers and their employers and a fair settling of the same. If such a court would stop the disturbances which have become so common and from which we all suffer, the plan is well worth attention. By talking about it we may help to secure it.

The Farm Home (18)

February 5, 1920

Co-operation is the keynote of affairs today and our lives seem to be governed mostly by the advice of experts. These both are greatly needed, and I heartily say, more power to them. But every good becomes evil when carried to excess by poor, faulty mortals. Thrift and economy overdone become miserliness; even religion may be carried so far as to become fanaticism and intolerance, the faith of love and gentleness causing hatred and persecution.

And if, just so, the power of cooperation and the privilege of having expert advice are not to become harmful, individual thinking and initiative must keep pace with them. We must still do our own thinking and act upon it, for even tho we make mistakes, experience is still the best teacher and thinking and experimenting develop character.

The more we think for ourselves, the less we shall need advice and high-priced experts would not need to waste their time and government money, which is really our money, in telling us things we should think out for ourselves.

I read an item a short time ago in a farm paper stating that government experts advised the use of oil on shoes to prolong their life and usefulness and in so doing beat the high cost of living. Full instructions were given for this treatment of shoes.

Now the weekly cleaning and greasing of the family shoes was a regular thing with the grandparents and the parents of most of us and they charged nothing for advising and instructing us in the process. In fact, there was at times a compelling quality about their advice that is lacking in that of government experts. But at least our grandparents and their "old-fashioned notions" are at last vindicated.

"Scrape off all that dirt and clean those shoes up good, then rub that grease into them," said they, perhaps a bit sharply.

"The shoes should be thoroly cleaned and warm oil then rubbed well into the leather," say the experts smoothly.

So you see that expert advice was given in our homes years ago. And after all that is the best place for teaching many things, first and most important of which is how to think for one's self.

The Farm Home (19)

February 20, 1920

The affairs of the world are moving swiftly and nowhere is the advance more rapid than in the field of invention. No sooner do we realize that an improvement is needed on something already in use than it comes to hand; no sooner is something entirely new and different desired than it appears as tho in answer to the waving of a magician's wand.

A great many of these are to the credit of Americans for Americans apparently have more inventive minds than people of other nations. No doubt this is because we are a younger nation and a people who were compelled to make a new country habitable. We were like the Yankee boy who had only his jack-knife but with it supplied himself with all the other playthings he cared for.

One problem, which has been given to the grownup Yankee boys to solve, was a threatened shortage in gasoline. Altho there is a present abundance, scientists and chemists have for years been trying to find a substitute, for they believe that we cannot go on forever using gasoline in ever increasing quantities without coming at last to the end of the supply.

Quite a few substitutes have been found tho nothing which combines all the various qualities, including efficiency and cost, of gasoline. The most promising substitute so far found is the benzol blend. Benzol is a by-product in the manufacture of coke from coal and was used during the war in the manufacture of the high explosive TNT. It was found that benzol could be made very cheaply but its explosive power was too great to permit it to be used in motor engines, and the problem was to so weaken its power that it would not injure the machine using it. To do this benzol is mixed with California naphthas, Oklahoma distillates, and other fractions of petroleum and is being sold as fuel for motors. The petroleum industry is making this fuel oil and it is being sold under trade names. It is said that the benzol mixture makes less carbon and gives more mileage than straight gasoline.

The making and selling of benzol is becoming a large business. One great steel company is making 1,250,000 gallons of benzol every month as a by-product in making from coal the coke needed for the furnaces of the plant. It is said that the manufacture of benzol in this way makes the cost only a few cents a gallon, probably not more than 5 cents and it has been selling at 18. Oil companies are buying it and without doubt are blending it with their gasolines. In fact, it is said, they have been doing so for the last two years.

Besides the invention of this substitute a new source of real gasoline has been discovered in natural gas and several millions of gallons have been made from it during the last six years.

Dr. Cottrell, the inventor of the process of precipitating the gases and floating particles in smoke fumes, thus abolishing the damage done by smoke from smelters and factories, has become a benefactor of inventors. When his invention had become a financial success he had an understanding with his backers that when the receipts had repaid the investment with interest, a large part of the patent rights should be turned over to some institution the receipts from which should be used to advance the work of invention. This is now being done, the Smithsonian Institution handling the fund.

The Farm Home (20)

March 5, 1920

When the days are growing longer and the sun shines warm, on the south slopes, with the promise of golden hours to come, my thoughts persist in arranging building plans; for always, in the springtime, I want to build a house.

The desire for changing the surroundings may be inherited from our wandering forefathers who always moved their tents to fresh hunting grounds with the coming of summer, or perhaps mankind, in common with the birds has an instinct to build nests when spring comes, but whatever the reason, I think most persons share with me the longing to plan and build at this season of the year.

But of late, stronger even than my love of planning has been my dissatisfaction with the usual manner of building, for when flimsy, short-lived materials are used in construction the joy of the creation is soon swallowed up in dismay at the quick process of deterioration and decay.

Wooden buildings need a great deal of repairing and their demand for paint is never satisfied. A short time ago a "paint up" campaign was put out in the papers of the country to promote the preservation of farm buildings.

I would like to take part in a build-up campaign to encourage the use of building materials that would be more lasting. I would like to see our farm homes built, not for the present generation only but for our children and our children's children.

Sometimes I wonder if the home ties would not be stronger if our homes were built with more of an idea of permanency.

There are so many beautiful ways of building without putting ourselves unreservedly in the hands of the lumber trust and paint manufacturers.

I have a fancy that the farm home should seem to be a product of the soil where it is reared, a permanent growth as it were, of conditions surrounding it, wherever this is possible, and nothing gives this effect more than a house built of rocks from the fields. Such a house, well built, will last for generations. Cement is another material of which lasting and beautiful buildings may be made. Even the common earth, the soil beneath our feet, can be used as building material and will last for hundreds of years. Tamped earth is one of the very oldest of building materials. In New Mexico and Arizona are walls made of it that are 4,000 years old, and it is still being used in various parts of the world.

This tamped earth is not adobe but is a mixture of either sand or clay with loam. It is used dry and must be tamped down in the forms until it rings. Treated in this way it becomes an earth stone that becomes harder with the passing years.

Because of the excessive cost of the usual building materials, the use of earth in this manner has been revived in England and is proving very successful. In various localities in our own country some experimenting would be necessary to determine the best mixture of the loam.

A house planned with loving thought and carefully built of any of these lasting materials would be a much better monument to one's memory than a costly stone in a cemetery, because it would be their embodied idea and the work of their hands, an expression of the mind and soul of the builder.

I never shall forget a drive thru a beautiful residence section of a Missouri town. The gentleman who accompanied me was a stone mason and builder. House after house that we passed, he told me he had built. Stone fences, with beautiful gateways were the work of his hands. Calling my attention to a fine house he said, "I built that house 20 years ago, and see how well and true it stands." Some of the fences had been built for 20, some for 15 and some for 10 years and were still perfect, not a stone loosened nor settled. He was very proud of his good work as he had every reason to be. "There," said he, "are my monuments. They will last long, long after I am gone."

The Farm Home (21)

March 20, 1920

"You are tired to death with work," I read. "Work with a little 'w' is killing the soul out of you. Work with a little 'w' always does that to men if they give it the whole chance. If you don't mix some big 'W' work in with it, then indeed your life will be disastrous and your days will be dead."

"What is it you mean by big 'W' work?" he asked. "Of course, that's the work you love for the work's sake. It's the work you do because you love the thing itself you're working for."

I closed the book. "That is plenty enough to think about for awhile," I said to myself. "I don't want any more ideas mixed with that until I thresh it out well."

We are all doing a great deal of little "w" work and it is necessary and right that we should. We must work for the pay or the profit that comes from it whether or not we love what we are working for, because we must live and lay by something for old age.

But it is sadly true that giving all our time and thought and effort to personal gain will cause us to become selfish and small and mean. If instead we devote ourselves a part of our time to work we love for itself, for what we are accomplishing, we grow stronger and more beautiful of soul.

Perhaps we all have been too intent on our own financial gain. From firsthand experience as well as the printed news, it would appear that no one is excessively fond of the work he is, or has been doing. Everyone is insisting on more money and less work or more profit and less return for it—little "w" work, all of it.

But there are encouraging signs in these somewhat discouraging times of grafters and grafting, of profits and profiteering, of distrust and suspicion, jealousy and strife. Sounds ugly, does it not? But those are the things to which our attention is called daily.

However, as I have said, there are hopeful signs. Only the other day a county officer refused a $900 raise in his salary, because, he said, knowing the condition of the county as he did, he knew that the money was needed so much worse for other things.

Altho it was a stormy day when I read of this man, it seemed as tho the sunshine was streaming over the world. A public official placing the welfare of the community before his private gain so far as to refuse more pay for his services is wonderfully encouraging to our hopes for our country. If there were enough of such public spirited men the difficulties which we are facing as a nation would soon disappear.

To work for the good of the community without full reward in money but because we love our fellows and long for the common betterment, is work with a big "W," work that will keep our souls alive.

Then there is the owner of the apartment house in New York who did not raise the rent! When at last his tenants had a meeting and voted to pay more rent, he refused to accept it, but when they insisted he took it and spent it all on improvements which made the tenants more comfortable.

And the little group of neighbor farmers who, after having made their own loans with the Federal Land Bank, gave their services, as appraisers for a year without pay, to help other farmers secure the same benefits.

There is also the young woman with the musical talent and the lovely singing voice, who uses it so freely for the pleasure and benefit of others; and the one who grows beautiful flowers because she loves them and delights in giving them away.

There is after all a great deal of work being done in the world, for the love of the thing worked for, with no thought of selfishness, and the lives of such workers are fuller and richer for it.

The Farm Home (22)

April 5, 1920

Politics looks "mighty curious" as the time draws near for women all over the country to take part in it for the first time.

Do you suppose that our ideas of housekeeping have been all wrong and we should have learned the milliner's trade in order to be a good cook and taught school in order that we may do the family washing properly? This seems to be the manner in which candidates for the managership of the biggest business in the world are being chosen.

The biggest business in the world? Why that's the United States of America! The expenses of the business run into billions of dollars a year.

The income is furnished by you and me and others like us, in many ways; by the taxes we pay directly, and goodness knows, they are coming high these days; by the tax on toilet articles; by the tax on legal papers; by duties on imports, which we pay in higher prices of the goods we buy; by an income tax if we are fortunate enough to have so much income. And all that not being enough, there is a bill now before Congress to put an excess profits tax on farm lands.

Besides the managing of these huge amounts of income and expense there is a vast volume of trade at home and with foreign countries that must be looked after and regulated in such a way as to be fair to us all, or as near as may be to that desired state.

There are disputes between labor and capital, between farmers and packers; of producers and consumers with profiteers. There are matters of international business and diplomacy that must be handled delicately yet with a sure hand and a certain knowledge of conditions at home and abroad.

Surely a man should be chosen as manager of such a business for his business, for his business ability, his qualities as an executive, his broad, comprehensive knowledge of world conditions and people as well as of the home problems of our own country, for in our buying and selling, even of our eggs and butterfat, in our taxes and wars, our peace and prosperity, even our health and our lives, we are closely united with the rest of the world, for better or worse until death parts us.

Our next President, who will be our business manager for four years, should be chosen for his fitness for the place as tho we were hiring him to attend to our own private business, for a lack of knowledge or disposition on his part will be felt in our homes, from the front door to the kitchen. It will make a difference in the amount of our egg money and the price of our new dresses.

In our own affairs we do not hire a person to take charge of an important work who has been carefully trained for something altogether different.

The Farm Home (23)

April 20, 1920

Out in the woods, the other day, I saw a tree that had branches on only one side. Evidently other trees had grown so near it that there had been room for it to grow in only the one way and now that it was left to stand alone its lack of good development and balance showed plainly.

It was not a beautiful thing. It looked lopsided and freakish and unable to stand by itself, being pulled a little over by the weight of its branches. It reminded me of a person who has grown all in one direction; in his work perhaps, knowing how to do only one thing, as those workmen in factories who do a certain thing to one part of a machine day after day and never learn how to complete the whole, depending on others to finish the job.

Or a woman who is interested in nothing but her housework and gossip, leaving her life bare of all the beautiful branches of learning and culture which might be hers.

Or that person who follows always the same habits of thought, thinking always along the same lines in the same safe, worn grooves, distrusting the new ideas that begin to branch out in other directions, leading into new fields of thought where free winds blow.

And so many are dwarfed and crooked because of their ignorance on all subjects except a very few, with the branches of their tree of knowledge all on one side!

Lives never were meant to grow that way, lopsided and crippled! They should be well developed and balanced, strong and symmetrical, like a tree that grows by itself in the open, able to stand safely against the storms from whatever direction they may come—a thing of beauty and satisfaction.

The choice lies with us, which we shall resemble. We may be like the young woman devoted to dress and fancywork, who when asked to join a club for the study of current events, replied, "What! Spend all the afternoon studying and talking about such things as that! Well, I should say not!"

Or, if we prefer, we may be like Mr. and Mrs. A. Mr. A. is a good farmer; his crops and livestock are of the best, and besides he is a leader in farm organizations. Mrs. A. is a good housekeeper; her garden is the best in the neighborhood and her poultry is the pride of her heart.

As you see they are very busy people but they keep informed on current affairs and, now that the son and daughter are taking charge of part of the farm work, are having more time for reading and study. Their lives are branching out more and more in every direction for good to themselves and other people, for it is a fact that the more we make of our lives the better it is for others as well as ourselves.

You must not understand me to mean that we should selfishly live to ourselves. We are all better for contact and companionship with other people. We need such contact to polish off the rough corners of our minds and our manners, but it is a pitiful thing when anyone cannot, if necessary, stand by himself, sufficient to himself and in good company even tho alone.

The Farm Home (24)

May 5, 1920

When Commodore Perry discovered the North Pole several years ago, it seemed there was no great field of adventure and discovery left. For some reason there never has been much interest taken in reaching the South Pole and the circumference of the earth was a well beaten track. What then was there left so intriguing to the imagination as to lead men on and on facing danger and death to discover?

But the imagination of mankind was not bounded by the whole round world. His fancy has literally taken flight above the earth and he is now exploring the vastness of the firmament above.

A very interesting article on this subject is, "Air 'Submarines' to Sound the Depths Beyond the Clouds." In reading it one learns that airmen are flying high, both actually and in a manner of speaking.

In this new field of discovery there is no monotony. The flyer's imagination is stirred by cutting adrift from the familiar earth and there are mysteries in the upper regions which excite his interest and lead him to greater efforts.

There are fierce winds encircling the earth and belts of mysterious gases and vapors, with other strange conditions that make a trip, to the outer edge of the atmospheric ocean which surrounds the earth, more alluring and adventurous than the voyages of those old navigators who set sail on an unknown sea in hopes of finding a short route to India.

As the aviator ascends the cold increases at the rate of 1 degree of temperature for every 300 feet of altitude. After the 4-mile level he has risen above the screen of atmospheric particles that we call the sky and entered the region of absolute silence, where the firmament becomes black and stars shine in the brightest day and where the cold is intense and terrible.

But the idea that the cold keeps on increasing with the altitude has been found to be a mistake. At 6 to 8 miles above the earth there is an "inversion of atmosphere," as it was called by its discoverer, Mr. De Bort, and from there up it constantly grows warmer. These facts were ascertained by means of small balloons with self-registering instruments.

Within the 6 to 8-mile limit the conditions are those with which we are all familiar. There thunders and lightenings play their accustomed parts and storms gather to descend upon the earth in rain or snow or sleet. The earth's atmosphere extends above the "weather strip," tho constantly thinning, for 20 to 30 miles.

Above the earth's "atmospheric envelope" investigators tell us, the great trade winds blow at the rate of 100 miles an hour, always from west to east. Still beyond this there are drifting ice clouds. Meteors and shooting stars flash across the void and then comes the boundary of the circle of inflammable air or pure hydrogen. After this is the stratum of helium which on earth is made from radium and treasured in test tubes.

During the last few months, interest has been increased in high flying by several record breaking flights. One of these being that of Major R. W. Schroeder, who flew to an altitude of more than 36,000 feet.

Aeronauts are now planning specially constructed airplanes to meet conditions at great heights and to lessen the dangers of high flying. The main feature of these new airships will be an enclosed cabin designed to protect the flyer. This cabin will be fitted with air compressors, oxygen tanks and heating arrangements.

And so perhaps someday a daring voyager may rise above the 5 mile limit of easy breathing to where the sky is black and the stars shine brightly even at noon, thru the region of clouds and storms, where the elements are forever striving, on beyond into the place of absolute silence where the fierce, great, trade winds blow forever higher and still higher into the stratum of inflammable air and thru this into the stratum of helium.

Will there some day be, I wonder, ships of the air making this voyage and bringing back cargoes of helium?

The Farm Home (25)

June 5, 1920

There is an old story about an argument between a Quaker and an infidel, in which the infidel, denying the existence of God and all things spiritual, exclaimed, "I don't believe in anything I can't see!"

To which the Quaker calmly replied, "Friend, does thee believe thee has any brains?"

I was reminded of this story recently when I read of the new system of electrical precipitation of dust by the use of the electric sieve.

This electric dust sieve is invisible without weight or substance, being woven of fine lines of electric force. It occupies no space, having no material body yet it will not allow the tiniest speck of dust to pass tho it does not interrupt the flow of gas.

The sieve has been extensively used in abating the dust nuisance in the making of cement and is now being put in use in blast furnaces to cleanse the gas of dust.

The manner of using electric force to sift the dust from gas is very simple. The gas is compelled to pass thru a vertical pipe, coming in at the bottom. In the exact center of the pipe and running the full length is an electric wire held tight by a weight at the bottom. When the current is turned on this wire the electric force repels the dust particles in the gas which is passing thru the pipe and in flying from the wire they strike against the sides of the pipe and adhere to it.

After the electric sieve has been in operation for from one to four hours the dust particles deposited on the sides of the pipe have lessened the distance between the electric wire and the pipe which causes electrical discharges to take place. The gas is then shut off by a damper, the electric current is cut off and the sides of the pipe are cleaned by being rapped by the hammer operated, of course, by machinery, and the dust is collected from the pipes.

There is enough potash in the dust, from the ores being treated in the furnaces, to make it a valuable by-product. It is sold to be used as fertilizer and it is said that it brings enough to pay the expenses of running the plant.

A considerable saving also is made in the operating expenses by the use of the electric sieve. It formerly required from four to six men to clean the dust from the stove walls, combustion chambers and boilers. Now the dust is caught and precipitated before it enters those places, by the invisible electric sieve which has no weight nor any material body and occupies no space.

Indeed if there is left in the world anyone who will not believe in things invisible, we are justified in the doubt expressed by the Quaker's question, "Friend! Does thee believe thee has any brains?"

For invisible forces are all about us. Of some we have an imperfect knowledge while of others we have as yet only the vaguest ideas.

The Farm Home (26)

July 5, 1920

Out in the berry patch, the bluejays scolded me for trespassing. They talked of a food shortage and threatened terrible things to profiteers who took more than their share of the necessaries of life. But I was used to their clamor and not alarmed even when one swooped down and struck my bonnet. I knew they would not harm me and kept right on picking berries. This is a parable. I give it to you for what it is worth, trusting you to draw your own comparisons.

When The Man Of The Place and I, with the small daughter, came to Missouri some years ago we tried to save all the wild fruit in the woods. Coming from the plains of Dakota where the only wild fruit was the few choke-cherries growing on the banks of the small lakes, we could not bear to see go to waste the perfectly delicious wild huckleberries, strawberries and blackberries which grew so abundantly everywhere on the hills.

By the way, did you ever eat choke-cherries? At first taste they are very good and the first time I tried them I ate quite a few before my throat began to tighten with a fuzzy, choking feeling. A green persimmon has nothing on a ripe choke-cherry, as I know. I have tried both. So when we came to the Ozarks we reveled in the wild fruit, for as yet there was no tame fruit on the place. Huckleberries came first and we were impatiently waiting for them to ripen when somebody told me that the green ones made good pies. Immediately I went out into the little cleared space in the woods where the low huckleberry bushes grew and gathered a bucket of berries. Company was coming to dinner next day and I took special pains to make a good pie of the berries for I did want my new neighbors to enjoy the visit. And the crust of the pie was deliciously crisp and flaky but after one taste, the visitors seemed to hesitate.

I took a mouthful of my piece and found it bitter as gall. I never tasted gall, but that is the bitterest expression I know and nothing could be more bitter than that pie.

"Oh!" I exclaimed. "They told me green huckleberries were good!"

"These can't be huckleberries," said Mrs. X, "for green huckleberries do make good pies."

Mr. X was examining the berries in his portion. "These are buckberries," he said. "They grow on a bush about the size of a huckleberry bush and you must have made a mistake when you gathered them."

And so I added to my knowledge the difference between huckleberries and buckberries and we have enjoyed many a green huckleberry pie since then. Used when quite small the berries not only taste delicious but give a bouquet of perfume to the pie that adds wonderfully to the pleasure of eating it.

When blackberries came on, chiggers were ripe also and there is nothing a chigger enjoys so much as feasting on a "foreigner." The blackberry patches are their home and we made many a chigger happy that season. We gathered the berries by bucketsfull; we filled the pans and pots and all the available dishes in the house, then hastily we bathed in strong soapsuds and applied remedies to the worst bitten spots. Then I put up the berries and cleared the decks for the next day's picking, for gather them we would no matter how the chiggers bit.

I was thinking of these experiences while the bluejays screamed at me in the berry patch—tame berries now. We never pick the wild ones these days because there are large tame ones in plenty. The apple trees that were little switches when we picked the wild fruit have supplied us with carloads of apples. Even the chiggers never bother us any more.

We are so accustomed to an abundance of fruit that we do not appreciate the fine cultivated sorts as we did the wild kinds that we gathered at the cost of so much labor and discomfort.

There is a moral here somewhere too, I am sure, and again I will leave it for you to discover.

The Farm Home (27)

July 20, 1920

Coming in from a successful round with the hay fork, helping The Man Of The Place to put a load of hay in the barn, I sat down to read a letter from the daughter, now Rose Wilder Lane, who is traveling in Europe, and this is what I read: "The farmers are cutting their hay already, usually women helping in the fields. I am one traveler in Europe who does not 'throw a fit' at sight of a woman helping in the hay."

She has seen it many a time at home, you know, besides she had long ago read, "Maud Muller on a summer's day raked the meadow sweet with hay" so she was well used to the idea both practically and with a glamor of romance.

It is rather amusing, is it not, that persons from this country, where farm women help so much with the out-of-doors work, should be so shocked at the sight of European women doing the same thing? To be sure they work in different ways but their methods of farming are so much different that naturally they would. After all it is only the old custom of time immemorial, the woman helping her man.

It is as easy to criticize other countries than ours as it is to find fault with other people than ourselves and both usually come from a lack of understanding. If we are looking for defects we are nearly certain to find them, while if we observe others with the purpose of learning and adapting for ourselves what is good in their lives and ways we gain much.

Just to illustrate my meaning: One soldier boy came home from France and, when asked about the ways of farming there, told of the antiquated, awkward machinery and slow, old-fashioned methods. Another boy back from the same place, remembered and told of the way in which the farmers raised much more to the acre than we do here. While we are in the lead with our machinery and ways of working, we could learn from them in the care of our soil and the growing of crops. One boy had seen the defects, while the other learned the helpful lessons.

There seems to be more beauty in the surroundings of country life in Europe than with us and here again we might learn, not to copy, but to adapt the idea to our circumstances.

Let me read you a little more from Rose's letter, written on the train as she was traveling from Paris to Geneva, Switzerland: "It's a very warm, sunny day and the country is lovely. Tilled fields look like broad ribbons on the hillsides. I don't know why, but the farmers cultivate all their land in long, narrow strips; one of oats, one of potatoes, perhaps; one of alfalfa, one of purple clover. The poppies are thick in the oats and wheat and they are the reddest things you ever saw and then there are strips perfectly yellow with wild mustard. So with the red-tiled roofs of the villages and white church spires and leafy green trees, there is lots of color in the landscape."

We would not cultivate our fields in their way for the sake of the color scheme but our farms might be planned to bring out and show their natural beauties. A determination that the beauty, as well as the utility, of our surroundings shall be considered will do wonders. It will prevent the new barn being placed where it will ruin the view from the kitchen window when it might as well be a little to one side. There are more inspiring views than a barn for a tired woman in a hot kitchen.

A craving for and delight in beauty is natural with us all, because it is necessary for our right development, for our well being in every way, mentally, spiritually and physically. Beautiful sounds in music have been known to cure illness; beauty for the eyes to feast upon is a help in the cure of mental disorders and nothing so lifts our souls Heavenward as some beautiful scene in nature.

From the spots on a butterfly's wing to the snows on a mountain top; from the still growth of a wild flower to the rush of a mountain torrent, every sight of nature is beautiful. From the sweet song of a bird to the roar of the mighty winds of a hurricane, every sound in nature has the beauties of harmony.

We Visit Arabia

August 5, 1920

Our ideas of Arabia have always been rather vague. It has been to us a land of romance, where swift camels and wild horsemen on fleet Arab steeds journey across the desert sands from oasis to green oasis. But in this land of mirage and mystery there has risen a new spirit and a new nation of Arabia is taking its place in the world.

A very interesting story of the country is told by Frederick Simpich in the Geographic Magazine. It seems that for several years a group of Arab students in Paris have been agitating for Arab independence and the idea was warmly supported by the more advanced Arabs everywhere. The war gave them their chance and Mohammedan troops joined the British under General Allenby fighting both Turkey and Germany, which was surprising as the Sultan of Turkey was the head of the Moslem faith. This joining with Christians to fight Turkey was brought about by the great Mohammedan leader Agha Khan who sent out a manifesto declaring that Turkey had forfeited its leadership of Mohammedans by becoming a tool of Germany. So Arabs joined the British soldiers in the march on Jerusalem, and Mohammedan and Christian fought side by side against the Turk in the last crusade which has freed Jerusalem from the infidel.

From Mecca, the holy city of Mohammedans, the Grand Shereef sent out a telegram to the leaders of Christian nations asking that "Arabia be admitted to the family of nations." This telegram opened that forbidden city so that Christians are safe there where formerly they were killed simply because they were Christians; it lets in the missionaries and the traders from Western nations and may forever prevent a "holy war" which has been a fear in the Christian world. British influence, which is very strong in Arabia, has brought this about.

The gateway to Mecca is the port of Jidda, squatting on its treeless hills at whose base rolls the oily waves of the Red Sea that once engulfed the hosts of Pharaoh. Jidda is further noted for having what is claimed to be the tomb of Eve. "Adam and Eve were big people, the Arabs say. Eve was so tall she could hold a grown lion in her lap and stroke it as we stroke a kitten." Needless to say the tomb is long. It is shaped like an airship hangar and made of stone.

Mecca is 45 miles east of Jidda. It is of great importance in both the political and religious worlds but it is small and ugly. Its chief business is living off travelers for it has the greatest tourist traffic of any city in the world, being the place of pilgrimage for Mohammedans, who are 12 per cent of all the people in the world.

The origin of the Arabian race is lost in the mists of antiquity but the Arabs were a nation with a king of their own long, long before the birth of Christ. Arabia once ruled from India to the Atlantic and its schools of science were world famous. Schools of healing were established in Bagdad and botany was studied as a branch of medicine. Many of our medicines and their use were known to the Arabs of that far away time and we still use many terms and signs taken from the Arab language. But education as we understand it is almost unknown in Arabia today. Learning is mostly confined to the classics of their literature and the Koran is learned by heart. There are no schools of any kind in small towns.

Arabs are divided by their manner of life into two classes, the Al Bedoo or Bedouins which means the Dwellers in the Open Land, and Al Hadr, or Dwellers in Fixed Localities. The Bedouins are the desert roamers and are better known than those who are settled in one place. Most of Arabia even outside the deserts is so dry that it is suitable only for grazing and sometimes, from lack of moisture, even the scanty grass will not grow so that the Bedouin Arab must move his family and his herds from place to place. Living this free, roving life out in "The Open Land" has made the Bedouin Arab bold and defiant and quick to fight. He is tall and graceful, dark complexioned and very handsome, being usually strong and healthy and of clean and simple habits.

The aristocracy of Arabia is found in the 80 per cent of the people who live in towns and villages. These families trace their ancestry back thru many generations. There is some admixture of African blood in the race which comes from intermarrying with freed slaves who have been brought from Africa. The Arabian people are very bright mentally, being the equal of any race in that respect.

The most important provinces of Arabia lie along the Red Sea coast. The valleys of these provinces produce coffee, figs, spices, hides and dates, but dates are the only crop of any importance. Grapes are grown, but the Mohammedan religion forbids drinking so no wine is made. The methods of farming are so primitive that they barely furnish food for the people.

The finest horses in the world are in Arabia and their pedigrees can be traced back to the Fifth Century. The Arabs value their horses more than their camels, but camels are the more useful, being worked and sheared for the camels' hair and when old killed and eaten. Goats and sheep are numerous but there are only a few cattle.

Wild animals are scarce. There are some tigers, panthers, wolves, foxes, hyenas and a few monkeys.

There are a few skilled workers in Arabia and tools are of the most primitive kind. The buildings are of mud or brick. The country has no factories and a few years ago 75 per cent of all cotton goods were shipped from the United States. At present, because of the war, Japanese and Indian cottons have taken their place. Kerosene, sewing machines, phonographs and cheap watches are imported from the United States.

In turn we buy many things from Arabia, chief among which is dates. When we open a package of dates in our kitchen we also open our minds to all the romance and mystery of the Orient, if we remember that the dates were picked and packed by dark skinned Arab women in the valleys by the Red Sea.

And by opening their country to us they have really said, "Come, let's get acquainted! Let's exchange ideas as well as goods and learn from one another."

The Farm Home (28)

August 20, 1920

The whole world was a deep, dark blue, for I had waked with a grouch that morning. While blue is without doubt a heavenly color it is better in skies than in one's mind, for when the blues descend upon a poor mortal on earth, life seems far from being worth the living.

I didn't want to help with the chores; I hated to get breakfast and the prospect of doing up the morning's work afterward was positively revolting. Beginning the usual round of duties—under protest, I had a great many thoughts about work and none of them was complimentary to the habit. But presently my mind took a wider range and became less personal as applied to the day just beginning.

First, I remembered the old, old labor law, "Six days thou shalt labour and do all thy work: But the seventh day is the Sabbath of the Lord thy God: In it thou shalt not do any work."[1]

It used to be impressed upon us as most important that we must rest on the seventh day. This doesn't seem to be necessary any longer. We may not, "Remember the Sabbath day to keep it holy,"[2] but we'll not forget to stop working. With our present attitude toward work, the emphasis should be put upon, "Six days thou shalt labor," and if we stick it out to work the six days, we will rest on the seventh without any urging. Given half a chance, we will take Saturday off also and any other day or part of a day we can manage to sneak, besides which the length of a work day is shrinking and shrinking for everyone except farmers, and they are hoping to shorten theirs.

But really the old way was best, for it takes about six days of work to give just the right flavor to a day off. As I thought of all these things, insensibly my ideas about work changed. I remembered the time of enforced idleness

1. Exodus 20:9–10.
2. Exodus 20:8.

when recovering from an illness and how I longed to be busily at work again. Also I recollected a week of vacation that I once devoted to pleasure during which I suffered more than the weariness of working while I had none of its satisfaction. For there is a great satisfaction in work well done, the thrill of success in a task accomplished.

I got the thrill at the moment that my mind reached the climax. The separator was washed. It is a job that I especially dislike, but while my mind had been busy far afield my hands had performed their accustomed task with none of the usual sense of unpleasantness, showing that after all it is not so much the work we do with our bodies that makes us tired and dissatisfied as the work we do with our minds.

We have been, for so long, thinking of labor as a curse upon man that, because of our persistently thinking of it as such, it has very nearly become so.

There always has been a great deal of misplaced pity for Adam because of his sentence to hard labor for life when really that was all that saved him after he was deported from paradise and it is the only thing that has kept his descendents as safe and sane even as they are.

There is nothing wrong with God's plan that man should earn his bread by the sweat of his brow. The wrong is in our own position only. In trying to shirk while we "let George do it," we bring upon ourselves our own punishment, for in the attitude we take toward our work we make of it a burden instead of the blessing it might be.

Work is like other good things in that it should not be indulged in to excess, but a reasonable amount that is of value to one's self and to the world, as is any honest, well-directed labor, need never descend into drudgery.

It is a tonic and an inspiration and a reward unto itself. For the sweetness of life lies in usefulness like honey deep in the heart of clover bloom.

Now We Visit Bohemia (1)

September 5, 1920

When you hear the word Bohemian what first comes to your mind? I'll venture to say it is some tale you have heard of what is called Bohemian life in New York, which is supposed to be the very free and freakish life led by artists and poets where ordinary conventions are disregarded. Or perhaps you remember hearing that Gipsies are Bohemians and are uncertain whether there is a country of that name. If you followed the news of the Great War closely you will know that Bohemian people were compelled, by

Austria, to go into its armies and that these soldiers deserted to the allies whenever there was a chance to do so.

I wish I could show you the picture postcards that Rose Wilder Lane has sent me from Prague, the capital of Bohemia. I'll share them with you anyway.

After seeing these pictures of wonderful, old places, the word Bohemian will always bring to mind a brave people who have kept their national ideals, culture and language thru 500 years of oppression by a brutal, conquering nation.

First there is the view of Prague as we approach it. On a high hill is the old city built by Queen Libussa in the year 600. The entire big hill is surrounded by great walls and on its highest point is the great castle and cathedral, in one building, built by the old Bohemian kings. The castle was taken by the Austrians under their Hapsburg rulers, but now since the World War, which freed Bohemia, it is again occupied by a Bohemian ruler, President Masaryk.

The original style of the castle-cathedral building was pure Gothic and the graceful heavenward pointing effect of the towers is very beautiful. One ugly square tower was added by the Hapsburgs and somewhat spoils the effect of the building but since the Bohemians control their own country again this is being changed to Gothic also.

Then there is the picture of the city clustering at the foot of the castle hill. Its buildings are all of stone with roofs of hand-baked tile and ornamented with carvings and mosaic work. They are the most wonderful colors of soft browns and yellows and grays with tints of red and shadows of blue.

A river runs thru the town with a beautiful stone bridge at every street crossing. The banks of the river are walled and gardened and there are many canals opening from it that are used as streets where all movement is by boat.

Spanning the river to Old Town is Charles Bridge built in the days of the old Bohemian kings. At each end of this bridge is a square stone tower with an arched opening thru which the street runs to the bridge. The towers, like all the stone buildings in the city, are ornamented with carvings and mosaic work.

In the city are many beautiful churches and public buildings made more beautiful by wonderful carvings of human figures and of warriors on horseback that show against the sky.

The National theater is on the river bank as is also a large old monastery. The old powder tower now about in the center of the city, used to stand over the inner end of the drawbridge that led to the city gate. Inside the archway are still the remnants of the portecullis that used to be let down over the entrance when the place was to be defended in the old wars. The moat, across which the drawbridge reached when let down, is now filled in and used as a street.

Adjoining the powder tower is the city's community meeting place. It has a splendid restaurant, big auditorium, dance halls and a little theater. Austria, the conqueror, gave Prague money to build a modern sanitary system but the city used it instead to build this community house. It was part of the effort to keep alive Bohemian culture and national spirit thru the 500 years of subjection to Austria when even the Bohemian language could be spoken only in secret.

The town hall is a wonderful building with Gothic towers and much carving.

It was in front of the town hall that, after conquering Bohemia at the battle of the White Mountain 500 years ago, the Austrian conqueror had all the aristocracy and all the learned men of Bohemia executed publicly, cutting out their eyes and tongues, cutting off their hands and feet and then beheading them as a symbol of the conquest of Bohemia and expecting by this to destroy the Bohemian national spirit.

The executions lasted all day and at night there was no one left in all Bohemia who could lead the people in a revolt against their enemies.

At the front of the town hall and a massive part of it is a clock made by a blind man in the Sixteenth Century. At a quarter before each hour the two little doors above open, the cock on the roof crows and the 12 apostles pass behind the open doors, each one stopping, turning to look at you and bowing.

The cock crows again three times when Peter passes and Judas comes last with a money bag and a rope. Meantime the clock strikes and the skeleton death at the right of the clock beats a slow roll on a drum. The clock tells the year, month, week and day, also position of the planets and sun.

Now We Visit Bohemia (2)

September 20, 1920

"Prague is the city of my heart," writes Rose Wilder Lane. "I arrived at noon and found the Sokol fete (a festival of celebration) in full blast. The streets were masses of flags and fully half of them were American. Bands played on every corner and the streets were glorious with color, everyone wearing the Bohemian costumes which are the loveliest things in the world—

embedded trousers and jackets and feathered caps on the men; the women wearing very full, short skirts, red and yellow and green, all gorgeous colors, and white waists solidly embroidered in colors with enormous sleeves. With this dress they wore aprons, of lace and silk, and short, black, velvet jackets. They wore head-dresses of jewels and embroidery, or enormous ones of white stuff with 3-foot stiff white bows behind." These are the old national costumes and must be stunning in more ways than one, but the description is not intended as fashion suggestions.

Rose Wilder Lane took tea with President Masaryk in the old castle on the hill. She also went into the tenements of the city such as those of the "East Side" in New York and of them she says, "We climbed up five flights of smelly stairs passing windows overlooking a courtyard where the rotting balconies were falling from the walls and garbage and sewage dripped and chickens and goats added to the scents. And all the women in sight were sitting on their doorsteps reading. Bohemia is the most literate country in the world. Everyone reads and reads good books.

"I only wish you could get an idea of Prague from the poor postcards I sent you. It is beyond words beautiful. Even the sidewalks—every single sidewalk in the city—are of mosaic and as you walk you see how the man who laid them played along as he went, making now a pattern of circles, getting tired of that and amusing himself by making a large and beautiful butterfly, going back to a new combination of circles, stopped to try a landscape that didn't succeed very well and putting in plain gray stones for awhile until his courage rose again and he tried the landscape once more with a larger assortment of colored stones and succeeded so nobly that in his joy he did zigzag lightning lines for quite a distance.

"There are old houses painted—the whole fronts painted—with marvelously colored pictures sometime in the fourteenth century, all the colors still bright and beautiful.

"On the hill are the enormous stone walls, with hundreds of people living in the rooms inside them, that were built by the good Queen Libussa in six hundred something, when she began the city of Prague.

"And oh, if you could see the Street of the Alchemists, the little street that is part of the great, old castle on the hill, the castle running along both sides of a deep, wooded canyon where the wild beasts were kept that ate prisoners thrown from the dungeons above.

"The Street of Alchemists looks as if it had been built by gnomes; its houses are so little and so quaint and so curiously colored. They make, of course, one long wall, but each is a little back or forward from the next, and all the roofs, that are hardly higher than your head, are slanted at a different angle or gabled or ornamented with a leering face. Inside there are only two rooms in each, the tiniest of little rooms where each alchemist worked at his experiments, and another just large enough for a tiny couch and a shrine, with a deep, small window overlooking the canyon and, in the days of the alchemists, the waiting wild beasts. The alchemists were maintained and the street for them built by King Rudolph, the last of the Bohemian monarchs when Bohemia was free and kings elected by the people. He was a patron of the arts and sciences, and greatly desired to be the king who should be honored by the discovery of the method of turning other metals to gold; the alchemists were honored and fatly fed, and expected to produce the secret. In time the king's patience wore thin and he earnestly desired them to produce it pretty quick, whereupon in despair some of them melted gold coins in their crucibles, and this was made known to the rejoicing king, and the alchemists fled wildly in the night, scattering all their belongings down the steep, highwalled road to the town below, and some got away and some were speared by guards, and some were haled back and thrown from their windows to the beasts, and that was the end of the street of the alchemists, which is now inhabited by watchmen of the palace. And the place of the wild beasts is inhabited by four Siberian bears that the Czechs in Russia brought back as gifts to President Masaryk who now occupies the palace."

The Farm Home (29)

October 5, 1920

Missourians again have cause to be proud of their state and their governor, for in the business of state government an example has been set which should be followed by the other states, and even by the United States Government at Washington.

When there is so much talk of extravagance and mismanagement, both public and private, it is very encouraging to know that our present state government has been so well managed that there is to be a lessening of the taxes because the state does not need so much income. On May 2 the balance in the state treasury was $11,006,898.94 and there were no outstanding debts.

There never before has been so much state money in the treasury. The revenue fund, from which the expenses of the state government are paid, has a balance to its credit of $2,150,666.13. The school fund has $2,510,168.59 of good money on hand, while the fund for good roads has a balance of $3,470,659.50.

This money has not been saved from the state revenues by letting any of the state institutions suffer in their necessary expenses, but instead by putting them on a business basis. As an example, under the present system of management the earnings of the state penitentiary during April were $439,698.99 and the expenses were $143,764.42.

Interest on the balance in the treasury is now bringing to the state $1,000 a day, which goes into the general revenue fund. As this is the fund that is used for the running expenses of the state government, the amount that must be collected by taxes is lessened by just that $1,000 a day.

The budget system, bringing expenses within the income with a margin over for savings, is quite as good for private use. It helps amazingly to keep down expenses as I know from experience. We all try to save and would be inclined to resent it if anyone should say we were not careful in our spending, but we are too much like the town woman who boycotted eggs because they were too high and then, without a protest, paid $36 for a pair of low shoes. Unless we figure carefully on both income and expenses, it is so easy to throw away with one hand what we save with the other.

The other day I sent to town for a toilet preparation, the price of which has always been 50 cents. When the Man of the Place brought it home, he said the price was $1 and the reason was plain when I had examined the goods. They were done up in a new style and very fancy package.

Now, it was the preparation I needed, not a fancy package, but that sporty container had doubled the price.

Everyone these days has a try at telling what is wrong with business conditions. I am sure that one thing causing us a great deal of trouble and making much higher the high cost of living is the extra price we pay for fancy packages.

The Farm Home (30)

October 20, 1920

There is a purple haze over the hill tops and a hint of sadness in the sunshine, because of summer's departure; on the low ground down by the spring the walnuts are dropping from the trees and squirrels are busy hiding away their winter supply. Here and there the leaves are beginning to change color and a little, vagrant, autumn breeze goes wandering over the hills and down the valleys whispering to "follow, follow," until it is almost impossible to resist. So I should not be too harshly criticized if I ramble a little even in my conversation.

We have been gathering the fruits of the season's work into barns and bins and cellars. The harvest has been abundant and a good supply is stored away for future needs.

Now I am wondering what sort of fruits, and how plentiful the supply, we have stored away in our hearts and souls and minds from our year's activities. The time of gathering together the visible results of our year's labor is a very appropriate time to reckon up the invisible, more important harvest.

When we lived in South Dakota, where the cold came early and strong, we once had a hired man (farmers had them in those days), who was a good worker, but whose money was too easily spent. In the fall when the first cold wind struck him, he would shiver and chatter and always he would say, "Gee Mighty! This makes a feller wonder what's become of his summer's wages!"

Ever since then, Harvest Home time has seemed to me the time to gather together and take stock of our mental and spiritual harvest, and to wonder what we have done with the wealth of opportunity that has come to us and the treasures we have had in our keeping. Much too often I have felt like quoting the hired man of other days.

Have we found a new friendship worth while? Have we even kept safely the old friendships, treasures worth much more than silver and gold? People in these history-making days hold their opinions so strongly and defend them so fiercely, that a strain will be put upon many friendships, and the pity of it is that these misunderstandings will come between people who are earnestly striving for the right thing. Right seems to be obscured and truth is difficult to find.

But if the difficulty of finding the truth has increased our appreciation of its value, if the beauty of truth is plainer to us and more desired, then we have gathered treasure for the future.

We lay away the gleanings of our years in the edifice of our character, where nothing is ever lost. What have we stored away, in this safe place during the season that is past? Is it something that will keep sound and pure and sweet or something that is faulty and not worth storing?

As a child I learned my Bible lessons by heart, in the good old-fashioned way, and once won the prize for repeating correctly more verses from the Bible than any other person in the Sunday school. But always my mind had a trick of picking a text here and a text there and connecting them together in meaning. In this way there came to me a thought that makes the stores from my invisible harvest important to me. These texts are familiar to everyone. It is their sequence that gives the thought.

"Lay not up for yourselves treasures upon earth, where moth and rust doth corrupt, and where thieves break thru and steal. But lay up for yourselves treasures in Heaven, where neither moth nor rust doth corrupt, and where thieves do not break thru nor steal."[3]

And then: "Why say ye, Lo here and lo there. Know ye not that the kingdom of Heaven is within you?"[4]

The Farm Home (31)

November 5, 1920

It is a rather general idea that the housewife's duties are narrowing to the mind, because of their samenesses—their "over and overishness" as one writer puts it.

If this is true it is not necessary, for there are many windows that open wide so we may pass thru them mentally, out into paths that lead on and on to far journeyings and interesting knowledge.

It doesn't occupy our brains to peel potatoes, to sweep and make beds or to darn the family hose. Our bodies learn to do the everyday tasks without much head-work, leaving our minds free to pass thru these windows and follow the fascinating ways that lead from them. The lightest touch of a thought is enough to set them wide that we may escape from any narrowing round of everyday work.

Thru my kitchen window, I saw the puppies playing and was reminded of an article I had read on training dogs for circus work. This brought to my mind the greatest circus man, our own P. T. Barnum, and that he once nearly bought the house where Shakespeare was born, to bring to America as an attraction. And that evening, with the help of magazines, I wandered thru the country where Shakespeare lived and worked and where the scenes of his plays and poems are laid.

Warwickshire, "Shakespeare's country," lies nearly in the heart of England and while there have been many changes, still a great deal is now as it was when Shakespeare saw it 300 years ago. The river Avon still flows gently thru the sweet meadows and leafy forests, spanned by its stone bridges which have been in use for hundreds of years. And on its banks are still many of the massive and wonderful old buildings of Shakespeare's time.

The Forest of Arden has disappeared and, where the poet's characters

3. Matthew 6:19–20.
4. Luke 17:21.

wandered among the trees in "As You Like It," there are now villages, farms, fine country houses and large parks.

Kenilworth Castle that Shakespeare saw in all its glory as a stately palace and at the same time a strong fortress, is now a mass of ruins. One of the parts still intact is Caesar's Tower, which still dominates the country around as it has for more than 400 years, its massive walls of stone 15 and 16 feet thick defying the march of the centuries. Kenilworth Castle was the scene of Sir Walter Scott's story "Kenilworth."

Warwick Castle was the same in Shakespeare's time as it is today; a castle fortress of medieval times whose stone towers and battlements and massive buttresses and windows high in the great walls bring to our minds pictures of ancient times and life.

Stratford-Upon-Avon is in the southern part of Warwickshire and here is the house where Shakespeare was born in 1564. It is now national property, having been bought by the British government in 1847, because of P. T. Barnum's proposition to buy it and remove it to America.

One mile from Stratford-Upon-Avon is the little, industrial town of Shottery which is celebrated as the home of Anne Hathaway who became Shakespeare's wife. The cottage where she lived when he wooed and won her still stands on the outskirts of the village and is just as it was at that time. It is a rather large building built of wood and plaster, covered with a thatched roof. The ceilings are low and the main room has a stone floor and a wide fireplace with a cozy chimney corner. Within the house are many relics of Anne Hathaway's time, among which is a hand carved bedstead. This cottage and contents also is owned by the British nation.

Shakespeare and Anne Hathaway were married in 1582 when he was 18 and she was 26. Three years later Shakespeare was obliged to leave the country and go to the city to seek his fortune. He left his family behind, probably in the Hathaway cottage, and for 27 years he lived in London visiting Stratford only once a year.

Stratford-Upon-Avon is a country town of 8,000 to 9,000 inhabitants. The town is mentioned in a Saxon charter of the eighth century and coins have been found there showing that it was inhabited in the far away times of Roman occupation of England. It has been an agricultural center and a manufacturing town but now owes its fame almost entirely to Shakespeare.

Here he was born and spent his youth; here he lived during the closing years of his life, dying in 1616 in his house called New Place, and here is his grave in the Church of the Holy Trinity, on the bank of the lovely river Avon. The church is on the site of a Saxon monastery. The central tower was built in the twelfth century and the building was completed about 500 years ago. Near the tomb of Shakespeare are those of his wife and daughter.

The Shakespeare memorial building, built in 1879, is on the bank of the river above the church. In this building is a theater where performances are given yearly, in April, and many Shakespearian treasures are kept here.

The Farm Home (32)

December 5, 1920

Among all the Americans who have crossed to France during the past few years probably no two saw the country alike at their landing, for no two persons in any place for the first time, are impressed by the same things. It is because of this that I venture to add to the many descriptions of Europe, these paragraphs from the letters of Rose Wilder Lane.

"I mailed my letter to you on shipboard," she wrote. "Then I went out and saw the green land lifted above the sea—a green land like the California foothills, all marked in little squares with hedges of trees and dotted with slanting-roofed houses of stone, and church spires.

"We came to Cherbourg at 1 o'clock. Long, solid walls of masonry reached out into the water and the harbor was buttressed with old, moss-grown masonry above which were banks of smooth, green lawn. Two or three buildings—guard houses or something of the sort—could be seen with hundreds of little slits of windows in the gray stone, and slanting roofs as green with moss as the lawn with grass. And the water all around was as blue as San Francisco Bay.

"The tender came out about 4 o'clock and took us off and while the baggage was being transferred we sat for hours, and watched a baby-blue-and-pink sunset. Then we went around the long stone piers and into the inner harbor of Cherbourg, where there was a long, wide, smooth promenade. It was paraded by holidaying soldiers and French women, and short-jacketed, barelegged, little boys and full-skirted, capped little girls rolling hoops, with nurses in peasant costumes knitting and watching them.

"Beyond were the lovely, old streets with stone houses. There isn't any use trying to describe them. I've read about French towns myself and never had the least idea how they looked. I can only say I stood on the deck and wept tears of joy. There isn't any way to express it. France just 'belongs,' that's all.

"Then came the customs! And I—with my typewriter, and my big suit case and my little suitcase and my week-end bag and my manuscript case and my roll of steamer rugs and pillows, and a bon voyage basket of fruit and candies, and my purse and my passport, and my (not) fluent French—was examined.

"However, all came thru unscathed except my purse. I had a porter carry the lot which was strung neatly on a rope and swung over his shoulders, and when he had them all into my compartment on the train I thought I'd pay him well and offered him 90 cents American money. He wept bitterly and beating his breast cried piteously. 'Pas beaucoup, not enough!' And I, having expected a sunshine burst of joy and gratitude was so stunned that mechanically I fed into his eager palm dime after dime and quarter after quarter until he had all the change I possessed, then he departed with bitter reproaches.

"Of course you have read about the continental trains but you don't know until you see them how strange they really are. There are two narrow seats, heavily upholstered in plush that run the length of the car, with a tall window between them at one end, and a half glass door between them at the other end. The walls are worked with scrolls and the most elaborate of chandeliers hangs overhead supporting two of the feeblest electric lights that ever enabled you to see how dark it was.

"Putting my face against the windowpane I could see snatches of blossomy orchards and tall stone gables of farm houses and a starry sky. During the night I made the acquaintance of a French girl who told me we were passing thru villages, and pointed out to me the rivers, which otherwise I should have thought were small irrigation ditches.

"Our train was supposed to start immediately upon the arrival of the boat, being a steamer special, but it did not leave until nearly midnight. The train was so filled with the charm of the spring night and 'apple blossom time in Normandy,' which was all about us, that it lingered along the way and arrived at Paris 7 hours late on a 6-hour run."

Dear Farm Women

January 5, 1921

For several years I have been talking and talking, hearing no reply, until I came to feel that no one was listening to me.

And to find that you are really there and will answer back is truly delightful.[1]

1. *Ruralist* editor John F. Case asked women readers to write Wilder on "Why I Should Like to Leave the Farm." Wilder had become concerned about reports of "lessened rural population" and felt the dissatisfaction of farm women might be a cause. This "First Prize Letter" is representative of the many she received:

> Mrs. A. J. Wilder—Give me just one logical reason why I should try to keep my boy and girl on the farm where all the odds are against them; where they are exploited in the market place; where they get less for their toil than in any other calling; where they have longer hours of harder work than do the folks in the city and get poorer pay for doing it?
>
> Why should I keep my boy and girl on the farm where they must attend the poorest schools on earth?
>
> Why should I desire them to remain thru life where they are made the butt of every stale joke sprung by every cheap joke-smith in the land, when the city offers a ten to one better chance to rise in the world than is afforded in the country?
>
> Why should I want them to remain among a class that by many is looked upon as a harmless group of "ignoramuses," a class who suspect their kind to such a degree that they will not take any measures to protect one another against the abuses that are heaped upon them by their exploiters?
>
> In the country we must travel over the worst roads in the world and where we are exposed to the worst weather conditions. We have poor churches and poorer schools; we cannot hear the best lectures, nor attend the best entertainments as can the folks in town.

Thank you all so much for the kind things you have said about my department. To know that I have helped you a little, or made a day brighter, will make my own work easier and cause the sun to shine on the dark days, for we all have them.

'Tis then a little place of sunshine, in the heart, helps mightily. And there is nothing that puts so much brightness there as having helped someone else.

We Visit Paris Now

January 5, 1921

Paris isn't only the place where fashions are made. It is very much more and in these word pictures drawn by Rose Wilder Lane the city seems to have come to life.

This is Paris as seen by one of ourselves:

"You never saw or dreamed of a city like Paris; it is perfectly beautiful! I have contended all these years that cities need not be ugly and crowded and crushing to death every human impulse worth having. I always knew there could be a Paris although I never could have imagined it as beautiful as it is.

"The broad streets lined with parks where children play, the curving, little, narrow streets lined with wonderful, old, stone buildings—there are not two roofs alike in all Paris, nor two streets that cross each other at right angles in the stiff way of American cities.

"There are almost no street cars—all traffic is underground or by taxi, and I wake in the mornings, in my hotel in the very heart of Paris, and hear nothing but birds as I would on Rocky Ridge Farm. Except the honks of the taxis, which have a funny, little hoarse sound and remind me of nothing so much as geese flying high and honking as they go.

We are told that many great men were born on the farm. But they did not become great on the farm. Every mother's son of them left the farm before he became great!

Why should I desire to remain on the farm where the men do not have time to keep posted on at least some of the news of the day and where women do not have time to clean their teeth; where men toil from 12 to 14 hours a day and grow crops that they must sell for less than the cost of producing them, and the women work from 12 to 18 hours a day, to care for babies and to cook for harvest hands, until when the supper work is over they are too tired to sleep.

Now can you, with a clear conscience, insist that I remain on the farm under its unfair terms? Mrs. W. M.

"The Champs Elysses is a broad, broad street with parks as broad along both sides; the loveliest, most graceful trees and lawns, and children playing there. Little girls all in little white dresses that show the legs half way above the knees and have no sleeves at all, with big bows in their hair and little white kid gloves; little boys in the least possible bit of clothing, a one-piece thing that ends just below their thighs and is low necked; no stockings for either girls or boys, just bare legs and arms except for little boots and gloves, always gloves. And with them are nurses, peasant women most of them, in embroidered aprons and wide-sleeved, black silk and velvet dresses and every one wearing a different sort of fantastic cap. I saw one Algerian nurse black as ebony. She wore a white sort of wrapped around robe and a turban of glorious reds and yellows. Under the trees are Punch and Judy shows, gaily painted and carved and gilded stages where Punch and Judy do things you could not believe possible of puppets, and the children yell with joy, packed all around in a crowd.

"I am very much surprised to find the Seine so small. I don't know why I had thought of it as such a large river, but I had some vague notion of its being like a river at home. It runs thru the city, you know, and is crossed every few blocks by beautiful stone bridges, and there are parks all along its edge and usually quite beautiful slanting-roofed or turreted stone buildings beyond them. At night when the colored lights shine from the bridges on the water, and the boats on it each carry a paper Japanese lantern swinging at the bow, it is like something you have dreamed about.

"The hotels in Paris have inner courts with grass and flowers. Every alleyway reveals the lovely, green vistas, alluring beyond words. Space is expensive but, by the bounty of God to the French, they know that hideousness is more so. They will tenderly nurse a tree and 16 square feet of flowers in land valued in hundreds of francs an inch.

"Little items are interesting. Door knobs are in the middle of doors instead of at the edge. Big doors, like hotel doors, open with long levers instead of handles.

"There are no traffic officers; everyone goes where he pleases, when he pleases, and if a pedestrian is run down he is arrested for blocking the traffic. That is perhaps one reason why there are almost no accidents. Another reason is the taxi drivers, who are the most reckless speed-maniacs on earth, who momentarily handle death at their finger ends and always escape.

"When you buy anything in a store you have to go with the clerk to the cashier's office where you wait while the purchase is recorded in the ledgers and then with the slip and the clerk you go to the next department, the treasurer I suppose, where you hand in your money and get the change and then to the wrappers where it is wrapped and given you."

The Roads Women Travel

February 1, 1921

All day I have been thinking about roads. There are so many of them. There is the dim trail that leads down thru the woods. It looks so fascinating, wandering away thru the patches of shade and sunshine that I long to follow it, but I happen to know that it bogs down in the soft ground at the creek bank where the cattle gather to drink. If I go that way I will sink in the mud over my shoe tops.

If I turned back from the mud, it would be hard to retrace my steps for the way that is such an easy descent becomes, on the return, a toilsome climb.

Then there is the lane between the rail fences, a pleasant way also. Sumac and hazel grow on either side and there are wild flowers in the fence corners. It's safe but narrow, so narrow persons cannot pass without getting out among the briars that mingle with the flowers at the roadside.

The main road to town is a broad, well-tended way. The roadbed is worked to an easy grade, stumps and rocks have been removed and the tracks are smoothed by the passing of many feet and rubber tires. But it is not pleasant for dust lies thick along that road and all the trees have been cut away from it so that travelers become hot and dusty in the summer's sun and cold and dusty in the winter wind.

There is another road that I love best of all. It is a less traveled way to town; a quiet road across a little, wooden bridge beneath which the water of the small creek ripples over the stone, then on a little farther passing under the spreading branches of a hickory tree. From there it climbs the hill, rather steeply in places, I'll admit. But there are forest trees along the way and tho the road is not very wide, still it is wide enough to pass, in a careful, friendly way, whomever one may meet. And when, after the effort of climbing, one reaches the hilltop there is a view of forest and fields and farmsteads and a wonderful skyscape for miles and miles, while on the slope at one's feet, the town is spread.

The view alone is well worth the effort required to overcome the obstacles on the way and one arrives at the beautiful outlook without confusion or dust tho perhaps a little weary and ready to rest.

From each of these roads there are other roads branching, some to the right, some to the left, leading into byways or toward other towns or back to some farm house among the hills. Some of them are full of ruts or of stumps and stones, while others are just dim tracks into the timber or thru the fields.

Roads have such an important part in our affairs! The visible roads are the pass-ways for most of the important events of our lives. Joy comes to us, light-footed, over them and again our happiness goes swiftly down the road away from us. We follow them out into every field of usefulness and endeavor and at times creep back over them to a place of refuge.

All day I have been thinking of roads—there are so many of them—so many ways thru life to choose from! Sometimes we take the path that leads into the bog with more or less mud clinging to our feet to make the toilsome ascent back, up the way that was so easy going down.

Sometimes we find ourselves in a way so narrow that it is impossible to meet others on a common ground, without being torn by brambles of misunderstanding and prejudice.

If we choose the way that "everybody does" we are smirched with their dust and confusion and imitate their mistakes. While the way to success, (not necessarily a money success) and a broad, beautiful outlook on life more often than not leads over obstacles and up a stiff climb before we reach the hill-top.

We Visit Poland

February 15, 1921

If one doesn't travel in interesting foreign places one's self, I'm sure the next best thing is to have a daughter who does. I have been so interested in what Rose Wilder Lane tells me about Poland that I feel sure you would like to hear it, too.

While in Poland she lived with other Red Cross workers at the Red Cross headquarters in a palace belonging to a Polish countess, who lived there at the same time with her family and servants. But so large was the palace that they never would have known she was there. The part of the palace occupied by the Red Cross people housed about 150 persons, with a great many servants.

In its outline Poland is much like Missouri, with mountains like the Ozarks in the southwest. There are plains all around Warsaw, which is a quaint old city, and the Vistula is much like the Missouri river except that it is very blue.

The country looks almost like Illinois. The farm houses are all of wood, with the same slant to the red roofs and the same weather boarding, and the same large barns. In the southern part, entering Poland from Czecho-Slovakia, there are even log cabins, and at the little stations men are lounging around just as they do at the little towns in Illinois. The land is fairly well cultivated, many beets and quite a few hops being grown. All over Poland there are any amount of potatoes and Poland China hogs.

After leaving the log cabin regions, one sees only Jews at the stations. All of them wear long, black coats and round caps and long hair and beards. You see there are as many kinds of Jews as there are of Protestants, and one of the subsidiary causes of the Jewish problem in Poland is that the Polish Jews belong to the branch that remains obstinately unmixed with other populations. It is the most rigidly religious branch, and the long coat, round cap and long hair are part of their religion and help to keep them distinct from the Poles.

The Jewish situation in Poland is truly a real problem. The Jews are the commercial class and owing to their strict religion, they are separate from the rest of the population. They control all the small business, commerce and industries and are about 40 per cent of the population of Poland. Their birth rate is much higher, and their infant mortality rate—due to their better care of children—much lower. If natural causes continue to operate they will simply eat up Poland. The feeling is aggravated now by the fact that there are many Russian Jews in Poland who welcomed the Russians when they advanced on Warsaw. Poles call them traitors and feeling runs high.

The Poles are very strong racially; I mean, that when one parent is a Pole the children are all Poles. I think it is not too much to say that the Polish blood shows visibly in the type of the middle western American.

The Poles themselves are amazingly like Americans of the Middle West. You see exactly the same sort of street crowds in Warsaw that you see in St. Louis or Kansas City. The resemblance is so striking that everyone sees it. I could not account for it until I found that there are 4 million Poles in our middle western states, most of them in the smaller towns and on the land, as they are an agricultural people.

Women and Real Politics

April 15, 1921

Women who feel that they had quite enough to do without taking part in politics and who are inclined to shirk the duties of full citizenship should be thankful they have escaped so easily and consider the situation of Polish women who seem to be eager to do more.

The women of Poland are working for—perhaps by this time have secured—a universal military service law for women. Their argument for this law is that all privileges carry duties with them; that if women vote they should feel that they owe a duty to the state. It is planned that their work during the year of military service will be not only military training but sanitary and other social welfare work also.

Rose Wilder Lane writes that the law was expected to pass without any serious opposition and continues:

AN INTERESTING CONGRESS

"The Diet, Poland's congress, was very interesting; they were making their constitution, when I visited them, and met in what was a girls' school before the war. Their offices were in the main building and the assembly in the church. When a member wanted to speak he went up into the pulpit and addressed the floor. The members were divided into right, left and center according to political beliefs; there were many priests on the right, the conservative side, in their black robes. There were some too in the center, or liberal division, and one Cardinal in his purple robe and scarlet cap. On the left, in the radical group, were many peasants in sheepskin jackets—worn wool side in with the outside embroidered in color—and long, tight, white wool trousers also embroidered.

"There are ten women in the Diet, most of them on the left, two in the center and one on the right. Poland is over 90 per cent organized. This is, I think, the first time in history that such a thing has been true; it is certainly the only place on earth now where it is. The peasants' party was organized by two women, who were revolutionists under the Russian Czar and had many adventures. The party now has practically all the peasants enrolled, some 300,000 and the two women are among its representatives in the Diet. They are said to be the best speakers in it.

"The industrial workers are equally well organized; they comprise the Socialist party in Poland and have 30 representatives. Their leader is vice-president of the Cabinet and a peasant is president. They have passed laws dividing the land; no one in Poland is allowed to own more than 400 acres; all the land is being surveyed and is to be sold to the peasants on long-time terms.

WOMEN HAVE MOST INFLUENCE

"Women have the greatest influence in Poland. It was the women who held the country together during the occupation by Germany, Russia, and

Austria. The partition of Poland, by the way, occurred because Poland had the first written constitution in history; the other nations jumped upon it as being dangerously radical and Poland was divided among the three neighboring monarchies.

"It was forbidden to teach Polish language or history in the schools and all boys were obliged to go thru government schools. The girls, being of no account, picked up learning in private schools and here the Polish traditions were kept alive. So the women were the real Poles, while the men became more or less German or Russian or Austrian. The women were therefore the leading spirits in revolutionary work, and naturally stepped into a great influence when Poland became a nation. All the cities have women aldermen and they are doing most of the social, educational and health work. There are women in the national labor department, and they manipulated the truce between capital and labor. As a rule they are very liberal but not radical, they call themselves for in Poland it is still radical to be liberal. They are passing a universal military law for women providing that all girls between 19 and 20 shall pass the year in military training and shall not be allowed to marry until it is finished.

"The outbreak of the war between Poland and Russia came in Lemberg when the Bolshevists withdrew and the Ukrainians took control. There is great jealousy between the Poles and the Ukrainians and Lemberg was largely a Polish city. The Polish men, however, were willing to wait and see what would happen but the women revolted. A few women stormed an arsenal and got arms; they attacked the Ukrainian troops who had the machine guns and there was fighting from behind barricades in the streets and from house to house until the Polish troops came and took the city. Then the war began in earnest.

"The streets of Warsaw and Krakow were full of women troops; the commanding general told me they were the most terrible fighters and the best soldiers behind the lines. Most of the male soldiers were under 20."

Pioneering on an Ozark Farm

A Story of Folks Who Searched—and Found Health, Prosperity and a Wild Frontier in the Mountains of Our Own State

June 1, 1921

The days of wilderness adventure are not past! The pioneer spirit is not dead![2]

We still have frontiers in our old, settled states where the joys of more primitive days may be experienced, with some of their hardships and now and then a touch of their grim humor.

Nestled in a bend of the Gasconade River 1¾ miles south of Hartville, the county seat of Wright county, is a little home which is gradually being made into a productive farm while losing none of its natural, woodland beauty. Its wild loveliness is being enhanced by the intelligent care it is receiving and the determination of its owners to take advantage of, and work with nature along the lines of her plans, instead of forcing her to change her ways and work according to man's ideas altogether—a happy co-operation with nature instead of a fight against her.

Mr. and Mrs. Frink, owners and partners in the farm, come of pioneer stock and never were quite content with town and village life. They often talked of the joys of pioneering and dreamed of going to the western frontiers somewhere.

And the years slipped by, leaving their imprint here and there a touch of snow in their dark hair; a few more lines around the eyes. Worst of all they found their health breaking. Mrs. Frink's nerves were giving way under the constant strain of teaching music and the combined efforts of each failed to pay the expenses of the many reverses, including doctor's bills with accompanying enforced idleness, and leave any surplus to be laid away for the old age that was bound to arrive with time.

THEN NATURE CALLED

All thru the sweet days of spring and summer as Mrs. Frink sat hour after hour, working with some dull music pupil, she heard the call of the big outdoors and would forget to count the beat as she dreamed of pioneering in some wild, free place where, instead of hearing the false notes of begin-

2. This article may be Laura's reply to those farm women who wrote saying they wanted to leave the farm.

ners on the piano, she might listen to the music of the wild birds' song, the murmur of the wind among the tree tops and the rippling of some silver stream. And Mr. Frink fretted at the confinement of his law office and longed for wider spaces and the freedom of the old West he had known as a boy. But still they knew deep down in their hearts that there is no more frontier, in the old sense.

By chance, Mr. Frink found the little nook, embraced by the bend of the river, tucked securely away in its hidden corner of the world and Mrs. Frink said, "This is our frontier, we will pioneer here!"

There were only 27 acres in the farm mostly woodland, some flat, some set up edgeways and the rest at many different angles as is the way of land in the Ozarks, where, as has been said, we can farm three sides of the land thus getting the use of many more acres than our title deeds call for.

I think at no time did Mr. and Mrs. Frink see the farm as it actually was, but instead they saw it with the eyes of faith as it should be later. What they bought were possibilities and the chance of working out their dreams. Mrs. Frink believed that here they could make their living and a little more. Mr. Frink was doubtful but eager to take a chance.

It required courage to make the venture for the place was in a bad state. There were some 6 or 7 acres of good bottom land in rather a poor state of cultivation and 7 acres of second bottom, or bench land, on which was an old thrown out, worn out field. The rest was woods land, a system of brush thickets a rabbit could hardly penetrate. The valleys and glens were overgrown with grape vines and poison ivy the abiding place of rattlesnakes and tarantulas. There were no fences worth the name.

The farm was bargained for in June, but negotiations were long and tedious for it was necessary to bring three persons to the same mind at the same time and it proved to be a case of many men of many minds instead. But at last the transaction was completed and one sunny morning in August, 1918, Mr. and Mrs. Frink gathered together their household goods and departed for the new home, on the frontier of the Ozarks, leaving Hartville without a mayor and its most prominent music teacher with one closed law and insurance office.

They went in a dilapidated hack, containing household goods and a tent, drawn by a borrowed horse. Hitched at the back of the hack was Mat, the Jersey cow, and Bessie Lee, her 9-months old calf. Dexter, a 4-months old colt, about 20 chickens, and three shoats had been sent ahead with a lumber wagon.

At four o'clock that afternoon the tent was pitched at Campriverside and the Frinks were at home on their own farm. As Mr. Frink says, "The great problem was solved; we would not live our whole lives on a ½-acre lot."

For supper they feasted on roasting ears and ripe tomatoes from their own fields. These were principal articles of fare for some time. The green corn later gave place to "grits" and finally these were replaced by their own grown corn meal.

The Frinks began their life on the farm in a small way and handicapped by debt. The price of the land was $600, but after paying off old indebtedness there was left of their capital, only $550 to pay for the land, build a house and buy a horse. For there was no house on the land and the tent must be the shelter until one could be built, while a horse was absolutely necessary to even a "one-horse farm."

Four hundred dollars was paid on the place and a note given for the balance of $200. Out of the remaining $150 a cabin was built and a horse bought. The material and labor in the house cost $120 and the horse cost $30.

Mr. and Mrs. Frink made up their minds at the start that the place must furnish fencing and building material as far as possible and really, log buildings seemed more in keeping with the rugged surroundings. The log house was built the first fall. It was 14 by 18 feet and a story and a half high. A shed for the stock, a chicken house and a good many rods of fence have been added since to the improvements.

From the first they lived from the proceeds of the little place. The land had been rented when bought and they were to have the owner's share from the 5 acres of corn on the bottom field. In the fall, the renter put 125 bushels of good, hard, white corn in the hastily constructed crib. The crop could have been cashed for $300.

The next fall there was 100 bushels of corn as their share from the rented field and a bunch of hogs raised on the place were sold for $125.

In 15 months after moving on the place the note for $200 and an old bill of $60 was paid off and a cream separator had been bought and paid for.

For the year of 1920 their share of corn was again 100 bushels, but because of the drop in prices, only $70 worth of hogs were sold. The income from cream and eggs averaged a little over a dollar a day for 10 months of the year. And from the little new-seeded meadow, 2 tons of clover hay were cut and stacked.

The stock has been increased. There are now at home on the place, 3 good Jersey cows, a team of horses, 2 purebred Poland China brood sows, 10 shoats, and 50 laying hens.

There is also on hand 600 pounds of dressed meat and stores of fruits and vegetables—the bulk of a year's provisions ahead. And best of all there are no debts but instead a comfortable bank account.

The expense of running the farm has been very little, about $25 a year for help. It is the intention that the eggs and cream shall provide money for running expenses, which so far they have done, leaving clear what money comes from selling the hogs, calves and surplus chickens.

The start in raising chickens was made under difficulties. Mrs. Frink was eager to begin stocking the place and early in the spring, when first the bargain was made for the farm, she wished to raise some chickens to take to it. At that time the law forbade selling hens, so she borrowed one from a neighbor and set her.[3] And that hen hatched out 11 roosters and only two pullets! Rather a discouraging start in the poultry business. But Mrs. Frink, while seeing the humor of the situation refused to admit failure. She took the 13 chickens out to the farm and put their coop up in a hickory tree beside the road. The roosters were fine, large Orpingtons and attracted the attention and admiration of the neighbors. Mrs. Frink refused to sell but offered to exchange for pullets and soon had a flock of 12 pullets and one rooster in the hickory tree. The pullets began laying in November, laid well all winter and raised a nice bunch of chicks in the spring.

The plans of these Ozark pioneers are not yet completed. Thirteen acres of the woodland are being cleared and seeded to timothy and clover. In the woods pasture the timber is being thinned, underbrush cleaned out and orchard grass, bluegrass and timothy is being sown.

Mr. Frink says, "There is much yet to be done. When the place is all cleared and in pasture it will support six cows, which means from $50 to $60 a month for cream and the fields in the bottom and on the bench will furnish grain for them and the hogs and chickens.

AND THEY'VE MADE GOOD

"We have demonstrated what can be done on a small piece of land even by renting out the fields. An able-bodied man could have done much better because he could have worked the fields himself and I would like to have more people know what a man with small means can accomplish."

Campriverside is located on the main fork of the Gasconade River, a section of country noted for its beautiful river and mountain scenery and Mrs. Frink's artist soul has found delight in the freedom and the beauties surrounding her. She says there is magic at Campriverside. An oak tree growing near the south side of the cabin, has the power, when atmospheric conditions are right, of seeming to talk and sing, being in some way a conductor of sounds of conversations and singing of neighbors living as far as a mile away. Among the branches of this tree, brushing the sides and roof of the house, birds of brilliant plumage and sweet song build their nests.

3. Perhaps an allusion to World War I commodity controls.

The rugged scenery and placid river had a greater charm for Mrs. Frink than the fertile soil of the bottom land and she took time each day to explore her little kingdom. Many were the beauty spots she discovered.

There were the basins in the rocks below the spring and Pulpit Rock which she desecrated by setting her tub upon it when she washed.

When the spring rises and makes a brook in the little glen, there are the Cascades and Wildcat Falls.

And there is Wild Cat Den where at rare intervals, the bobcat screams, calling the mate who has been the victim of encroaching civilization, while just below is Fern Glen where magnificent sword ferns grow.

As if these were not enough natural beauties for one small farm, there are the Castle Rocks and the Grotto and the dens where the woodchucks and minks live.

And there are wild flowers everywhere—"wild flowers that mark the footsteps of the Master as He walks in His garden and the brilliant coloring of the autumn foliage speaks again of His presence."

As a Farm Woman Thinks (1)

June 15, 1921

Did you ever hear anyone say, "I don't know what the world is coming to; people didn't use to do that way; things were different when I was young," or words to that effect?

Is it possible you ever said anything of the kind yourself? If so, don't be deluded into thinking it is because of your knowledge of life nor that the idea is at all original with you. That remark has become a habit with the human race, having been made at least 900 years ago and I suspect it has been repeated by every generation since.

An interesting article in "Asia" tells of a book of old Japan that is being translated by the great Japanese scholars Mr. Aston and Mr. Sansome. The book was written by a lady of the court, during the reign of the Japanese Emperor Ichijo, nearly a thousand years ago.

Among other interesting things in the article, I found this quotation from the old book—"'In olden times' said one of her Majesty's ladies, 'even the common people had elegant tastes. You never hear of such things nowadays'."

Doesn't that have a familiar sound? One's mind grows dizzy trying to imagine what things would have been like in the times that were "olden times" a thousand years ago, but evidently things were "going from bad to worse" even then.

"Distance lends enchantment to the view," looking in one direction as well as in another and that is why, I think, events of olden times and of our childhood and youth are enveloped in such a rosy cloud, just as at that time the future glowed with bright colors. It all depends on which way we're looking. Youth ever gazes forward while age is inclined to look back. And so older persons think things were better when they were young.

"WHEN I WAS A CHILD—"

Not long ago, I caught myself saying, "when I was a child, children were more respectful to their parents;" when as a matter of fact I can remember children who were not so obedient as some who are with us today and I know, when I am truthful with myself, that it always, as now, has taken all kinds of children to make the world.

Sometimes we are inclined to wish our childhood days might come again but I am always rescued from such folly by remembering a remark I once heard a man make—"Wish I were a boy again!" he exclaimed, "I do not! When I was a boy I had to hoe my row in the corn-field with father and the hired man; I must keep up too and then while they rested in the shade I had to run and get the drinking water."

And so quite often the rather morbid longing for the past will be dispelled by facing the plain facts.

There are abuses in the world, today, surely; there have always been. Our job is to face those of our day and correct them.

We have been doing a great deal of howling over the high prices we have to pay and the comparatively low prices we get and we should do more than cry aloud about it, but we would have suffered worse in those good old times after the civil war when the coarsest of muslin and calico cost 50 cents a yard and banks failed over night, leaving their worthless money in circulation.

Prices have not been so high after this much greater war and our money has been good. It is a frightful thing that our civilization should be disgraced by the conditions of the world today, but in the former Dark Ages of history there was no Red Cross organization working to help and save.

Abuses there are, to be sure, wrong to be righted, sorrows to be comforted; these are obstacles to be met and overcome. But as far back as I can remember the old times were good times; they have been good all down thru the years, full of love and service, of ideals and achievements—the future is in our hands to make it what we will.

Love and service, with a belief in the future and expectation of better things in the tomorrow of the world is a good working philosophy; much better than, "in olden times—things were so much better when I was young." For there is no turning back nor standing still; we must go forward, into the future, generation after generation toward the accomplishment of the ends that have been set for the human race.

The notes of the great bell over a Buddhist temple in Japan are said to announce the transience of life and to say as it tolls—

"All things are transient,
They, being born, must die,
And being born are dead,
And being dead are glad to be at rest."

But however fleeting and changeable life may appear to be on the surface, we know that the great underlying values of life are always the same; no different today than they were a thousand years ago.

From a Farm Woman to You

July 1, 1921

When Rose Wilder Lane wrote me about the street of the alchemists in the old city of Prague, it gave me a sense of shock that people, not so very long ago, should have credited anyone with the powers which alchemists were popularly supposed to possess. No wonder the poor things failed to live up to their reputation and were thrown to the wild beasts! It was really too much to demand that they should change common metals into gold.

But I have found an alchemist who is successful in doing what was then attempted in vain. She is just a farm woman like ourselves and would be very much surprised if she were accused of practicing alchemy. But she has a clear right to the title for she is continually transmuting the dross of common things into pure gold, or the most precious things in life.

To her, the every day work is not drudgery but a labor of love, to help the husband who works so hard, to make the dear ones comfortable and happy, to keep the home bright and beautiful outside and in.

Discouragements do not dishearten her because she sees always some advantage, some blessing in them, changing by her magic arts their dark hues to brightness. I bewailed the fact that the freezing weather had killed the fruit, she replied: "Well, we will get a rest from putting up this year and how good it will be next year and how we'll enjoy working with it. Besides we all have a good supply left over. There are bright spots, let's look at them!"

Indeed why not enjoy the vacation from the work, instead of making ourselves miserable over the loss! Complaints and wailings don't help matters and we may as well get joy and happiness out of circumstances as to choose gloom and discontent.

As a Farm Woman Thinks (2)

July 15, 1921

It is hot in the kitchen these days cooking for the men in the hay harvest fields. But perhaps we are making ourselves more warm and tired than necessary, by fretting and thinking how tired and warm we are. We would be much cooler and less tired if, instead of thinking of the weather and our weariness, we would try to remember the bird songs we heard in the early morning, or notice the view of the woods and hills, or valley and stream. It would help us to think of the cooling breeze on the porch where we rest in the evening's lengthening shadows when the long, hot day is over.

There are pleasant things to think about and beauty to be found everywhere and they grow by dwelling on them. If we would but open our eyes to the beauty of our surroundings we would be much happier and more comfortable. The kingdom of home, as well as the Kingdom of Heaven, is within us. It is pleasant and happy or the opposite according as our minds and hearts atune themselves to the beauty and joy around us, or vibrate to thoughts of ugliness and discomfort.

Which leads me to conclude our lives are like coal tar. This sounds rather unpleasant, but I'm sure I'll be pardoned for using the simile when it is clearly understood that I have no intention of blackening anyone's character. Coal tar is not altogether what it appears to be. A great many things can be taken from it. That's like life, isn't it—everybody's life?

Until recently I always thought of coal tar as a black, sticky, unpleasant substance, fit only for use as a roofing paint. But it is a wonderful combination of elements out of which may be made what one wills. The most beautiful colors, delightful perfumes and delicious flavors are contained within its blackness and may be taken from it. It also contains valuable food elements, and the most dreadful poisons. From it also are made munitions of war, and the precious medicines that cure the wounds made by those same munitions.

And so our lives are similar in that we may make of them or get out of them what we choose—beauty and fragrance and usefulness or those things that are ugly and harmful. It is necessary to understand chemistry to extract from coal tar its valuable properties and we must practice the "creative chemistry" of life to get the true values from life.

Just as the chemist in his laboratory today is carrying on the work of the old time alchemist, so we may practice magic arts. We may change unloveliness into beauty and from the darkness of life evolve all the beautiful colors of the rainbow of promise by developing the bright rays of purity and love, the golden glow of constance, the true-blue of steadfastness and the ever-green home of immortality.

When Grandma Pioneered

August 1, 1921

Grandma was minding the baby—"Oh, yes, she is sweet," she said, "but she is no rarity to me. You see there were ten of us at home and I was the oldest save one and that a boy. Seems like I've always had a baby to take care of. There were the little ones at home then when I was older I used to go help the neighbors at times and there was always a new baby, for women them days didn't hire help unless they were down sick. When I was married I had 11 of my own; now it's the grandchildren—No indeed! Babies are no rarity to me! I was just a child myself when father and mother drove an ox team into the Ozarks. Father stopped the wagon in the thick woods by the big road; cut down some trees and made a rough log cabin. But mother never liked the house there; father was away so much and she didn't like to stay alone with the young ones so near the road. The Ozarks was a wild, rough country then and all kinds of persons were passing, so father built another house down by the spring out of sight and we lived there.

"The woods were full of wild turkeys and deer; when we children hunted the cows at night we thought nothing of seeing droves of them. Snakes were thick, too, and not so pleasant to meet, but none of us ever got bit tho we went barefoot all summer and until freezing weather.

"Father used to tan the hides of deer and cattle and make our shoes but later we had 'boughten' shoes. Then the men of the settlement would drive their ox teams south into the pineries in the fall and haul in logs to the mills. When they had hauled a certain number of loads they were paid with a load of logs for themselves. These they had sawed into lumber and hauled the lumber to Springfield or Marshfield 75 or 100 miles, and sold it to get their tax money and shoes for the family.

"The men worked away a good deal and the mothers and children made the crops. Neighbors were few and far apart but we were never lonely, didn't have time to be. We raised wheat and corn for our bread; hogs ran loose in the woods and with venison and wild turkey made our meat; we kept some sheep for the wool and we raised cotton.

"After we had gathered the cotton from the fields we hand picked it from the seeds. We carded the cotton and wool and then spun them into yarn and thread and wove them into cloth; we made our own blankets and coverlets and all the cloth we used, even our dresses.

"We worked long days. As soon as we could see, in the morning, two of us would go into the woods and drive up the oxen for the day's work. Then we girls worked all day in the fields while mother worked both in the house and out. Soon as supper was over we built a brush fire in the fireplace to make light and while one tended the fire to keep it bright the others spun and wove and knit and sewed until 10 or 11 o'clock. Passing a house after dark, any time before midnight you could always hear the wheel a whirring and the loom at work. We cooked in the fireplace too, and I was 16 years old before I ever saw a cook stove.

"When the crops were raised, mother and we children did the threshing. The wheat was spread on poles with an old blanket under them to catch the grain as it dropped thru and we flailed it out with hickory poles, then blew the dust out in the wind, and it was ready to take to mill.

"We were taught to be saving. The shoes bought in the fall must last a year and we were careful with them. When they got calico into the country it cost 25 cents a yard and if we had a calico dress we wore it for very best. When we took it off we brushed off all the dust, turned it, folded it and laid it carefully away.

"I never got much schooling. There was three months school in the year beginning the first Monday in September but that was molasses making, potato digging, corn picking time and we older children had to stay home and do the work. The little ones went and by the time they were older we had things in better shape so they got lots more learning. But it was too late for us.

"Now school comes before the work at home and when children go to school it takes all their time; they can't do anything else.

"I wish folks now had to live for a little while like we did when I was young, so they would know what work is and learn to appreciate what they have. They have so much they are spoiled, yet every cent they get they must spend for something more. They want cars and pianos and silk dresses—Why when I was married all my wedding clothes were of my own spinning and weaving, but my husband was so proud he wouldn't let me wear my linsey dresses but bought me calico instead.

"Ah, well, times have changed! I'm an old woman and have worked hard all my life but even now I can work down some of the young ones."

Mother, a Magic Word

September 1, 1921

The older we grow the more precious become the recollections of childhood's days, especially our memories of mother. Her love and care halo her memory with a brighter radiance, for we have discovered that nowhere else in the world is such loving self-sacrifice to be found; her counsels and instructions appeal to us with greater force than when we received them, because our knowledge of the world and our experience of life have proved their worth.

The pity of it is that it is by our own experience we have had to gain this knowledge of their value, then when we have learned it in the hard school of life, we know that mother's words were true. So, from generation to generation, the truths of life are taught by precept and generation after generation we each must be burned by fire before we will admit the truth that it will burn.

We would be saved some sorry blunders and many a heart-ache if we might begin our knowledge where our parents leave off instead of experimenting for ourselves, but life is not that way.

Still mother's advice does help and often a word of warning spoken years before will recur to us at just the right moment to save us a misstep. And lessons learned at mother's knee last thru life.

But dearer even than mother's teachings are little, personal memories of her, different in each case but essentially the same—mother's face, mother's touch, mother's voice:

Childhood's far days were full of joy,
So merry and bright and gay,
On sunny wings of happiness,
Swiftly they flew away.
But oh! By far the sweetest hour,
Of all the whole day long,

Was the slumber hour at twilight
And my mother's voice in song—
"Hush my babe, lie still and slumber,
Holy angels guard thy bed,
Heavenly blessings without number
Gently resting on thy head."

Tho our days are filled with gladness,
Joys of life like sunshine fall,
Still life's slumber hour at twilight
May be sweetest of them all.
And when to realms of boundless peace,
I am waiting to depart
Then my Mother's song at twilight
Will make music in my heart.
"Hush, my babe, lie still and slumber,
Holy angels guard thy bed."—
And I'll fall asleep so sweetly,
Mother's blessings on my head.[4]

A Homey Chat for Mothers

Are You Your Children's Confidant?

September 15, 1921

A letter from my mother, who is 76 years old, lies on my desk beside a letter from my daughter, far away in Europe. Reading the message from my mother, I am a child again and a longing unutterable fills my heart for mother's counsel, for the safe haven of her protection and the relief from responsibility which trusting in her judgment always gave me.

But when I turn to the letter written by my daughter, who will always be a little girl to me, no matter how old she grows, then I understand and appreciate my mother's position and her feelings toward me.

Many of us have the blessed privilege of being at the same time mother and child, able to let the one interpret the other to us until our understanding of both is full and rich. What is there in the attitude of your children toward yourself that you wish were different? Search your heart and learn if your ways toward your own mother could be improved.

4. Perhaps one of Laura's own poems.

In the light of experience and the test of the years you can see how your mother might have been more to you, could have guided you better? Then be sure you are making the most of your privileges with the children who are looking to you for love and guidance. For there is, after all, no great difference between the generations; the problems of today and tomorrow must be met in much the same way as those of yesterday.

During the years since my mother was a girl to the time when my daughter is a woman, there have been many slight, external changes, in the fashions and ways of living, some change in the thought of the world and much more freedom in expressing those thoughts. But the love of mother and child is the same, with the responsibility of controlling and guiding on the one side and the obligation of obedience and respect on the other.

The most universal sentiment in the world is that of mother-love. From the highest to the lowest in the scale of humanity, and all thru the animal kingdom it is the strongest force in creation, the conserver of life, the safeguard of evolution. It holds within its sheltering care the fulfillment of the purpose of creation itself. In all ages, in all countries it is the same—a boundless, all-enveloping love; if necessary, a sacrifice of self for the offspring.

Think of the number of children in the world, each the joy of some mother's heart, each a link connecting one generation with another, each a hope for the future. There are more than 20 million school children in the United States; they would fill four cities the size of New York or eight the size of Chicago. We are told that if placed in an unbroken line four abreast, they would reach across the continent from San Francisco to the city of Washington, and there still would be several thousand children waiting to get into line.

It stuns the mind to contemplate their numbers and their possibilities, for these are the coming rulers of the world—the makers of destiny, not only for their own generation but for the generations to come. And they are being trained for their part in the procession of time by the women of today. Surely, "The hand that rocks the cradle is the hand that rules the world."

As a Farm Woman Thinks (3)

November 1, 1921

Mrs. A. was angry. Her eyes snapped, her voice was shrill and a red flag of rage was flying upon each cheek. She expected opposition, and anger at the things she said but her remarks were answered in a soft voice; her angry eyes were met by smiling ones and her attack was smothered in the softness of courtesy, consideration and compromise.

I feel sure Mrs. A had intended to create a disturbance but she might as well have tried to break a feather pillow by beating as to have any effect with her angry voice and manner on the perfect kindness and good manners which met her. She only made herself ridiculous and in self-defense was obliged to change her attitude.

Since then I have been wondering if it always is so, if shafts of malice aimed in anger forever fall harmless against the armor of a smile, kind words and gentle manners. I believe they do. And I have gained a fuller understanding of the words, "A soft answer turneth away wrath."[5] Until this incident I had found no more in the words than the idea that a soft answer might cool the wrath of an aggressor, but I saw wrath turned away as an arrow deflected from its mark and came to understand that a soft answer and a courteous manner are an actual protection.

Nothing is ever gained by allowing anger to have sway. While under its influence we lose the ability to think clearly and the forceful power that is in calmness.

Anger is a destructive force; its purpose is to hurt and destroy, and being a blind passion it does its evil work not only upon whatever arouses it, but also upon the person who harbors it. Even physically it injures him, impeding the action of the heart and circulation, affecting the respiration and creating an actual poison in the blood. Persons with weak hearts have been known to drop dead from it and always there is a feeling of illness after indulging in a fit of temper.

Anger is a destroying force. What all the world needs is its opposite—an uplifting power.

As a Farm Woman Thinks (4)

November 15, 1921

The season is over, the rush and struggle of growing and saving the crops is past for another year and the time has come when we pause and reverently give thanks for the harvest. For it is not to our efforts alone that our measure of success is due, but to the life principle in the earth and the seed, to the sunshine and rain—to the goodness of God.

5. Proverbs 15:1.

We may not be altogether satisfied with the year's results and we can do a terrific amount of grumbling when we take the notion. But I am sure we all know in our hearts that we have a great deal for which to be thankful. In spite of disappointment and weariness and perhaps sorrow, His goodness and mercy does follow us all the days of our lives.

As the time approaches when we shall be called upon by proclamation to give thanks, we must decide whether we shall show our thankfulness only by overeating at the Thanksgiving feast. That would seem a rather curious way to show gratitude—simply to grasp greedily what is given!

When a neighbor does us a favor we show our appreciation of it by doing him a favor in return. Then when the Lord showers favors upon us how much more should we try to show our gratitude in such ways acceptable to Him, remembering always the words of Christ, "Inasmuch as ye have done it unto one of the least of these, ye have done it unto me."[6]

6. Matthew 25:40.

As a Farm Woman Thinks (5)

January 1, 1922

With the holidays safely past, it is a good time to make resolutions not to overeat. It is easy to do so just after eating too much of too many good things.

We do eat too much! Everyone says so! But we keep right on eating. I remember a neighborhood dinner I attended recently. You who have been to such dinners know how the table was loaded. There were breads and meats, vegetables and salads, pies of every kind, with flakey crusts and sweet, juicy fillings, cakes—loaf, layer, cup, white, yellow, pink, chocolate, iced and plain, pickles, preserves and canned fruit and such quantities of it all! We ate all we could and then some.

Then I learned of a dinner prepared for guests in the mountains of Albania[1] to which the neighbors were bidden. The food was coarse cornbread, made without leavening, sweet and nutty and so precious that the tiniest crumb, if dropped on the floor or table, must be picked up, kissed and the sign of the cross made over it, lean pork, stripped of every scrap of fat, broiled on sticks over the fire.

In Albania it is etiquette to leave a great deal of the food and it was sent away while the guests were still hungry. Then a wooden bowl filled with cubes of fat pork fried crisp was brought. This was also removed before hunger was satisfied and water was brought for washing the hands. The stranger guests ate first, then the neighbors ate and after them, the family who entertained.

1. Laura's daughter, Rose, wrote of Albania in *The Peaks of Shala* (New York and London: Harper and Brothers, 1923).

"In Albania it is not good manners to show eagerness for food," said the guide, "Albanians are not greedy."

As a Farm Woman Thinks (6)

February 1, 1922

A wonderful way has been invented to transform a scene on the stage, completely changing the apparent surroundings of the actors and their costumes without moving an article. The change is made in an instant. By an arrangement of light and colors the scenes are so painted that with a red light thrown upon them, certain parts come into view while other parts remain invisible. By changing a switch and throwing a blue light upon the scene, what has been visible disappears and things unseen before appear, completely changing the appearance of the stage.

This late achievement of science is a good illustration of a fact we all know but so easily forget or overlook—that things and persons appear to us according to the light we throw upon them from our own minds.

When we are down-hearted and discouraged, we speak of looking at the world thru blue glasses; nothing looks the same to us; our family and friends do not appear the same; our home and work show in the darkest colors. But when we are happy, we see things in a brighter light and everything is transformed.

How unconsciously we judge others by the light that is within ourselves, condemning or approving them by our own conception of right and wrong, honor and dishonor! We show by our judgment just what the light within us is.

What we see is always affected by the light in which we look at it so that no two persons see people and things alike. What we see and how we see depends upon the nature of our light.

A quotation, the origin of which I have forgotten, lingers in my mind: "You cannot believe in honor until you have achieved it. Better keep yourself clean and bright; you are the window thru which you must see the world."[2]

2. From George Bernard Shaw's play *Man and Superman*.

As a Farm Woman Thinks (7)

March 1, 1922

Officially, winter is over and spring is here. For most of us, it has been a hard winter, despite the fact that the weather has been pleasant the greater part of the time. There are things other than zero weather and heavy snow falls that make hard winters.

But we know all about those things and so I'll tell you of something else—something as warming to the heart as a good fire on the hearth is to a chilled body on a cold day.

I often have thought that we are a little old-fashioned here in the Ozark hills; now I know we are, because we had a "working" in our neighborhood this winter. That is a blessed, old-fashioned way of helping out a neighbor.

While the winter was warm, still it has been much too cold to be without firewood and this neighbor, badly crippled with rheumatism, was not able to get up his winter's wood; with what little wood he could manage to chop, the family scarcely kept comfortable.

So the men of the neighborhood gathered together one morning and dropped in on him. With cross-cut saws and axes they took possession of his wood lot. At noon a wood saw was brought in and it sawed briskly all the afternoon; by night there was enough wood ready for the stove to last the rest of the winter.

The women did their part, too. All morning they kept arriving with well filled baskets and at noon a long table was filled with a country neighborhood dinner.

After the hungry men had eaten and gone back to work, the women and children gathered at the second table, fully as well supplied as the first, and chatted pleasant neighborhood gossip while they leisurely enjoyed the good things. Then when the dishes were washed, they sewed, knit and crocheted and talked for the rest of the afternoon.

It was a regular old-fashioned, good time and we all went home with the feeling expressed by a new-comer when he said, "Don't you know I'm proud to live in a neighborhood like this, where they turn out and help one another when it's needed."

"Sweet are the uses of adversity" when it shows us the kindness in our neighbors' hearts.

As a Farm Woman Thinks (8)

March 15, 1922

Reading of an agricultural conference in Washington, I was very much interested in the address of Mrs. Sewell of Indiana on the place of the farmer's wife in agriculture. She drew a pathetic picture, so much so as to bring tears to the eyes of the audience.

Now I don't want any tears shed over my position, but I've since been doing some thinking on the farm woman's place and wondering if she knows and has taken the place that rightfully belongs to her.

Every good farm woman is interested as much in the business part of farm life as she is in the housework and there comes a time, after we have kept house for years, when the housekeeping is mostly mechanical, while the outside affairs are forever changing, adding variety and interest to life.

As soon as we can manage our household to give us the time, I think we should step out into this wider field, taking our place beside our husbands in the larger business of the farm. Co-operation, mutual help and understanding are the things that will make farm life what it should be.

And so, in these days of women's clubs from which men are excluded, and men's clubs that permit women to be honorary members only, I'm glad to know of a different plan whereby farm men and women work together on equal terms and with equal privileges. To a woman who has been an "auxiliary" until she is tired of the word, it seems like a start toward the promised land.

Nowhere in the constitution or by-laws of this club is any distinction made between men and women members. Meetings are held once a month at homes of members and are all day sessions. The morning is devoted to business of the club and a program. After dinner comes an inspection of farm, garden and stock and the day ends with music and discussion.

The men are interested and take part in the indoor program and the women assist in the inspection of the farm.

As in Days of Old

April 15, 1922

It is curious how nearly alike are the instructions given farmers in the year 1730, in the land of the "Heathen Chinee" and the advice given by our agricultural teachers to the farmers today.

"The preparation of the seedbed is most important," I have just read in one of our farm papers. "When the plowing is ended, the entire plot is broken up with the iron-toothed harrow. The harrow has the effect of making the soil fine, so that the seeds can send roots into it. Therefore people say: 'Fine harrowing is the completion of the work'." This sounds as tho I might still be quoting from our farm paper, but instead it is from the commentaries on the "Pictures of Plowing and Weaving" written by order of the Emperor Chien Lung nearly 200 years ago.

As reproduced in "Asia," these old pictures and the commentaries on them are very interesting and in one particular they are a model of good farm articles—they are so very plain, simple yet comprehensive, covering the entire process of the work in so few words.

As an instance consider this note under the picture of sowing in the old Chinese book.

"When the ground is entirely prepared, the watered seeds are placed in a 10-quart vessel. This is suspended from the left elbow, while the right hand takes out the seeds and scatters them. The seeds are sown, the sower always going forward, about a handful to three steps. For a mou of land, one needs 3 quarts of seeds. The most important thing in sowing is evenness so that the shoots will not be too close nor too far apart."

Could more full, yet concise and simple directions for the work be given? Following them an inexperienced farmer could make no mistake, tho they do rather remind me of a recipe for cooking I once read which said to "mix the ingredients in a yellow bowl."

These pictures, each with its footnote minutely describing the pictured process, cover the season's work in the raising of rice and the making of silk, from the beginning to the completion, and the last is a picture of the Thanksgiving service. The footnote reads: "When the work in the field is finished and the innumerable treasures have been gathered, the protection of the Divinity must not be forgotten."

And so, after the harvest, Thanksgiving was celebrated those hundreds of years ago, in far away China, while not with our own observances still with the same thankfulness of heart.

Curious is it not that down thru the centuries there should be so little change and strange that the minds of such different peoples should run so nearly in the same channels?

But nature's processes continue in the same way, giving of the bounties of the earth to those who labor understandingly wherever their home may be and the Chinese farmers, like ourselves, work hard thru the season and thank God for the harvest. And it is a pleasant thought that when we get acquainted we find our neighbor nations, like our farmer neighbors, to be pretty good folks after all despite their peculiarities.

As a Farm Woman Thinks (9)

May 1, 1922

Some small boys went into my neighbor's yard this spring and with sling shots, killed the wild birds that were nesting there. Only the other day, I read in my daily paper of several murders committed by a 19-year-old boy.

At once there was formed a connection in my mind between the two crimes, for both were crimes of the same kind, tho perhaps in differing degree—the breaking of laws and the taking of life cruelly.

For the cruel child to become a hard-hearted boy and then a brutal man is only stepping along the road on which he has started. A child allowed to disobey without punishment is not likely to have much respect for law as he grows older. Not that every child who kills birds becomes a murderer nor that everyone who is not taught to obey goes to prison.

The Bible says, if we "train up a child in the way he should go, when he is old, he will not depart from it."[3] The opposite is also true and if a child is started in the way he should not go, he will go at least some way along that road as he grows older. It will always be more difficult for him to travel the right way even tho he finds it.

The first laws with which children come in contact are the commands of their parents. Few fathers and mothers are wise in giving these, for we are all so busy and thoughtless. But I am sure we will all agree that these laws of ours should be as wise and as few as possible, and, once given, children should be made to obey or shown that to disobey brings punishment. Thus they will learn the lesson every good citizen and every good man and woman learns sooner or later—that breaking a law brings suffering.

If we break a law of nature we are punished physically; when we disobey God's law we suffer spiritually, mentally and usually in our bodies also; man's laws, being founded on the ten commandments, are really mankind's poor attempt at interpreting the laws of God and for disobeying them there is a penalty. The commands we give our children should be our translation of these laws of God and man, founded on justice and the law of love, which is the Golden Rule. And these things enter into such small deeds. Even insisting that children pick up and put away their playthings is teaching them order, the law of the universe, and helpfulness, the expression of love.

The responsibility for starting the child in the right way is the parents'—it can not be delegated to the schools nor the state, for the little feet start on life's journey from the home.

3. Proverbs 22:6.

As a Farm Woman Thinks (10)

June 15, 1922

Gnawing away at the mountains of shale near Denver, is a machine that eats rocks, transforming them into oil, paraffin, perfumes, dyes, synthetic rubber—in all 155 different products, including gasoline and lubricating oils. The separating of the shale rock into these elements is done by heat generated by oil burners, and there is absolutely no waste, for the refuse, dumped out at the back of the machine is made up of hydro-carbons of great commercial value.

The story of this rock eating monster is worthy of a place with the tales brought to Europe by travelers in India who first saw cotton and sugar cane. They told that in that strange land were "plants that bore wool without sheep and reeds that bore honey without bees."

The first cotton cloth brought to Europe came from Calicut and was called calico. Only kings and queens could afford to wear it.

Arabs brought the lumps of sweet stuff, like gravel, that they called "sukkar." This was so scarce and precious in Europe that it was prescribed as medicine for kings and queens when they were ill.

From the days when sugar and cotton were such wonders to the time when a machine crushes rocks and from them distils delicate perfumes and beautiful colors has not been so very long when measured by years, but measured by the advance of science and invention it has been a long, long way. Looking forward, we stand in awe of the future wondering if the prophecy of Berthelot, the great French chemist will be fulfilled. He says the time will come when man by the aid of chemistry, will take his food from the air, the water and the earth without the necessity of growing crops or killing living creatures; when the earth will be covered with grass, flowers and woods among which mankind will live in abundance and joy.

This is far in the future and almost impossible of belief, but that which is the wonder of one age and hardly believable is the commonplace of the next. We go from achievement to achievement, and no one knows the ultimate heights the human race may reach.

As a Farm Woman Thinks (11)

July 1, 1922

My neighbor, who came from a city where her husband worked for a salary, said to me, "It is difficult for any one who has worked for wages to get used to farming. There is a great difference between having a good pay check coming twice a month, or having only the little cash one can take in on a small farm. Why we have scarcely any money at all to spend!"

"You spent the paycheck for your living expenses did you not," I asked?

"All of it," she answered. "Every bit! We never could save a cent of it."

"And you have your living now, off the farm," said I.

"Yes and a good one," she replied, "with a little left over. But it was great fun spending the pay check. If we'd had a little less fun, we might have had more left."

All of which brings us to the question the little girl asked: "Would you rather have times or things"—good times to remember or things to keep, like bank accounts, homes of our own and such things?

Things alone are very unsatisfying. Happiness is not to be found in money or in houses and lands, not even in modern kitchens or a late model motor car. Such things add to our happiness only because of the pleasant times they bring us.

But times would be bad without some things. We can not enjoy ourselves if we are worried over how we shall pay our bills, or the taxes, or buy what the children need.

And so we must mix our times and things, but let's mix 'em with brains, as the famous artist said he mixed his paints, using good judgment in the amount we take.

How the Findleys Invest Their Money

These Missouri Parents Figure That Education of Their Boys and Girls Pay Bigger Dividends Than Pretty Clothes and Frivolous Pastimes

August 1, 1922

"We are putting what we earn into our children's minds, instead of into houses and clothes," said little Mrs. Findley as she smoothed the hair of small Ben who leaned against her knee. "We think it a better investment."

"Oh yes, my husband agrees with me! He didn't at first. He said we couldn't educate the children because we were poor, but now he is as ambitious for them as I am."

"Tell me about it," I said and this is the story she told me as we sat on the shady porch one pleasant afternoon.

"When I was a child we lived back in the woods and father was poor. My own mother was dead and while my stepmother did the best she could for me, there were smaller children to take care of and always so much to do. Father wanted me to go to school, but when I was needed at home to help, he could never see any other way but that I must stay and work. Then, too, he hadn't money to buy my school books.

IT WAS AN UPHILL PULL

"When I was twelve years old, my brother and I chopped a load of wood, hauled it to town and sold it for money to buy a grammar and history. We hacked the wood up some, but we got it into sticks and we got the books.

"It was that way when I needed the first book for my children, Glen and Joette; there was no money to buy the book, so I took in a washing and got the money. I've always been ashamed of that work. It was not well done, because I was in such poor health that I had to hold myself up by the tub while I scrubbed, but that book just had to come and it came.

"You see, after I married, we lived in Joplin and my husband worked in the mines. Jess had been earning $4.50 a day but it took it all to live, so when we came back to the hills we had only our bare hands.

"Well, I started the children to work in their new book and every day we had lessons. I taught them first a word, then the letters in it and they had them ready for use in another word. When they learned a name, I showed them the object; when they learned an action word, we acted it; for instance, when they read the word 'jump' we jumped and how they did enjoy saying their lessons to daddy in the evening, especially when he'd let them beat him.

STARTING THE CHILDREN AT HOME

"When Glen was 7 years old and Joette 6, I started them to school ready for the fourth grade work. The superintendent could not think it possible and insisted that they begin in the third grade, but after only one day there they were promoted to the fourth.

"The first year they went to school only two months, then finished their grades at home. The next year they went two months and finished at home. The next year they went four months and were obliged to stop because of sickness, but again they finished the grades at home. Since then they have gone regularly and at 13 and 14 years old have finished the first year in high school and the fifth set in book-keeping.

"Violet and Ben have had the same training at home that the older children had and now at 6 and 8 years old are ready to start to school in the fourth grade.

"Violet has been more difficult to teach than the others, because she likes to sew and play with her dolls better than to study. People said she was stupid and that I never would be able to push her as I had the others, but she was only different and just as smart if not smarter. She just would not keep her mind on her books until she found she must and would be punished if she didn't. I know what her talent is, but she has to have her books, too, and she will sew all the better for having 'book learning.'

"Besides I had made up my mind that thru my children I would raise the standard of the family. It couldn't be bettered morally but it could be raised educationally and so Violet, as well as the rest, must study her books. I knew her well and gave her special attention so she is going right along with the others.

"I believe it would be much better for everyone if children were given their start in education at home. No one understands a child as well as his mother and children are so different that they need individual training and study. A teacher with a roomful of pupils cannot do this. At home, too, they are in their mother's care. She can keep them from learning immoral things from other children. At home the expense is much less, for in school there are a great many expenses that are difficult for poor people to meet.

"It was great fun teaching the children, but soon after I began I saw that if they were going to be educated, I must do something more to help, for Jess's wages would not support us and pay school expenses.

"I thought I could earn something raising chickens so I got an incubator from my brother to use on shares, then I did washing to pay for the eggs to fill it. Jess couldn't see the way out on it for I knew nothing about incubators or raising chickens for profit, but I read up on it in the farm papers and I had a 90 per cent hatch the first time.

"I bought my brother's share of these chicks and gave my note at the bank to pay for them. Then I did washing to pay that note. I set the incubator again and from the two hatches I raised more than 400 chicks.

"It surely took scratching to feed them but soon they were big enough to fry and I told Glen we could take them to market in his little red wagon. 'Oh mama,' he said, 'people will laugh at us.' But I told him it was our business and we would attend to it.

"The wagon was small and we had to make several trips. People did stare as we went down street, but we sold the cockerels at a good price. The money bought feed for my pullets and I raised 200 layers from them.

"We paid strict attention to business and did not take time to go to picnics, nor spend money for ice cream, melons and the like. Even tho the neighbors were rather offended we stuck to it caring for the chickens and teaching the children.

"We watched every expense, too, and spent very little on the table or our clothes. Some of the neighbors thought I ought to dress better; they said I'd lose my husband's love if I went shabby. But I said, 'If love is only dress deep let it go.' Not that I didn't love pretty things for I did and before I married, when I had a good position in Springfield, I had as many pretty clothes as anyone. But I was willing to give them up for real things, for the doing of things worth while.

"The chickens seemed to appreciate what I did for them for soon we were carrying big baskets of eggs to town. The egg money more than supported the family and we banked some of it and all of Jess's wages. My, but he was pleased over it! He was prouder than I because he had not thought I could do it. But I've always found that when anything has to be done, it can be done.

"Don't think we sacrificed our pleasures by shutting ourselves away from the world to work and teach the children. We enjoyed so much being with them that we did not need to go out to hunt pleasure. It came to us. We had old-fashioned, happy, home times.

"But I knew we could not always stay at home. Soon the children must take part in school affairs and go out with other children. We were going to need a car when they were older. When I told Jess about it he said, 'We can't buy a car, we must save our money! Suppose we should die, we wouldn't have enough to pay for burying.'

"I told him we had friends and they'd help him bury me, and if he died not to worry, I'd get him buried. I never did have any patience with this looking for a rainy day all one's life.

"Well we bought the car but it was a costly piece of tin. We worked and saved for six years to pay for it, then we kept it only three weeks and Jess sold it at a profit. I was proud of him and I'm proud of other things he has done, too. He has made an attachment for a churn that some day he'll get patented. The little model works fine. He studies about such things in his spare time, but he hasn't much of that, for all this time he has been working hard.

STARTING AS A FARM HAND

"He hired out as a farm hand for $22.50 a month the first year; the next year he was raised to $25, the next to $27.50 and then he was offered $30 a month or a share of the crop. He took the share and we had a bumper crop.

"He is farming on shares now, and gets pay for what work he does outside of making the crop, and half the cream for taking care of the cows. Our share of the cream brings us about $6 a week.

"You see it's much easier not; we have a beautiful place to live and we dress better; we have another car. It's paid for and the hens lay the gasoline. We get so much good out of the car! I'm not very strong and a drive rests me when I'm tired, while we all enjoy the beauties of nature on our little trips along the river.

"But best of all the children are well started in getting their education. None of the family has ever graduated from high school, but my children will and some of them will go to college, too.

IS THE AIM TOO HIGH?

"Jess says I aim too high, but I tell him I'll shoot straight, for when a thing has to be done, it's done. And if people say the Jess Findley family were poor, they'll say, too, that the children were well educated, for that is where we are putting our life's work—into their heads.

"We are doing something worth while, for in raising the standard of our children's lives we are raising the standard of four homes of the future and our work goes on and on raising the standard of the community and of future generations."

When Mrs. Findley had finished her story I mentally took note of one thought which has escaped so many of us. It was not the old story of an education always being within the grasp of those who really seek it, but in raising the standard of the Findley home, the standard of four homes of the future had been elevated to the point which we like to think of as a representative "American Home." Here, mother love had combined with the vision of future usefulness in the country's citizenship, with the result the finest service, perhaps that any parent can aspire to.

As a Farm Woman Thinks (12)

August 15, 1922

It has become quite the customary thing for farms to be given a distinguishing name. It adds much to the interest of a farm home, especially as the name usually calls attention to some feature of the place that marks it as different from the farms surrounding it.

Naming the home place is an old, old custom, but the people who lived at such places used to have a family motto, also. Families as well as farms have distinguishing traits of character, and there is always some of these on which a family prides itself. Only the other day I heard a man say, "My father's word was as good as his note and he brought us children up that way."

Why not have a family motto expressing something for which we, as a family, stand?

Such a motto would be a help in keeping the family up to standard by giving the members a cause for pride in it and what it represents; it might even be a help in raising the standard of family life and honor.

If the motto of a family were, "My word is my bond," do you not think the children of that family would be proud to keep their word and feel disgraced if they failed to do so?

Suppose the motto were, "Ever ready," would not the members of that family try to be on the alert for whatever came?

Perhaps it would be possible to cure a family weakness by choosing a motto representing its opposite as an ideal for the family to strive toward. We might keep our choice a family secret until we had proven ourselves and could face the world with it.

Tho, in these days, we would not put the motto upon our shield as did the knights of old, but we could use it in many ways. If carried only in our hearts, it would draw the family closer together.

Let's have a family motto as well as a farm name!

As a Farm Woman Thinks (13)

September 1, 1922

It is said that "money is the root of all evil," but money that is at the root of any evil in itself represents selfishness.

The old proverb slanders good, clean money and it would be nearer the truth to say that selfishness is the root of evil and the over-valuation of money only one manifestation of it.

Money hasn't any value of its own; it represents the stored up energy of men and women and is really just some one's promise to pay a certain amount of that energy.

It is the promise that has the real value. If no dependence can be put on the promises of a nation, then the currency of that nation, which is its promise to pay, is worthless. Bank notes depend for their value on the credit of the bank that issues them and a man's note is good or not according to whether his promise to pay can be relied on.

So it comes to this, that, as the business of the world is done on credit, a man's word backed by his character is the unit of value and that character is the root of good or evil, making his word, good or worthless.

If there were only one thing of any value in this world and it were in our possession, how precious it would be to us. How carefully we would guard it from all smirching or damaging, defending it with our lives if necessary! There would be no carelessness in the keeping of it, no reckless giving of it here and there as tho it amounted to nothing.

Listen then to this Eastern proverb: "In this world a man's word is all he has that is of real value; it is at the bottom of all other values."

As a Farm Woman Thinks (14)

October 15, 1922

I was told to go into a certain community and get the story of the most successful person in it.

"There are no successes there," I said, "just ordinary people, not one of whom has contributed to the progress of the world. I can get no story there worth anything as an inspiration to others."

Then came the reply: "Surely someone has lived a clean life, has good friends and the love of family. Such a one must have contributed something of good to others."

Rearranging my standard of "success" to include something besides accumulated wealth—achieved ambition of a spectacular sort—I thought of grandpa and grandma Culver, poor as church mice, but a fine old couple, loved by everybody and loving everybody. Home meant something to their children who return there year after year. I went to see them.

"No," Grandma told me over the jelly she was making for the sick, "Pa and I never have been well-off in money, but oh, so very rich in love of each other, of family and friends.

"We've tried to see every little submerged virtue in each other, in the children and in everybody. I had the gift of cheerfulness, Pa had patience; we cultivated these traits.

"Every day we have tried to be of a little use to somebody, never turning down a single opportunity to help some one to a glimpse of things worth while. What we have lacked in money and brilliance, we have tried to make up in service."

But ever the world has let the flash of more dazzling successes blind it to the value of such lives as these.

As a Farm Woman Thinks (15)

November 1, 1922

Some time ago I read an Irish fairy story which told how a mortal, on a fairy steed, went hunting with the fairies. He had his choice whether the fairy horse should become large enough to carry a man-sized man or be small enough to ride the horse as it was.

He chose to become of fairy size and, after the magic was worked, rode gayly with the fairy king, until he came to a wall so high he feared his tiny horse could not carry him over, but the fairy king said to him, "Throw you heart over the wall, then follow it!" So he rode fearlessly at the wall, with his heart already bravely past it, and went safely over.

I have forgotten most of the story and do not remember the name of the author, tho I wish I did, but often I think of the fairy's advice. Anyone who has ridden horses much, understands how the heart of the rider going over, fairly lifts the horse up and across an obstacle. And I have been told, by good drivers, that it holds true in taking a motor car up a difficult hill.

But the uplift of a fearless heart will help us over other sorts of barriers. In any undertaking, to falter at a crisis means defeat. No one ever overcomes difficulties by going at them in a hesitant, doubtful way.

If we would win success in anything, when we come to a wall that bars our way we must throw our hearts over and then follow confidently. It is fairy advice, you know, and savors of magic, so following it we will ride with the fairies of good fortune and go safely over.

As a Farm Woman Thinks (16)

November 15, 1922

Among all the blessings of the year have you chosen one for which to be especially thankful at this Thanksgiving time, or are you unable to decide which is the greatest?

Sometimes we recognize as a special blessing what heretofore we have taken without a thought, as a matter of course, as when we recover from a serious illness, just a breath drawn free from pain is a matter for rejoicing. If we have been crippled and then are whole again, the blessed privilege of walking forth free and unhindered seems a gift from the Gods. We must needs have been hungry to properly appreciate food and we never love our friends as we should until they have been taken from us.

As the years pass, I am coming more and more to understand that it is the common, everyday blessings of our common everyday lives for which we should be particularly grateful. They are the things that fill our lives with comfort and our hearts with gladness—just the pure air to breathe and the strength to breathe it; just warmth and shelter and home folks; just plain food that gives us strength; the bright sunshine on a cold day and a cool breeze when the day is warm.

Oh, we have so much to be thankful for that we seldom think of it in that way! I wish we might think more about these things that we are so much inclined to overlook and live more in the spirit of the old Scotch table blessing.

"Some hae meat wha canna' eat
  And some can eat that lack it.
But I hae meat and I can eat
  And sae the Laird be thankit."[4]

Reminiscences of Fair Time

December 1, 1922

While visiting our county fair this fall I was impressed anew with the variety of a farm woman's duties and the good work she is doing. Thru the poultry department, past the display of garden products and cookery and the fancy work still I sauntered and, instead of these material objects, I saw exhibited the industry and thrift, the imagination and love of beauty of women on the farms of the country today.

What endless work and patience it takes to make poultry keeping a paying part of the farm business, yet women are doing it in connection with gardening which supplies the greater part of the family's living the year around.

It is all a part of their routine, together with the wonderful cooking they do without a thought that they are practicing the finest arts of chemistry.

Not content with all this, farm women show their love of beauty as well as their thrift, in the fancy work with which they adorn their homes.

4. From the poem "The Selkirk Grace" by Robert Burns.

Looking at the beautiful quilts and rugs made from scraps, especially one rug woven from burlap bags, one could almost believe that, despite the old saying to the contrary, a "silk purse could be made out of a sow's ear."

The work of grandmother's patient fingers displayed beside the very latest in hand embroidery shows that, thru a long life, the love of beauty and habit of industry still persists.

A farm woman who is successful with her garden, poultry and homemaking has mastered several difficult trades, proved herself a good executive as well as business woman and is a link between the old and the new ways of life, preserving what is worth while from the days of her grandmother and adding to this the improvements and knowledge of her later day.

She has good reason to be proud of her work and her place in the scheme of things.

As a Farm Woman Thinks (17)

January 1, 1923

With the coming of another new year we are all more or less a year older. Just what does it mean to us—this growing older? Are we coming to a cheerful, beautiful old age, or are we being beaten and cowed by the years as they pass?[1]

Bruised we must be now and then, but beaten, never, unless we lack courage.

Not long since a friend said to me, "Growing old is the saddest thing in the world." Since then I have been thinking about growing old, trying to decide if I thought her right. But I cannot agree with her. True, we lose some things that we prize as time passes and acquire a few that we would prefer to be without. But we may gain infinitely more with the years, than we lose in wisdom, character and the sweetness of life.

As to the ills of old age, it may be that those of the past were as bad but are dimmed by the distance. Tho old age has gray hair and twinges of rheumatism remember that childhood has freckles, tonsils and the measles.

The stream of passing years is like a river with people being carried along in the current. Some are swept along, protesting, fighting all the way trying to swim back up the stream, longing for the shores that they have passed, clutching at anything to retard their progress, frightened by the onward rush of the strong current and in danger of being overwhelmed by the waters.

1. Although no author is given for this column, the assumption is that Mrs. Wilder wrote it.

MOVING WITH FAITH

Others go with the current freely, trusting themselves to the buoyancy of the waters knowing they will bear them up. And so with very little effort they go floating safely along, gaining more courage and strength from their experience with the waves.

As New Year after New Year comes, these waves upon the river of life bear us farther along toward the ocean of Eternity, either protesting the inevitable and looking longingly back toward years that are gone, or with calmness and faith facing the future serene in the knowledge that the power behind life's currents is strong and good.

And thinking of these things, I have concluded that whether it is sad to grow old depends on how we face it, whether we are looking forward with confidence or backward with regret. Still in any case it takes courage to live long successfully, and they are brave who grow old with smiling faces.

Hitching Up for Family Team Work

The Oettings of Wright County, Building on the Sure Foundation of Faith and Industry, Have Made Ozark Farming Pay

January 15, 1923

While we are all preaching farmer co-operation and trying so hard to practice it, it is encouraging to find an example of successful, family cooperation on a farm. If the lesson can be learned at home it will be easier to apply its principles in a larger field.

The Fred Oetting farm, near Mansfield, shows what can be accomplished by a few working together for the common good. It is a pleasant place to visit; the cheerful friendliness of the family makes visitors feel welcome. There is such quiet efficiency indoors and out, no confusion and seemingly no hurry. Still the work goes on with neatness and dispatch, while the condition of the farm and the sleek, contented livestock shows that nothing is neglected.

This, of course, indicates good management, but I am sure a great deal is due to the good understanding of Mr. and Mrs. Oetting with their sons and daughters, their co-operation in the work and sharing in the profits of the farm.

From the time the children were old enough to hunt hen's nests and gather the eggs they had a share in the income from the farm. You may be sure it was a wise old hen who could manage to keep her nest hidden. Mr. Oetting says, "Giving the children a share is good for both them and me, for the more I get, the more they get and so they take an interest in their work." And with the intelligent, interested help of the whole family Mr. Oetting has made a success.

Mr. Oetting came to Wright county, Missouri, in 1885 from Iowa where he had worked as a farm hand since coming over from Germany five years before. In Iowa he learned how Americans farm and how to combine these new ways with the old country's thrift and thoroness. Then in Missouri he found things done in still a different fashion and combined his knowledge with the experience of soil, climate and conditions which the native farmers of the Ozark Hills had incorporated in their ways of farming. He says he made a great many mistakes in the first years but his willingness to learn from others and thus adapt his knowledge to his surroundings saved him many losses he otherwise would have had.

Mr. Oetting soon learned that no great success could be made by raising corn and wheat enough for his bread, and hogs enough for his meat as so many were content to do at that time. His first departure from the routine was in truck gardening. The truck could be grown, but marketing it was the problem. It had to be hauled to Marshfield and the trip took three days and nights. He nearly killed himself with overwork but he had promised to pay the note, and there was no other way to get the money so he stuck it thru the season, paid the note and then looked around for some easier way of making the farm pay.

Raising strawberries was the thing he decided to try and this went better. The children, tho small, could pick berries enough to help a great deal without working too hard. Still, hauling the berries to town interfered with the regular farm work and the children grew tired of picking them. So with the consent of everyone concerned, strawberries were abandoned and the Oetting family started a dairy.

It began with Mrs Oetting taking first prize for butter at the county fair, which led to a contract to deliver butter at 15 cents a pound. But after a few deliveries, the customer calmly informed Mr. Oetting that he did not want any more as he could buy butter for 10 cents a pound. Soon after this a company was formed and a creamery started in Mansfield. That made a great difference in the price of cream and butter.

Mr. Oetting says that the hardest thing he had to learn in the dairy business was to control his own temper. He had to learn it for he found that cows do not respond with large yields of milk to being beaten with the milk stool or even to rough words, or loud, unusual talking. So he learned to grit his teeth and not kick the cow when things went wrong.

Becoming convinced that a good, warm barn to protect the cows in cold or rainy weather saves feed and increases the yield of milk, Mr. Oetting built such a barn for 12 cows about eight years ago. A 50 ton silo is inside the barn. He put the Babcock tester in the separator room and proceeded to test out his cows. To his surprise he found that one he had thought his best cow was the poorest of all. Tho the quantity of milk was large, the butterfat content was small. By testing he found that the boarders in his herd were eating up the profits and decided he must have better dairy stock.

Since then Mr. Oetting has weeded out the poor individuals and gradually acquired purebred Jerseys to take their place. His first purebred was too old for best results but she gave him some excellent calves.

Three years ago he bought four registered Jersey heifers and tho the price paid was from $70 to $200 each he feels well repaid, for with his system of testing and culling he is building up a herd of which to be proud. One cow produces 54 pounds of butterfat in 30 days off pasture only; another gives 47 to 48 pound of milk at a milking; another gives 8,000 pound of milk a year and still another gives 11,000 pound of milk a year.

The separator room is in the barn and each cow's milk is weighed and tested carefully. There are still a few grade cows in the herd, but in a couple of years there will be only purebreds.

Mr. Oetting's experience has shown him that to get the greatest returns from his cows he must make a good use of the skim milk and so with the dairy business he combines hog and poultry raising. Four years ago he shipped the first purebred Poland China hog into Wright county from the Springfield fair. This hog soon died and the next venture in the purebred hog line was with Duroc Jerseys, which breed still is handled.

It is interesting to look over Mr. Oetting's farm account books and note the amounts he has received from his cows and hogs during the past few years. From $112.63 for cream from seven cows in 1911, his receipts went as high as $1,413.68 in 1919. In 1921, with the lower prices for produce the receipts were $986.76.

The amount received for cream during the last eight years is $6,925.71; for cattle during the last six years $2,346.14 and for hogs $4,047.20. Besides this there has been an average of from $3 to $4 a week from the poultry.

Mrs. Oetting and the children raised the poultry and for their help the children's share was 1 cent a dozen for all eggs sold. This amounted to quite a little when two cases of eggs a week were sold.

As soon as they were old enough to milk the share allowed each child for helping care for the cows and milking was 10 per cent of the cream check. The girls were not expected to do this work, but one of them took her father's place at milking time during his absence for the short term at the Missouri College of Agriculture. On his return she asked to be allowed to continue and receives 10 per cent of the cream check for herself.

The two older boys now at home have been taken into partnership in the hog business and at present the three large sows are making a yearly profit of $100 each, besides furnishing the family's meat.

The Oetting success has not been made without the practice of intelligent economy. The home-made dry-house in the orchard saves a great deal of fruit that otherwise would go to waste and there is a good cellar for the storage of fruit and vegetables for winter use. It is built above ground, has double walls of oak lumber with sawdust between and a space between the ceiling and the roof to pack sawdust, hay or leaves. The cellar never freezes but is kept quite cold by an arrangement of two ventilator shafts. They are placed side by side one being about 20 inches lower than the other. The higher opening draws off the warm air, while cold air comes in thru the lower to take its place.

The waste of feed from keeping poor cows was eliminated from the dairy and the saving and increased profits made by building the barn were enough, in six years, to build the comfortable farm house.

The building of the silo is a story in itself. One of that size would have cost Mr. Oetting $150. He hadn't the money to invest and so made his silo after a plan of his own. He built the concrete base with walls 2 feet high and the silo itself, resting on these walls, was made of matched flooring, 16 feet long, making the silo 18 feet high. It is 14 feet in diameter.

The hoops binding the flooring were made of siding put on the thick edge up. Over that another hoop of the same size was placed, breaking joints with the first and with the thick edge down, making the completed hoop an inch thick. The hoops were well nailed to the body of the silo. Tho built eight years ago, the silo is in perfect condition. Its entire cost was only 40 dollars. Thus these things we should remember—co-operation, like charity, begins at home, and bringing up the family "on it" means clearer sailing for agriculture in the days to come.

As a Farm Woman Thinks (18)

April 1, 1923

Just how much does home mean to you? Of what do you think when it is mentioned? Is it only the four walls and the roof within the shelter of which you eat and sleep or does it include the locality also—the shade trees around the house, the forest trees in the woodlot, the little brook that wanders thru the pasture where the grass grows lush and green in spring and summer, the hills and valleys, and the level fields of the farm lands over which the sun rises to greet you in the early morning and sets in glorious waves of color as you go about your evening tasks?

When I think of home, the picture includes all these things and even the farm animals that are our daily care, our vexation and our pride and so I know I can never be a "Tin Can Tourist," for a shelter on wheels moving from place to place cannot furnish all I require of a home.

But if home to you is only a shelter, then you might be happy with this modern Gipsy band. According to World Traveler magazine, the "Tin Can Tourists of the World" was organized in 1917 at Tampa, Fla., of a few tourists who made traveling in motor cars their principal business. In 1922 there were 200,000 of them.

These people live in their motor cars and tents, spending the summer in the north and going south for the winter.

NO RESPONSIBILITY OR CARE

"Labor—physical or mental—if it is not taboo in their creed, is reduced to the smallest possible proportions, likewise it follows that expenditures are put upon their most economical basis. Care, responsibility, and ambition—these things have no longer a place in the life of a Tin Can Tourist," says Norman Borchardt.

At first these tourists went back to farms and work when winter was over but now at least 30 per cent of them live in their cars the year around and the number who do this is increasing fast.

There are families of children being raised in these traveling homes, and, since reading the article, I have been wondering just what this all will mean to us in the future.

A DANGER TO CUSTOMS

It seems to me that such a class of careless, unresponsible drifters will be a danger to our customs and our country, for where the home is eliminated an important part of our social structure is missing. No shelter on four wheels, continually on the move, can really be a home, tho children reared to know no better would not understand the difference.

I am jealous for the farm home and fearful of anything that seems to threaten it so I hope we will do what we can to counteract the effect of so many choosing a homeless life by letting our love of home grow into a strong and beautiful sentiment, embracing the whole of the farm lands and all that goes to make life possible and pleasant upon them.

We can teach this love of home to the children and it will help to hold them steady when their time comes. They may need such help more than you think, for the greater number of the "Tin Can Tourists" are from farms of the Middle West.

As a Farm Woman Thinks (19)

April 15, 1923

With the birds singing, the trees budding and, "the green grass growing all around," as we used to sing in school, who would not love the country and prefer farm life to any other? We are glad that so much time can be spent out-of-doors while going about the regular affairs of the day, thus combining pleasure with work and adding good health for full measure.

I have a favorite way of doing this, for I have never lost my childhood's delight in going after the cows. I still slip away from other things for the sake of the walk thru the pasture, down along the creek and over the hill to the farthest corner where cows are usually found as you can all bear witness.

Bringing home the cows is the childhood memory that oftenest recurs to me. I think it is because the mind of a child is peculiarly attuned to the beauties of nature and the voices of the wildwood and the impression they made was deep.

"To him who, in the love of nature, holds community with her visible forms, she speaks a various language,"[2] you know. And I am sure old Mother Nature talked to me in all the languages she knew when, as a child, I loitered along the cow paths, forgetful of milking time and stern parents waiting, while I gathered wild flowers, waded in the creek, watched the squirrels hastening to their homes in the tree tops and listened to the sleepy twitterings of birds.

Wild strawberries grew in grassy nooks in spring time. The wild plum thickets, along the creek yielded their fruit about the time of the first frost, in the fall. And all the time between there were ever varied, never failing delights along the cow paths of the old pasture. Many a time, instead of me finding the cows they, on their journey home unurged, found me and took me home with them.

2. From the poem "Thanatopsis" by William Cullen Bryant.

The voices of nature do not speak so plainly to us as we grow older, but I think it is because, in our busy lives, we neglect her until we grow out of sympathy. Our ears and eyes grow dull and beauties are lost to us that we should still enjoy.

Life was not intended to be simply a round of work, no matter how interesting and important that work may be. A moment's pause to watch the glory of a sunrise or a sunset is soul satisfying, while a bird's song will set the steps to music all day long.

As a Farm Woman Thinks (20)

May 15, 1923

"The days are just filled with little things and I am so tired doing them," wailed a friend recently. Since then I have been thinking about little things, or these things we are in the habit of thinking small, altho I am sure our judgment is often at fault when we do so.

"FEEDING THE WORLD"

Working in the garden, taking care of the poultry, calves and lambs, milking the cows, and all the other chores that fall to the lot of farm women may each appear small in itself, but the results go a long way in helping to "feed the world." Sometimes I try to imagine the people who will eat the eggs I gather or the butter from my cream and wear the clothes made from the wool of the lambs I help to raise.

Doing up cut fingers, kissing hurt places and singing bedtime songs are small things by themselves but they will inculcate a love for home and family that will last thru life and help to keep America a land of homes.

Putting up the school lunch for the children or cooking a good meal for the family may seem a very insignificant task as compared with giving a lecture, writing a book or doing other things that have a larger audience, but I doubt very much if in the ultimate reckoning they will count as much.

If, when cooking, you will think of yourself as the chemist that you are, combining different ingredients into a food that will properly nourish human bodies, then the work takes on a dignity and interest. And surely a family well nourished with healthful food so that the boys and girls grow up strong and beautiful while their elders reach a hale old age, is no small thing.

It belittles us to think of our daily tasks as small things and, if we continue to do so, it will in time make us small. It will narrow our horizon and make of our work just drudgery.

There are so many little things that are really very great and when we learn to look beyond the insignificant appearing acts themselves to their far reaching consequences we will, "despise not the day of small things." We will feel an added dignity and poise from the fact that our everyday round of duties is as important as any other part of the work of the world.

And just as a little thread of gold, running thru a fabric, brightens the whole garment, so women's work at home, while only the doing of little things, like the golden gleam of sunlight runs thru and brightens all the fabric of civilization.

As a Farm Woman Thinks (21)

July 1, 1923

At a gathering of women the other day, a subject came up for discussion on which I knew the opinions held by several present as they had expressed to me privately.

It happened that a woman who held the opposite opinion to theirs led off in the talk and a number followed her lead; then these women who differed, fell in with what they thought was the popular side and by a few words let it be understood that they were in accord with the opinion stated and so what might have been an interesting and profitable discussion became merely a tiresome reiteration of the same idea.

I knew those women had been false to themselves but was not surprised, for I have been observing along that line recently and have seen so much of the same thing. As people are pretty much the same everywhere I do not think that this spirit is shown in one community alone.

For fear of giving offense many persons agree to anything that is proposed when they have no intention of doing it and will find an excuse later. They join in with what they think is popular opinion until it is almost impossible to tell where anyone stands on any subject or to do anything, because one cannot tell upon whom to depend. This disposition is found everywhere from social affairs to the man who agrees to come and work.

Have you not found it so? Of course it is easier, for a time, to go with the current but how much more can be accomplished if we would all be honest in our talk. And how much wasted effort would be saved! We all despise a coward but we sometimes forget that there is a moral as well as a physical cowardice and that it is just as contemptible.

I am sure that moral cowardice is responsible for a great deal of the trouble and confusion in the world. It gives unprincipled persons an opportunity to "put things over" that they would not have if others had the courage of their convictions. Besides it is weakening to one's personality and moral fiber to deny one's opinions or falsify one's self, while it throws broadcast into the world just that much more cowardice and untruth.

We all know who is the father of lies and a lie can be acted as well as spoken, while an untruth is often expressed by silence. It is not necessary to be unpleasant if we disagree; an opinion supported by a good reason kindly stated should not offend, neither should a pleasant refusal to join in anything proposed. We may be friendly and courteous and still hold frankly to our honest convictions. But—

> "This above all to thine own self be true
> And it will follow as the night the day,
> Thou canst not then be false to any man."[3]

As a Farm Woman Thinks (22)

August 1, 1923

Out in the meadow, I picked a wild sunflower and, as I looked into its golden heart such a wave of homesickness came over me that I almost wept. I wanted mother, with her gentle voice and quiet firmness; I longed to hear father's jolly songs and to see his twinkling blue eyes; I was lonesome for the sister with whom I used to play in the meadow picking daisies and wild sunflowers.

Across the years, the old home and its love called to me and memories of sweet words of counsel came flooding back. I realized that all my life the teachings of those early days have influenced me and the example set by father and mother has been something I have tried to follow, with failures here and there, with rebellion at times, but always coming back to it as the compass needle to the star.

So much depends upon the homemakers. I sometimes wonder if they are so busy now, with other things, that they are forgetting the importance of

3. From William Shakespeare's *Hamlet* 1.3.

this special work. Especially did I wonder when reading recently that there were a great many child suicides in the United States during the last year. Not long ago we never had heard of such a thing in our own country and I am sure that there must be something wrong with the home of a child who commits suicide.

Because of their importance, we must not neglect our homes in the rapid changes of the present day. For when tests of character come in later years, strength to the good will not come from the modern improvements or amusements few may have enjoyed, but from the quiet moments and the "still small voices" of the old home.

Nothing ever can take the place of this early home influence and, as it does not depend upon externals, it may be the possession of the poor as well as the rich, a heritage from all fathers and mothers to their children.

The real things of life that are the common possession of us all are of the greatest value; worth far more than motor cars or radio outfits; more than lands or money; and our whole store of these wonderful riches may be revealed to us by such a common, beautiful thing as a wild sunflower.

As a Farm Woman Thinks (23)

November 1, 1923

While driving one day, I passed a wornout farm. Deep gullies were cut thru the fields where the dirt had been washed away by the rains. The creek had been allowed to change its course, in the bottom field, and cut out a new channel ruining the good land in its way. Tall weeds and brambles were taking more strength from the soil already so poor that grass would scarcely grow.

A STRANGER'S OPINION

With me, as I viewed the place, was a friend from Switzerland and as he looked over the neglected farm he exclaimed, "Oh, it is a crime! It is a crime to treat good land like that!"

The more I think about it the more sure I am that he used the exact word to suit the case. It is a crime to wear out and ruin a farm and the farmer who does so is a thief, stealing from posterity.

We are the heirs of the ages, but the estate is entailed as large estates frequently are, so that while we inherit the earth the great round world which is God's Footstool, we have only the use of it while we live and must pass it on to those who come after us. We hold the property in trust and have no right to injure it nor to lessen its value. To do so is dishonest, stealing from our heirs their inheritance.

The world is the beautiful estate of the human family passing down from generation to generation, marked by each holder while in his possession according to his character.

Did you ever think how a bit of land shows the character of the owner? A dishonest greed is shown by robbing the soil; the traits of a spendthrift are shown in wasting the resources of the farm by destroying its woods and waters, while carelessness and laziness are plainly to be seen in deep scars on the hillsides and washes in the lower fields.

It should be a matter of pride to keep our own farm, that little bit of the earth's surface for which we are responsible in good condition passing it on to our successor better than we found it. Trees should be growing where otherwise would be waste places, with the waters protected as much as possible from the hot sun and drying winds, with fields free from gullies and the soil fertile.

As a Farm Woman Thinks (24)

November 15, 1923

We are inclined to think of Thanksgiving day as a strictly American institution and so, of course, it is in date and manner of celebrating. But a harvest feast with the giving of praise and thanks to whatever gods were worshiped is a custom much older than our Thanksgiving that has been and still is observed by most races and peoples.

It seems to be instinctive for the human race to give thanks for benefits bestowed by a Higher Power. Some have worshiped the sun as the originator of blessings thru its light and heat, while others have bowed the knee to lesser objects. Still the feeling of gratitude in their hearts has been the same as we feel toward a beneficent providence who has given us the harvest as well as countless other blessings thru the year. This is just another touch of nature that makes the whole world kin and links the present with the far distant past.

Mankind is not following a blind trail; feet were set upon the true path in the beginning. Following it at first by instinct, men stumbled from it often in the darkness of ignorance even as we do today, for we have much to learn. But even more than for material blessings, let us, with humble hearts, give thanks for the revelation to us and our better understanding of the greatness and goodness of God.

What Makes My County Great

And Why I'm Proud to Be a Citizen

December 1, 1923

When we came to Missouri in 1894, we were looking for a place where the family health might make a good average, for one of us was not able to stand the severe cold of the North, while another could not live in the low altitude and humid heat of the Southern states.

It was before the days of "Tin Can Tourists" and we traveled with a team and covered wagon. It was rather unpleasant journeying in the heat of the summer, but as we climbed into the hills this side of Springfield, the air grew fresher and more invigorating the farther we went until in Wright County we found the place we were seeking, far enough south so that the winters are mild; high enough for the air to be pure and bracing; sheltered in the hills from the strong winds of the west, yet with little breezes always blowing among them; with plenty of wood for fuel and timber and rocks for building; with low lands for cultivation and upland bluegrass pastures for grazing; with game in the woods and fish in the rivers; and springs of pure, cold, mountain water everywhere.

"ATOP THE OZARKS"

Here on the very peak of the Ozark watershed are to be found good health, good homes, a good living, good times and good neighbors. What more could anyone want?

Wright county is the highest part of the state south of the Missouri river. Its surface is a broad plateau broken by hills rising from it and by valleys and ravines thru which flow the numerous spring branches, creeks and rivers seeking the waters of the Missouri and the Mississippi.

The rolling hills and fertile valleys are beautifully wooded, except where cleared for agricultural purposes. The trees are of many different kinds, Black oak, White oak, blackjack, maple, cherry, ash, elm, sycamore, gum, hickory, walnut, butternut, persimmon, redbud and linden give great variety to the forest foliage and furnish timber for every use. A peculiarity of the country is that springs break out near the tops of the hills as well as on lower ground and wells of good water on the high lands are only from 40 to 60 feet deep.

In the early days all the large game lived here, except buffalo. Deer fed on the hills and in the valleys; bears and panthers denned in the many caves, while wolves and foxes hunted their prey where they might find it. Even yet a panther or wildcat appears now and then while at times wolves are reported killing the sheep.

There is no record of an Indian settlement in Wright county, but the Delawares, Shawnees and Pinkashaws wandered over it hunting and fishing. Their stone arrowheads and clubs are still frequently found.

The first Americans to settle in Wright county came from Tennessee, Kentucky and the Carolinas. The first settlement was made in 1836 and there were seventy slaves in the county at the beginning of the Civil war.

Wright County was organized January 29, 1841 and the court house was built in December, 1849. The county was named for Silas Wright, a leading New York politician, and the guiding spirit of the life of Bart Baynes, the hero of "The Light in the Clearing,"[4] which many Ruralist readers will recall.

The first vote of the county was taken in 1844, the total number of ballots being 583; 97 for Henry Clay and 486 for James K. Polk.

The first church was organized in 1842 and the first school in 1848. The first road thru the county was the old trail from Union to the Fullbright settlement and the pioneer newspaper was The Southwest News, established at Hartville in 1869.

There are many amusing stories told of Wright county's earlier law courts, one being of a certain judge who adjourned without observing the proper formalities and when one of the lawyers protested, exclaiming, "You can't do that! You can't do that!" replied, "Well, by ——— I have done it!"

This is the spirit in which many things have been done in Wright county until what seemed impossible of accomplishment has become a commonplace.

We were told that motor cars could never be used in our hills, now nearly every farmer owns and runs one.

We were told that we never could have good roads, but there are now 53 miles of state road in good condition and more building. The very best of materials for permanent roads lie all along the highways and are being used in the construction of these roads.

We have no large city within our boundaries, but our towns are good trad-

4. A novel by Irving Bacheller (Indianapolis: Bobbs-Merrill, 1917).

ing points and are developing on a sound basis with the country around them.

Hartville, the county seat, is an inland town, on the beautiful Gasconade river. It is an old town with a history that includes several battles of the Civil war. The fine court house and tree shaded court house square give the town its distinctive character.

Mountain Grove, Mansfield, Norwood and Cedar Gap and Macomb are railroad shipping points.

Mansfield is the heaviest shipping point, save one, for cream between Springfield and Memphis, shipping in the last three months 2,812 cans of cream. Other farm products are shipped in proportion.

In three months, there were shipped from Mountain Grove 68 cars of eggs, valued at $275,000; 14 cars of poultry, $48,000; 45 cars lumber, $60,000; 47 cars ties, $13,000; 26 cars hogs, cattle and mules, $30,000; 1 car apples, $6,000; 1 car butter, $8,000; making a total of $404,600.

There are several farmers exchanges in the county and the one at Mountain Grove did a business last year of $182,640, paying dividends and interest back to the farmers of more than $11,000. For the first half of this year they have returned $5,400 to the 400 members.

The soil of Wright County is a deep, gravelly, clay loam, with a red clay subsoil, having an admixture of gravel which makes it porous and gives good drainage for plant roots.

On the lowlands along the Gasconade river and its branches, Beaver, Elk, Whetstone and Clark's Creek, are many fine bottom farms, while on the uplands cattle are grazing on a thousand hills rich in many kinds of grasses.

Conditions in the whole county are ideal for the raising of poultry and fruit.

"LAND OF THE BIG, RED APPLE"

Wright county is in the heart of the "Land of the Big Red Apple" and, besides apples, grows peaches, pears, plums, cherries, persimmons, grapes, strawberries, huckleberries, dewberries and currants. We have fruit the year around, for apples keep well, in the cellar, until strawberries are plentiful and then there is a great variety as well as an unbroken succession of fresh fruit.

In 1921 there were 157,755 bearing fruit trees in Wright county.

At the Missouri Fruit Experiment station, located at Mountain Grove, there are being produced 550 varieties of apples, 40 different kinds of peaches, 50 kinds of pears, 40 different kinds of strawberries and 180 varieties of grapes, the largest collection of varieties of different fruits in the United States.

At Mountain Grove is also located the Missouri Poultry Experiment station. The fact that this station, during the years of 1921 and 1922 turned into the state treasury $19,800 from the sale of poultry and eggs, shows that this is a good place to raise poultry.

There are many poultry farms in the county. One deserving of mention is that of Roy Clodfelter near Hartville. Mr. Clodfelter's plant is modern in every way even to Delco lighting in the hen house. He raises White Leghorns and keeps on hand 1,200 laying hens, raising 3,000 chicks each spring.

Mrs. Rippee near the same town raises Barred Plymouth Rocks bred for laying as well as size. She has some 200 egg hens in her flock.

Then there is Mrs. Wilson of the Wilson Farm who specializes in Mammoth Bronze turkeys, making a profit of more than $1,000 a year from them, but who does not believe in putting all the farm business eggs in one basket, even tho they are turkey eggs, and so keeps 100 head of purebred Shorthorn cattle for which the Wilson Farm is known all over the Middlewest.

There are several herds of purebred Jerseys in the county. Near Mansfield, herds are owned by Joe Westbrook and Fred Oetting. Mr. Oetting was selling $300 worth of cream a month from his cows last summer.

One particularly attractive thing about our county is that while so much has been done and tho, by date of settlement, it is an old county, still it is practically a new country, for its resources and possibilities have only been touched. There is still plenty of opportunity for young and old, on the land and in the openings for factories and manufacturing plants to care for our products and furnish us the things we need.

There are several wholesale houses and a few manufacturies in our towns and at Cedar Gap are the Erb Fruit Farms, with their own packing house, cold storage and vinegar plant. These and our canning factories, busily canning and shipping tomatoes and fruits, show what can be done along these lines and point the way to larger things.

The growing of tomatoes and grapes is on the increase, the conditions of soil and climate being particularly favorable for them and also for the growing of sorghums; our sorghum molasses having an especially fine flavor.

And besides all these things, Wright county has valuable mines of lead, zinc, coal and onyx, which tho not fully developed are worked at times.

With such diversity of products, so many different branches of agriculture, Wright county offers to everyone a chance to follow their own especial taste in farming—poultry, dairying, fruits, beef cattle, horses and mules, sheep, goats, hogs, grain, hay and bees—one can make his own choice of what he will specialize in, or by raising all on the same place, as is usually done, there is the finest sort of diversified farming one could wish and each member of a family may work at the thing he likes best.

While attending to other growing things, the children of Wright are not neglected, our schools are good.

There are fine high schools in Hartville, Mansfield, Mountain Grove and Norwood. Each year for five years there has been a school fair at the Hartville High School, at which each school in the county makes an exhibit from the year's work in manual training, agriculture and home economics.

There are also two schools for disabled ex-service men, one teaching poultry raising, the other the Braille alphabet, typewriting, rug and basket weaving and poultry raising to men with failing eyesight. These schools are located at Mountain Grove.

The chance for home building in Wright county is something of which I am particularly proud for nowhere can such healthful, comfortable and beautiful, farm homes be built with less trouble and expense. There are on our land all the materials for building, either with stone or timber, and the abundance of water in springs and wells and streams makes it possible to put running water in nearly every farmhouse.

We play as well as work in Wright county and do it with as much enthusiasm, having all the materials at hand for this also.

Our diversity is not confined to our agriculture and amusements, but extends to our people. From Wright county have gone many who have distinguished themselves in various ways. Among these are Cleveland Newton who was sent to Congress where he made good and from there went to his law office in St. Louis where he still is making good; William H. Hamby noted writer of books, magazine stories and photo plays; Rose Wilder Lane, writer and world traveler whose books and short stories are published in the United States and England and have been translated into foreign languages; and Carl Mays, famous pitcher for the Yankees who has been called the greatest pitcher in the world.

Not all of us can become famous, but nowhere are there better neighbors or truer friends. If misfortune, sickness or sorrow comes to one, the neighbors rally to help, with a whole hearted good fellowship that makes living worth while and dying easier.

If you have thoughtfully read this little story, you will know that I am proud of Wright county because of its healthful, pleasant climate and its natural features which make possible a happy combination of work and play; because of what has been accomplished and its promise for the future and because of the spirit of its people, which is the American, pioneer spirit of courage, jollity and neighborly helpfulness.

As a Farm Woman Thinks (25)

January 1, 1924

Standing on the shore with the waves of the Pacific rolling to my feet, I looked over the waters as far as my eyes could reach until the gray of the ocean merged with the gray of the horizon's rim. One could not be distinguished from the other. Where, within my vision, the waters stopped and the skies began I could not tell so softly they blended one into the other. The waves rolled in regularly, beating a rythm of time, but the skies above them were unmeasured—so vast and far reaching that the mind of man could not comprehend it.

A symbol of time and of eternity—time spaced by our counting into years, breaking at our feet as the waves break on the shore, and eternity, unmeasurable as the skies above us—blending one into the other at the fartherest reach of our earthly vision.

As the New Year comes, seemingly with ever increasing swiftness, there is a feeling that life is too short to accomplish the things we must do. But there is all eternity blending with the end of time for the things that really are worth while.

We are so overwhelmed with things these days that our lives are all more or less cluttered. I believe it is this, rather than a shortness of time, that gives us that feeling of hurry and almost of helplessness in the face of them. Everyone is hurrying and usually just a little late. Notice the faces of the people who rush past on the streets or on our country roads! They nearly all have a strained, harassed look and any one you meet will tell you there is no time for anything any more.

Life is so complicated! The day of the woman whose only needed tool was a hairpin is long since passed. But we might learn something from her and her methods even yet, for life would be pleasanter with some of the strain removed—if it were no longer true, as some one has said, that "things are in the saddle and rule mankind."

Here is a good New Year's resolution for us all to make: To simplify our lives as much as possible, to overcome that feeling of haste by remembering that there are just as many hours in the day as ever, and that there is time enough for the things that matter if it is rightly used.

Then, having done the most we may here, when we reach the limit of time we will sail on over the horizon rim to new beauties and greater understanding.

As a Farm Woman Thinks (26)

January 15, 1924

In her late book, "Beginning Again at Ararat," Mabel E. Elliot M. D., Near East Relief worker, says that among the refugees, in the tumble-down, crowded, filthy Turkish interior cities there "appeared once more that magic of the American woman's home-making ability, surprisingly revealed by the war and the peace.

"American women are the only women in the world who, far from home, in primitive countries, without familiar materials, set to work with whatever they can lay hands upon and make a home. Somehow they curtain windows, create couches and tables and chairs from packing-cases, make leather cushions of sheep's skins, table covers of peasant's petticoats; then they set a flowering almond branch in a pottery jar—and there, triumphantly, is an American living-room, tasteful, charming, comfortable. In every language of Europe and Asia men marvel at this."

This is the reputation of American home-makers. I had not realized how far our fame had traveled. But I long ago discovered that making a reputation is one thing and living up to it another story.

Are our living rooms "tasteful, charming and comfortable"? If not why not "set to work with whatever we can lay hands upon" and make them so?

BRIGHTENING UP

It is remarkable what an improvement a little paint will make used where paint should be applied. Varnish in its proper place makes all the world look brighter. An added window in a dark corner, letting the sunlight in, will change the whole character of a dull room making of it a cheerful place and helping to brighten our lives.

If there is too much of sameness and monotony in farm life, it is perhaps mostly our own fault. The same things in the same places, the same colors in the same rooms and exactly the same way of living become tiresome in time. A different arrangement of the furniture, a small moving from one room to another will bring to the house a newness and a freshness that will relieve tired nerves and restlessness almost as much as the seeing of new places.

What I think the greatest compliment that Rocky Ridge Farm house ever has received was given it by a neighbor who, seeing for the first time the interior of the house, stood where he could look it over and said, "I like your house—I do like your house! It is not so monotonous!"

The Fairs That Build Men

Where Citizens of Tomorrow Are Trained

January 15, 1924

We accept, without thinking about it, the fact that happy nations do not appear in history. But only lately I have realized that events of greatest importance are least noticed, even while they are occurring under our very eyes.

I realized this when I walked down the steps of the Hartville high school building, thinking of the fair I had just seen and comparing it with others I remembered. There was the unforgettable World's Fair in San Francisco, the several great state fairs at Sedalia, the land congress fairs, county fairs, stock fairs, poultry fairs—all of them interesting and admirable. But this fair I had just seen, this small fair unknown outside Wright county, mentioned only in the Hartville papers, seemed to me more important than any of them.

The great World's Fairs show what has been builded by nations; the small rural school fairs are building the nation itself, for the training which these children are getting in co-operation and honorable competition will make of them useful and possibly great citizens of the nation and the world. It means much to a child, in character building, to learn to be an honest winner or a good loser in whatever contest he takes part, whether it be a World War or a poultry show.

This fair was a fair of children, and—under guidance—by and for children. School children made nearly half of the record-breaking attendance of 2,500 who crowded the school building and grounds.

GIRLS COOK AND CAN

The children of the Hartville school cooking class served luncheon to them all, and were kept rather more than comfortably busy preparing the quantities of toothsome dishes. If it had been possible to use the food exhibited there would easily have been an abundant supply of the best quality. It made one's mouth water to gaze on the quantities of beautiful canned fruit and rosy-cheeked apples, the nuts and grains and vegetables.

The growth, care and selection of all these exhibits must have made farm work, thru the year, intensely interesting to the pupils of the 24 schools represented.

There were 44 varieties of canned fruit exhibited by New Mountain Dale school. There were 15 varieties of grasses and 78 kinds of native woods shown by Rodgers School. There were 18 varieties of forest leaves collected by the Hall School. These exhibits were in addition to those of the regular school work, agricultural and manual training displays, among which was a special model of a milking stool designed by one of the Rodgers school class.

Little Creek School brought 27 varieties of forest leaves, 21 varied grains, 22 kinds of seeds, 14 species of insects, 10 noxious weeds, 70 kinds of native woods. Little Creek school by this astounding total won second prize for exhibits.

Pleasant Hill school carried off first prize with a large display of turnips, pumpkins, potatoes, melons, grains, grasses, weeds, knots, agricultural maps, general school work, fancy work, patchwork, potted flowers, 37 varieties of canned fruit, 11 varieties of apples, a roomful of chickens, and a calf, with an overflow into the school yard of two pens of hogs.

Blanchard School won third prize for exhibits.

Lone Star School, with 100 per cent attendance, accompanied by their entire school board, for the second time won the attendance prize.

The teachers of these schools, Emmett Jones, Pleasant Hill; J. M. Vestal, Little Creek; Homer Smith, Blanchard; and Mrs. James Shelby, Lone Star, certainly deserve honorable mention. And what a training all these rural teachers have been giving their pupils in observance of the world around them, in seeing and knowing leaf and weed and insect and all the varied, interesting things on the farm.

MANY OTHER FEATURES

Reading contests and singing contests were features of the last day of the fair. The song contest was won by Pleasant Hill School. Glenette McGowan, of Blanchard School carried off the prize in the reading contest.

Basket ball and other athletic games, played on the campus in a spirit of friendly rivalry and good temper, were a pleasure to witness.

Good speaking during the fair added much to the interest of the occasion.

In the exhibits and school work, health, agriculture, poultry and dairy farming were emphasized and much interest was shown by farm folks attending, in the definite lessons presented on feeding dairy cows, poultry and hogs by Professor Hess's vocational class and also in the soil exhibit showing methods of fertilization and testing for the need of lime, while the model poultry house and the model farm with its impressive lesson in the necessity of crop rotation to maintain soil fertility were much talked about.

All this can not fail in affecting for the better the farming methods of the county and being an education for parents as well as children.

The Wright County School Fair for 1923 was a remarkable success and much of the credit for this is due Professor Hess of the Hartville School, University Extension workers and County Superintendent Ray Wood, who with his hard working rural teachers, backed by the business and professional men of Hartville, worked together for that object.

Turkeys Bring $1,000 a Year

Where Secret of Success Is "Love Them"

February 1, 1924

It was late afternoon at the Wilson Farm and the coolness of the evening was very pleasant after the warmth of the spring day. The cows were lowing on their way to the barn and milking time. Among the other sounds of evening on the farm came a call with a hint of wildness in it—"Turrk! Turrk!" it said. The turkeys were coming up, followed by their little ones scurrying thru the grass, slipping from cover to cover like shadows, but following their mothers' call—"Turrk! Turrk! Turrk!"

"The one that runs in the orchard isn't there," said Mrs. Wilson. "I must go hunt her. Make yourself comfortable until I get back," she called, as she hurried away. But she did not find the stray in the orchard, and some others that ranged along the river did not appear, so down to the river went Mrs. Wilson hunting them. Brother-in-law Jim, riding the little pony, searched in the far meadow. The Airedale puppy broke from his imprisonment in the barn to join in the hunt, and I brought up the rear. I was slow and awkward, unable to keep up with the pup, not used to hunting turkeys, but I did help drive up the strays and feed and pen each flock in its small house. Such pretty, wild little things, and dozens and dozens of them! "Cheep, Cheep, Cheep!" they said, as they pecked at their supper of eggs and cheese spread on boards at the door of each house.

I saw them again just before Thanksgiving. It was noon, this time. "Oh, they'll come whenever I call them," Mrs. Wilson said, walking out into the yard with a basket of corn on her arm. She gave her turkey call, which I will not attempt to reproduce, and turkeys materialized where apparently no turkeys had been before. She kept calling, and the woods seemed alive with turkeys, all flying and running toward her. One hundred eighty-five, she said were there, and I know that, as we say in the vernacular, "the woods was full of 'em." It was a pretty sight to see them gather around her, their beautiful bronze feathers glistening in the sun.

GIVES THEM ATTENTION

Mrs. Wilson's turkeys know her so well that if they are frightened in the night her voice will quiet them; they will answer when she speaks, and will eat from her hand. And Mrs. Wilson loves her turkeys. When the time comes to kill them she runs and hides to cry while they are being butchered.

It takes time and patience, gentleness and tact, to be successful in raising turkeys. "They are very fond of attention," said Mrs. Wilson, "and like to be talked to. It makes no difference what you say, just so your tone is quiet and your voice gentle." Turkeys are nervous, shy, wild things by nature, and Mrs. Wilson treats them accordingly. Sometimes, however, when a turkey is very bad she is punished. I saw Mrs. Wilson switch a quarrelsome mother-turkey to make her stop fussing with her neighbor and go to her crying babies at her own house-door.

Mrs. Wilson began raising turkeys ten years ago with three hens and a tom. Not knowing anything about turkeys, she let them follow their own sweet wills. Consequently, not being worried by being followed about nest-hunting, they nested in underbrush near the house. The three hens laid sixty eggs the first clutch, and, from these Mrs. Wilson raised 55 to maturity. She was so elated by this success that she confidently set the mark at 200 for the next season.

Eager to find all the eggs from which to raise the 200, she followed her best hen so closely at nesting time that the hen at last became seriously annoyed. The last Mrs. Wilson ever saw of her was when she rose with a spread of her strong wings and flew away into the woods.

Now difficulties multiplied. Crows and black snakes took the eggs; overfeeding killed the poults. At the end of the season Mrs. Wilson had only 35 turkeys, instead of the 200 she had confidently expected to raise. A lesser person would have quit the turkey business right there. But Mrs. Wilson has pluck and perseverance, and it is hard for anyone or any circumstances to beat her. Instead of quitting, she began to learn how to raise turkeys. She learned it well, for the flock I saw gave her $1,005 net profit for the year.

A DISASTROUS SEASON

She had a pen made, 20×60 feet, 7 feet high, and covered with poultry netting. By being quiet and gentle with her turkeys she tamed them so that every morning they would follow her into this pen, listening to her voice as she talked to them and eating from her hands. Day after day, Mrs. Wilson enjoyed this early morning visit with her turkeys. Then she went to her other work, while they ranged the fields. At nesting-time she shut them into the pen for an hour every morning. The hen that had made her nest showed it by her uneasiness, and they were so accustomed to her presence that she could let the hen out and by following it cautiously could locate the nest. Thus one by one every turkey was watched until she betrayed her nesting place. Every year since then Mrs. Wilson has used this method of finding the nests. When a nest is found she does not go near until the hen has left it, and no hen is ever shut in the pen after her nest is found, for the less they are bothered the better. If they are made nervous they will change their nest place.

In the hen's absence her eggs are carefully taken from the nest and given to common hens to hatch, in order to protect them from snakes and crows. The turkey hens are left setting on the nest with just enough eggs to keep them there until the poults are hatched, when they are given to their turkey mothers. Mrs. Wilson has learned from experience that 20 poults are as many as a turkey hen can properly hover after they are three or four weeks old, and that they must be well covered or they may drown if caught out in a hard rain.

HOW SHE FEEDS THEM

For their first feeding, 48 hours after hatching, Mrs. Wilson gives hard-boiled eggs chopped very fine; for 20 poults and mother, one egg three times a day. After the first day of feeding, lettuce, dandelion, sow thistle or onion tops, finely chopped, are added to the egg. In fine weather, when the poults can run, she feeds the same amount daily for two weeks; if they are kept in the coops she adds a little bread, soaked in sweet milk until it crumbles. When they are two weeks old, and out on range, they are fed twice a day, two eggs at a feed for twenty poults and mother. After this age, Mrs. Wilson sometimes substitutes an equal amount of cottage cheese for the eggs, at one feeding a day, and they are always given plenty of milk. Green food and milk can be given at any time, but the rest of the ration is never exceeded, as there is danger in over-feeding.

The hens are turned out for a few hours every fine day, but are carefully watched, for when the poults are young the mothers will hide them if possible. The coops, one for each brood, are 3 by 6 feet, 3½ feet high in front and 2½ feet in back, built of common boarding with shingled roof. The whole front is of screen wire, with a door that slips in and fastens with two buttons. The doorway must be so large that it will not touch the hen as she goes in and out. At night the hens and their broods are shut into these coops where they are safe from "varmints," and during bad weather they may be kept in several days. They range as much as possible, however, for Mrs. Wilson finds they grow faster when allowed to run.

Healthy, vigorous parent stock is most important in raising turkeys, Mrs. Wilson says, and she does not use parent stock under two years old. For one of her toms she paid $200, and went herself to New York to get it. She counts it a profitable investment, for she sells young toms at $20 each, and eggs for hatching at $10 each. Most of her year's profit—usually about $1,000—comes however, from the sale of fat turkeys for Christmas dinner-tables.

But no investment in money will make success in turkey raising. Only ceaseless expenditure of time, attention and genuine interest in her turkeys has made Mrs. Wilson's success possible. It is no wonder that confidential relations are established between her and her turkeys, for from the time of hatching they know her care. She has each one in her hands at least once a week while it is young, examining it for lice or signs of sickness; she vaccinates every one of them against blackhead; she makes a pet of each one, and as long as a turkey is on her farm she has it in her arms at least once a month.

As a Farm Woman Thinks (27)

February 1, 1924

The lotus is the sacred emblem of Buddhism, because in its rise from the bottom of ponds to the light and sweet air above where it puts forth its large green leaves and beautiful blossoms "it symbolizes triumph over self, extinction of the fires of passion, abnegation and self control." It is a beautiful example of the growth of good with darkness and evil left behind. But this is accomplished only by a reaching upward and a striving toward the light—a longing for the pure air and sunshine.

The lotus gardens of Japan are renowned for their beauty. The plants have large corded, green leaves 2 feet across and wonderful blossoms that float above the water with the birds and butterflies in the sunshine. It is here that the women of Japan delight to spend their summer afternoons.

One cannot imagine the lotus sprouts crawling around on the bottom of the ponds without making the effort to rise higher into all this beauty and fragrance leaving the mud behind. There is a lesson for us all in this symbol of an old, old religion.

If we wish to help make beauty and joy in the world, living in it and becoming lovely ourselves, also, we must follow the example of the lotus and strive toward light and purity into the sunshine of the good.

As a Farm Woman Thinks (28)

March 1, 1924

"I would rather have made that pie than to have written a poem," said Rose Wilder Lane, pausing midway of the triangular piece upon her plate. It was just a plain, farm apple pie, the kind we all make in Missouri. But listen! "Oh these Missouri pies," exclaimed the other New York writer. "Never before have I seen such wonderful pies."[1]

So it seems that the center of pie fame as well as the center of population has traveled westward for pie, you know, was a New England dish, not known anywhere else in the world. To this day it is made only in America. And speaking of pies and poems, the first pie as we know pie, invented by a New

1. Well-known writers such as Sinclair Lewis and Dorothy Thompson, Lewis's wife, visited Laura's home in the Ozarks at the invitation of Rose.

England woman, was a poem of love and service, full of imagination, spicy with invention. Oh, of course, what it was really filled with was something very common and homely, but I'll tell you the tale as 'twas told to me and you shall decide if my description of that first pie as a poem does not hold good.

In one of the New England states away back in Colonial times, a pioneer woman one Saturday was cooking the Sunday dinner. She wanted a sweet meat for the ending but had nothing of which to make anything of the kind she ever had seen. But she did want to please and satisfy the good man and the children, so using her imagination and Yankee invention, she made a dough with bear's grease for shortening, spread it in a pan and filled it with a mixture of vinegar and water thickened with flour, sweetened with maple sugar and flavored with a bit of spice bush.

FIRST AMERICAN PIE

She baked it and behold, the first American pie! In fact, it was the first pie, spicy and sweet, of custard-like consistency and crispy crust, a poem in cookery. Its originator was truly an artist as tho she had written a poem or painted a picture for she had used her creative instinct and imagination with a fine technic. Thinking of pies and poems, I am more content with pie making for surely it is better to make a good pie than a poor poem.

As a Farm Woman Thinks (29)

April 1, 1924

The topic that had been given me for my club lesson was music. Now the only instrument I can play is the phonograph and I venture to sing only in a crowd where I can drown my voice in the volume of sound. To be sure I have a little music in my feet, but that would not answer for a club paper, so it seemed rather hopeless, but never yet have I been "stumped." I began to dig up just plain facts about music and seldom have I found anything so interesting.

The simple fact, of how music came to have written form, takes us away into the days of chivalry, in the 16th Century. To guide the choir boys in following the melody when singing masses, the monks wrote the Latin words, not in a straight line but up and down to indicate their place in the musical scale. Later, to shorten the time and labor of writing, the words were replaced by circles and the horizontal lines of the staff were added to more clearly indicate their position. Slowly, from time to time, the different forms of notes were made and music was standardized into the base and treble cleffs, so that our music of today takes its printed form directly from the manuscripts so laboriously written by hand in the monasteries of the 16th Century.

This is only one of the many things I learned about music, but I learned also that it isn't what one already knows that adds interest to the preparation of a club paper so much as the learning something new in order to be able to go on with it.

Learning things is most fascinating and I think it adds joy to life to be continually learning things so that we may be able to go on with it creditably.

As a Farm Woman Thinks (30)

May 15, 1924

The man of the place was worried about the weather. He said the indications were for a dry season and ever since I have been remembering drouths. There were dry years in the Dakotas when we were beginning our life together. How heart breaking it was to watch the grain we had sown with such high hopes wither and turn yellow in the hot winds! And it was back breaking as well as heart breaking to carry water from the well to my garden and see it dry up despite all my efforts.

I said at that time that thereafter I would sow the seed but the Lord would give the increase if there was any, for I could not do my work and that of Providence also by sending the rain upon the gardens of the just or the unjust.

But still I suppose our brains were given us to use, by the same Providence that created the laws of nature and what we accomplish by the use of them is in a certain sense, Its work. Just as all good is for us, if we but reach out our hand and take it, so in the higher atmosphere around our earth there is a great supply of moisture. It is there for our use if, with the brains which God has given us, we can find a way to tap it. This is what a California man claims to have done.

Hatfield, the rain maker, lives in Glendale, Cal., near Los Angeles. He claims to be able to make rain by projecting into the atmosphere, from a high scaffolding, certain chemicals which attract and precipitate moisture. There are always storms in movement and storm formations pass high over a country without ever condensing and causing rain. The way he operates, he'll make that storm give up its water as it comes along.

In 1915 there was a very severe drouth in Southern California, especially in San Diego County, where the water situation became critical. As a last resort the San Diego Chamber of Commerce decided to try out this man Hatfield. A contract was made by which he was to receive $10,000, if he brought down water enough to fill the great irrigation reservoir. Shortly after he began operations the rain began to fall in such quantities that the reservoir not only filled but burst its dam and the Chamber of Commerce, instead of paying him $10,000, brought suit against him for damages in destroying the dam.

A DRY SEASON

This year also has been an exceptional year in California. There was a long dry spell thru the winter and in the district around Hanford, orchardists have sent for Hatfield. He is operating there with considerable success and fulfilling his contract to bring 4 inches of rain.

Engineers say they believe Hatfield's method is sound enough, but they doubt if, operating from a scaffold, he can reach the higher strata of atmosphere where there always is sufficient moisture to produce rain.

In Europe they are experimenting along the same lines, but are operating from airplanes, at elevations from 10,000 to 20,000 feet.

As a Farm Woman Thinks (31)

June 1, 1924

"Mother passed away this morning" was the message that came over the wires and a darkness overshadowed the spring sunshine; a sadness crept into the birds' songs.[2]

Some of us have received such messages. Those who have not, one day will. Just as when a child, home was lonely when mother was gone, so to children of a larger growth, the world seems a lonesome place when mother has passed away and only memories of her are left us—happy memories if we have not given ourselves any cause for regret.

Memories! We go thru life collecting them whether we will or not! Sometimes I wonder if they are our treasures in heaven or the consuming fires of torment when we carry them with us as we, too, pass on.

2. Caroline Quiner Ingalls, "Ma" Ingalls, 1839–1924.

What a joy our memories may be or what a sorrow! But glad or sad they are with us forever. Let us make them carefully of all good things, rejoicing in the wonderful truth that while we are laying up for ourselves the very sweetest and best of happy memories, we are at the same time giving them to others.

As a Farm Woman Thinks (32)

June 15, 1924

When one is tired with the season's sewing, the remodeling of old garments or making of new because the styles have changed, one thinks what a joy it would be to wear a national costume that never changes as is done by some of the people of Europe.

In the Federated Socialist Soviet Republics that we used to call Russia, of which there are more than 30, the division is racial and the general costume of all women is a rather short, very full skirt, tight fitting bodice or jacket, an apron and a cap.

This costume differs as to detail from section to section, even from village to village. In some places knee high boots are worn. Kirghis women especially are renowned for their high boots of apple-green leather, finer than kid gloves, soft as silk and appliqued all over with the same leather in bright colors.

The men wear high boots, trousers rather like hunting breeches, a blouse quite like a shirt worn outside, a cape or cloak and a headdress which in style shows the place from which they come.

Georgian women wear full skirts and tight bodices of dark colors and embroidered aprons. Their own hair is always completely concealed and over each ear, hanging on the breast, they wear a thick curl of artificial hair. Over their heads they wear veils of white lace or embroidered net. Over this is worn a little crown of black velvet adorned with coins, or if wealthy, diamonds. Over all is a veil of black lace, or black embroidered net. Both black and white veils are large, folded cornerwise and have fancy edging. They give a beautiful effect, framing the face and hanging down the back.

When one remembers that all the lace and embroidery are hand-made, it doesn't seem so simple after all and I've no doubt the endless stitching of making it would be more tiresome than the summer's sewing.

As a Farm Woman Thinks (33)

December 15, 1924

The snow was scudding low over the drifts of the white world outside the little claim shanty. It was blowing thru the cracks in its walls and forming little piles and miniature drifts on the floor and even on the desks before which several children sat, trying to study, for this abandoned claim shanty that had served as the summer home of a homesteader on the Dakota prairies was being used as a schoolhouse during the winter.

The walls were made of one thickness of wide boards with cracks between and the enormous stove that stood nearly in the center of the one room could scarcely keep out the frost tho its sides were a glowing red. The children were dressed warmly and had been allowed to gather closely around the stove following the advice of the county superintendent of schools, who on a recent visit had said that the only thing he had to say to them was to keep their feet warm.[3]

This was my first school, I'll not say how many years ago, but I was only 16 years old and 12 miles from home during a frontier winter. I walked a mile over the unbroken snow from my boarding place to school every morning and back at night. There were only a few pupils and on this particular snowy afternoon they were restless for it was nearing 4 o'clock and tomorrow was Christmas. "Teacher" was restless too, tho she tried not to show it for she was wondering if she could get home for Christmas Day.

It was almost too cold to hope for father to come and a storm was hanging in the northwest which might mean a blizzard at any minute. Still, tomorrow was Christmas—and then there was a jingle of sleigh bells outside. A man in a huge fur coat in a sleigh full of robes passed the window. I was going home after all!

When one thinks of 12 miles now, it is in terms of motor cars and means only a few minutes. It was different then, and I'll never forget that ride. The bells made a merry jingle, and the fur robes were warm, but the weather was growing colder and the snow was drifting so that the horses must break their way thru the drifts.

We were facing the strong wind, and every little while he, who later became the "man of the place," must stop the team, get out in the snow, and by putting his hands over each horse's nose in turn, thaw the ice from them

3. Laura Ingalls Wilder, *These Happy Golden Years* (New York: Harper and Row, 1971), chapters 8–9.

where the breath had frozen over their nostrils. Then he would get back into the sleigh and on we'd go until once more the horses could not breathe for the ice.

When we reached the journey's end, it was 40 degrees below zero, the snow was blowing so thickly that we could not see across the street and I was so chilled that I had to be half carried into the house. But I was home for Christmas and cold and danger were forgotten.

Such magic there is in Christmas to draw the absent ones home and if unable to go in the body the thoughts will hover there! Our hearts grow tender with childhood memories and love of kindred and we are better thruout the year for having in spirit become a child again at Christmas-time.

Spic, Span—and Beauty

How a Home Responds to Springtime Touches

April 1, 1931

"In the spring a young man's fancy lightly turns to thoughts of love," says the poem, but a housekeeper turns to thoughts of housecleaning, and not so lightly either.

Even when the whole place is in order, we feel that something more should be added to the charm of its freshness and sweetness. We want beauty within to accord with the springtime beauty outside.

If we have plenty of money to use in the work it is easier to accomplish this, but even with a little much may be done in redecorating and beautifying our homes.

Old furniture may be made to look like new by painting it with a quick-drying varnish stain, which comes in all colors or clear. The grain of the wood shows thru the clear varnish and used over a freshly sand-papered piece of old furniture renews its youth.

If the floors are in good shape, they may be waxed. There are good waxes on the market, but one may be made at home as good and much cheaper. Use one-third melted parowax with two-thirds coal oil or gasoline. Melt the wax, then add the gas or oil, being very careful to keep them away from the fire. After mixing, apply to floors, linoleums, congoleums, etc. In a few minutes the gas will have evaporated; then polish with a woolen cloth, which for convenience may be put over a dust mop. The use of this wax will both preserve and beautify the floors.

HOME-MADE THROW RUGS

If floors are in bad condition, it may be necessary to paint them and cover mostly with rugs. There are so many rugs on the market that one may buy at a price to suit the purse, but home-made ones are very pretty and quite the thing just now.

Paints or other like preparations may be used to freshen the walls, but printed wallpapers are especially good this spring and not expensive.

One of the most important things in the beautifying of our homes is the treatment of the windows and a beautiful effect is obtained by a view, thru two or more rooms and a window at the end, to the outdoors.

Windows entirely covered with lace curtains are out of place in the country, for we want the view of hills and woods, of prairie and stream to add to the beauty of our homes and to give them an effect of space and distance. We want our windows to be moving pictures of storms and sunshine, of sunrise and sunset, of moonlight and sunshine and the ever changing seasons. And so, while they must be more or less draped, the less they are draped the more we shall love them.

If the walls are plain, cretonnes or prints are good draped at the sides and across the very tops, but if there is figured paper on the walls then a plain color or white is better for the windows.

I once made some very pretty window curtains out of unbleached muslin, edged with crochet lace. The soft cream color of the muslin and the effect of the lace were charming when the curtains were hung.

COOL AND INVITING

In winter we give our homes a feeling of warmth and coziness by the use of warm materials and warm, bright colors and by a snug grouping of the furniture.

In warm weather, however, we want to suggest coolness, to give a sense of lightness, airiness and restfulness. To secure this effect it is better not to have too much in a room, for a cluttered room is stuffy and gives a feeling of confusion which is tiring. The furniture should be rather scattered, with chairs and couches arranged to take full advantage of the fresh air from open windows.

A few good pictures on the walls are better than many and the bright colored bindings of books give a pleasing note of color in a darker corner.

The quality of quietness and coolness should be especially emphasized in the treatment of our bedrooms, thus helping to induce a restful sleep when hot weather comes. One of the quilts, from some beautiful, old pattern that everyone has been making lately, is a lovely cover for a bed and several cushions, of different patterned blocks, go nicely with it. A tiny block, of the same pattern as the quilt, in the corner of white window curtains and dresser scarf gives a touch of quaintness to the whole.

BIBLIOGRAPHY

Mrs. A. J. Wilder's Articles and Columns in the *Missouri Ruralist*

"According to Experts." February 5, 1917, p. 9.

"All in the Day's Work: Just a Neighborly Visit with Folks at Rocky Ridge Farm." February 5, 1916, p. 20.

"All the World Is Queer." September 20, 1916, p. 9.

"The American Spirit." December 20, 1918, p. 11.

"And a Woman Did It." July 20, 1917, p. 10.

"And Missouri 'Showed' Them: From A To Z—Alfalfa to Zinc—the 'Show Me State' Won Honors at 'Frisco's Exposition." December 5, 1915, pp. 3, 7.

"Are We Too Busy?" October 5, 1917, p. 12.

"Are You Going Ahead?" February 20, 1917, p. 13.

"Are You Helping or Hindering?" July 5, 1918, p. 21.

"As a Farm Woman Thinks" (1). June 15, 1921, p. 17.

"As a Farm Woman Thinks" (2). July 15, 1921, p. 16.

"As a Farm Woman Thinks" (3). November 1, 1921, p. 24.

"As a Farm Woman Thinks" (4). November 15, 1921, p. 21.

"As a Farm Woman Thinks" (5). January 1, 1922, p. 20.

"As a Farm Woman Thinks" (6). February 1, 1922, p. 26.

"As a Farm Woman Thinks" (7). March 1, 1922, p. 28.

"As a Farm Woman Thinks" (8). March 15, 1922, p. 26.

"As a Farm Woman Thinks" (9). May 1, 1922, p. 14.

"As a Farm Woman Thinks" (10). June 15, 1922, p. 22.

"As a Farm Woman Thinks" (11). July 1, 1922, p. 20.

"As a Farm Woman Thinks" (12). August 15, 1922, p. 27.

"As a Farm Woman Thinks" (13). September 1, 1922, pp. 20–22.

"As a Farm Woman Thinks" (14). October 15, 1922, p. 27.

"As a Farm Woman Thinks" (15). November 1, 1922, p. 20.
"As a Farm Woman Thinks" (16). November 15, 1922, p. 26.
"As a Farm Woman Thinks" (17). January 1, 1923, p. 20.
"As a Farm Woman Thinks" (18). April 1, 1923, p. 30.
"As a Farm Woman Thinks" (19). April 15, 1923, p. 32.
"As a Farm Woman Thinks" (20). May 15, 1923, p. 22.
"As a Farm Woman Thinks" (21). July 1, 1923, p. 16.
"As a Farm Woman Thinks" (22). August 1, 1923, p. 18.
"As a Farm Woman Thinks" (23). November 1, 1923, p. 22.
"As a Farm Woman Thinks" (24). November 15, 1923, p. 16.
"As a Farm Woman Thinks" (25). January 1, 1924, p. 34.
"As a Farm Woman Thinks" (26). January 15, 1924, p. 20.
"As a Farm Woman Thinks" (27). February 1, 1924, p. 39.
"As a Farm Woman Thinks" (28). March 1, 1924, p. 31.
"As a Farm Woman Thinks" (29). April 1, 1924, p. 31.
"As a Farm Woman Thinks" (30). May 15, 1924, p. 16.
"As a Farm Woman Thinks" (31). June 1, 1924, p. 16.
"As a Farm Woman Thinks" (32). June 15, 1924, p. 16.
"As a Farm Woman Thinks" (33). December 15, 1924, p. 16.
"As in Days of Old." April 15, 1922, p. 36.
"An Autumn Day." October 20, 1916, p. 9.
"Before Santa Claus Came." December 20, 1916, p. 3.
"A Bouquet of Wild Flowers." July 20, 1917, p. 13.
"Buy Goods Worth the Price." April 5, 1917, p. 17.
"Chasing Thistledown." June 20, 1917, p. 12.
"Dear Farm Women." January 5, 1921, p. 7.
"Does 'Haste Make Waste'?" April 20, 1917, p. 16.
"A Dog's a Dog for A' That: Intelligent Pets Sometimes Seem Almost Like Real Folks." August 20, 1916, p. 5.
"Doing Our Best." June 5, 1917, p. 13.
"Do Not Waste Your Strength." September 5, 1916, p. 11.
"Do the Right Thing Always." June 20, 1918, p. 11.
"Each in His Place." May 5, 1917, p. 9.
"Early Training Counts Most." October 20, 1918, p. 13.
"Economy in Egg Production." April 5, 1915, p. 21.
"Everyone Can Do Something." November 20, 1917, p. 16.
"Facts Versus Theories." June 20, 1916, p. 9.
"The Fairs That Build Men: Where Citizens of Tomorrow Are Trained." January 15, 1924, p. 23.
"The Farm Home" (1). May 5, 1919, p. 26, 35.
"The Farm Home" (2). May 20, 1919, p. 21.

"The Farm Home" (3). June 5, 1919, p. 23.
"The Farm Home" (4). June 20, 1919, p. 19.
"The Farm Home" (5). July 5, 1919, p. 19.
"The Farm Home" (6). July 20, 1919, p. 29.
"The Farm Home" (7). August 5, 1919, p. 20.
"The Farm Home" (8). September 5, 1919, p. 32.
"The Farm Home" (9). September 20, 1919, p. 44.
"The Farm Home" (10). October 5, 1919, p. 23.
"The Farm Home" (11). October 20, 1919, p. 22.
"The Farm Home" (12). November 5, 1919, p. 17.
"The Farm Home" (13). November 20, 1919, p. 34.
"The Farm Home" (14). December 5, 1919, p. 33.
"The Farm Home" (15). December 20 1919, p. 27.
"The Farm Home" (16). January 5, 1920, p. 41.
"The Farm Home" (17). January 20, 1920, p. 45.
"The Farm Home" (18). February 5, 1920, p. 35.
"The Farm Home" (19). February 20, 1920, p. 40.
"The Farm Home" (20). March 5, 1920, p. 36.
"The Farm Home" (21). March 20, 1920, p. 38.
"The Farm Home" (22). April 5, 1920, p. 34.
"The Farm Home" (23). April 20, 1920, p. 27.
"The Farm Home" (24). May 5, 1920, p. 39.
"The Farm Home" (25). June 5, 1920, p. 27.
"The Farm Home" (26). July 5, 1920, p. 27.
"The Farm Home" (27). July 20, 1920, p. 29.
"The Farm Home" (28). August 20, 1920, p. 33.
"The Farm Home" (29). October 5, 1920, p. 31.
"The Farm Home" (30). October 20, 1920, p. 34.
"The Farm Home" (31). November 5, 1920, p. 27.
"The Farm Home" (32). December 5, 1920, p. 25.
"Favors the Small Farm: It Lessens the Investment, Improves Country Social Conditions, Makes the Owner More Independent of Poor Help, Promotes Better Farming Methods and Reduces the Labor of Housekeeping." February 18, 1911, p. 1.
"A Few Minutes with a Poet." January 5, 1919, p. 19.
"Folks Are 'Just Folks': Why Shouldn't Town and Country Women Work and Play Together?" May 5, 1916, pp. 12–13.
"Friendship Must Be Wooed." March 5, 1919, p. 44.
"From a Farm Woman to You." July 1, 1921, p. 12.
"Get the Habit of Being Ready." October 20, 1917, p. 13.
"Getting the Worst of It." March 5, 1917, p. 9.

"Giving and Taking Advice." January 20, 1917, p. 9.
"Good Times on the Farm: It's Easy to Have Fun if You Plan for It." February 5, 1914, p. 9.
"Haying While the Sun Shines." July 20, 1916, p. 9.
"Hitching Up for Family Team Work: The Oettings of Wright County, Building on the Sure Foundation of Faith and Industry, Have Made Ozark Farming Pay." January 15, 1923, p. 3.
"A Homemaker of the Ozarks: Mrs. Durnell Reclaimed a Farm, Built a House in the Wilderness and Learned the Secret of Contentment." June 20, 1914, pp. 3, 8.
"A Homey Chat for Mothers." September 15, 1921, p. 14.
"How About the Home Front?" May 20, 1918, p. 10.
"How the Findleys Invest Their Money: These Missouri Parents Figure That Education of Their Boys and Girls Pay Bigger Dividends Than Pretty Clothes and Frivolous Pastimes." August 1, 1922, p. 1.
"If We Only Understood." December 5, 1917, p. 14.
"Join 'Don't Worry' Club: Conservation of a Woman's Strength Is True Preparedness." March 20, 1916, pp. 10–11.
"Just a Question of Tact: Every Person Has Said Things They Didn't Mean." October 5, 1916, p. 11.
"Just Neighbors." May 20, 1917, p. 9.
"Keep Journeying On." March 5, 1918, pp. 10–11.
"Keep the Saving Habit." March 20, 1919, p. 25.
"Kin-folks or Relations?" August 5, 1916, p. 9.
"Learning to Work Together." December 5, 1916, p. 11.
"Let's Revive the Old Amusements." January 20, 1919, p. 24.
"Let Us Be Just." September 5, 1917, p. 16.
"Life Is an Adventure: Voyages of Discovery Can Be Made in Your Rocking-chair." March 5, 1916, p. 14.
"Look for Fairies Now." April 5, 1916, p. 11.
"Magic in Plain Foods: All the World Serves a Woman When She Telephones." November 20, 1915, pp. 12–13.
"Make a New Beginning." January 5, 1918, p. 2.
"Make Every Minute Count." March 20, 1918, p. 13.
"Make Your Dreams Come True." February 5, 1918, p. 12.
"Making the Best of Things." June 20, 1915, p. 9.
"Mother, a Magic Word." September 1, 1921, p. 20.
"Mrs. Jones Takes the Rest Cure." February 5, 1919, p. 34.
"My Apple Orchard: How a "Tenderfoot" Knowing Nothing about Orcharding Learned the Business in Missouri—Quail as Insect Destroyers."

June 1, 1912, p. 5. (Probably written by Mrs. Wilder but credited to Mr. Wilder.)
"New Day for Women." June 5, 1918, pp. 12–13.
"Now We Visit Bohemia" (1). September 5, 1920, p. 30.
"Now We Visit Bohemia" (2). September 20, 1920, p. 30.
"Opportunity." November 5, 1918, p. 26.
"Our Fair and Other Things." November 5, 1916, p. 12.
"Overcoming Our Difficulties." August 20, 1918, p. 11.
"The People in God's Out-of-Doors." April 15, 1911, p. 12.
"Pioneering on an Ozark Farm: A Story of Folks Who Searched—and Found Health, Prosperity and a Wild Frontier in the Mountains of Our Own State." June 1, 1921, p. 3.
"A Plain Beauty Talk: Women Can Afford to Spend Time on Their Looks." April 20, 1914, p. 9.
"Put Yourself in His Place." August 5, 1917, p. 20.
"Reminiscences of Fair Time." December 1, 1922, p. 22.
"The Roads Women Travel." February 1, 1921, p. 17.
"San Marino Is Small but Mighty." December 5, 1918, p. 22.
"Santa Claus at the Front." January 20, 1918, p. 16.
"Shorter Hours for Farm Women: The Woman Who Manages the Farm Home Should Have Every Means of Saving Labor Placed at Her Disposal. Simple Conveniences within Reach of All." June 28, 1913, pp. 3, 10.
"Showing Dad the Way: Mansfield Has a Boys' Good Road Club That Works and Plays." August 5, 1916, pp. 12–13.
"Sometimes Misdirected Energy May Cease to Be a Virtue." February 20, 1916, p. 11.
"So We Moved the Spring: How Running Water Was Provided in the Rocky Ridge Farm Home." April 20, 1916, p. 19.
"Spic, Span—and Beauty: How a Home Responds to Springtime Touches." April 1, 1931, pp. 5, 12.
"The Story of Rocky Ridge Farm: How Mother Nature in the Ozarks Rewarded Well Directed Efforts after a Fruitless Struggle on the Plains of the Dakotas. The Blessings of Living Water and a Gentle Climate." July 22, 1911, p. 3. (Probably written by Mrs. Wilder but credited to Mr. Wilder.)
"Swearing Is a Foolish Habit." August 5, 1918, p. 10.
"Thanksgiving Time." November 20, 1916, p. 13.
"'Thoughts Are Things.'" November 5, 1917, p. 23.
"To Buy or Not to Buy." September 20, 1917, p. 18.

"Turkeys Bring $1,000 a Year: Where Secret of Success Is 'Love Them.'" February 1, 1924, pp. 26–27.
"Victory May Depend on You." February 20, 1918, p. 13.
"Visit 'Show You' Farm: Prosperity and Happiness Is Found on a 25-Acre Plot." March 20, 1918, pp. 20–21.
"We Must Not Be Small Now." April 20, 1918, p. 11.
"We Visit Arabia." August 5, 1920, pp. 22–23.
"We Visit Paris Now." January 5, 1921, p. 23.
"We Visit Poland." February 15, 1921, p. 29.
"What Days in Which to Live." September 20, 1918, p. 13.
"What Makes My County Great: And Why I'm Proud to Be a Citizen." December 1, 1923, pp. 3, 12.
"What's in a Word." January 5, 1917, p. 9.
"What the War Means to Women." May 5, 1918, p. 10.
"What Would You Do?" April 5, 1918, p. 12.
"When Grandma Pioneered." August 1, 1921, p. 20.
"When Is a Settler an Old Settler?" June 5, 1916, p. 15.
"When Proverbs Get Together." September 5, 1918, p. 11.
"Who'll Do the Women's Work?" April 5, 1919, p. 36.
"Without Representation." July 5, 1917, p. 8.
"Women and Real Politics." April 15, 1921, p. 19.
"Women's Duty at the Polls." April 20, 1919, p. 36.
"Work Makes Life Interesting." February 20, 1919, p. 42.
"Your Code of Honor." October 5, 1918, p. 26.

INDEX